New Movements in the Study and Teaching of Geography

In the series

NEW MOVEMENTS IN THE STUDY AND TEACHING OF HISTORY
edited by Martin Ballard

Contents

Introduction

1 Introduction

NORMAN GRAVES

The problems of teaching geography to school students are well known to teachers and, in the past, there has been no shortage of texts giving guidance to teachers about the best methods to put into practice in the classroom. Such texts have been informed by the long years of experience of their writers, either in the classroom or in teacher training. They have contained sound practical advice about the management of classes, the handling of equipment, the drafting of lessons on geography indicating various ways in which the subject might be presented to pupils in an interesting way. Few, however, have gone deeply into the theoretical issues involved in the teaching of geography, looked at either from the point of view of the subject or from the educationist's standpoint. At this stage in the evolution of geography it was thought useful to take a more penetrating look at the path the discipline was taking and at the problems this presented for its teaching at the secondary school (11–18 year) level.

What in fact has happened to geography which merits this sort of close examination? Many might argue that nothing much had changed and some would insist that what had changed was for the worst. Perhaps what has changed most is the attitude of many who call themselves geographers, particularly the younger geographers. Many who, like myself, were trained in the UK in the immediate post-war years or earlier, were initiated into a tradition which stemmed largely from the writings of Vidal de la Blache and his followers. Those of us who joined the teaching profession saw ourselves essentially as the means whereby our charges might learn something about the world they lived in through the 'explanatory descriptions of landscapes'. We were concerned to see that our pupils acquired an understanding of the many interacting influences which led to a region acquiring a particular 'cachet' or 'personality'. True, we also taught something about the processes of denudation and something about elementary meteorology, but we always assumed this to be subservient to our main aim. In so doing we were accepting unwittingly the idea of geography as an 'art subject', one in which the felicitous phrase or the elegant description was perhaps more valuable than the quantitative assessment of data when describing a particular area. We came to accept, again perhaps not critically enough, the idea that regional description would present a nice synthesis of the information available about an area.

We had our worrying moments. We were told in 1949 by no less an authority than Professor Wooldridge, that we were in danger of 'taking the GE out of geography'. As a result some redressed the balance by teaching a good deal of geomorphology. Then the world kept changing. As fast as we tried to keep up with iron-ore development on the Quebec–Labrador border, so new deposits were found in Mauretania and then in the Hamersley Range in Western Australia. We developed a permanent guilt complex about being somewhat less up to date in our facts than we felt we ought to be. Then, those who were exploring the frontiers of our subject were steadily producing a mounting output of research papers dealing both with areas and with systematic studies. As the length of time grew between the year when we graduated and the present, so we became no doubt more proficient practitioners in the classroom, but what we taught bore less and less resemblance to what current university geographers were doing. Perhaps this was of no consequence, yet there was in the back of our minds the sneaking suspicion that even if we were not out of date with our facts, then we were out of date with our concepts.

It seemed as though by the early 1960s we had got ourselves into a vicious circle. The more we tried to keep up with our facts the less time we had to deal with new ideas, concepts or theories. How could we break out of it? The answer to this question seemed deceptively simple: the concepts were more important than the facts, the nomothetic aspects (or general principles) of geography were more important than the ideographic (or particular) descriptions of areas. What mattered most was to give our pupils a conceptual understanding of geography rather than an encyclopaedic knowledge of the world. Undoubtedly this was the way many geographers at university level had been thinking for some time. In some university departments of geography, regional description had gradually been declining in relative importance, whilst the study of theory relating to various aspects of human and physical geography had been increasing in importance.

If this were true, then it posed anew the old question 'What is geography?' If it was not the explanatory description of landscapes, then what was it? In the past this question was answered in the main by geographers, who were trying to find something unique about geography as a subject. In Chapter 2, Terence Moore and I make an attempt *not* to find out what is unique about geography, or to argue a case for what ideally geography ought to be, but rather to look at what geographers have written and submit this to philosophical analysis and so find out the kind of knowledge that geography in fact conveys. It would seem of some value to understand the fundamental knowledge-structure of the subject if one is to teach it in an appropriate manner. Further, if the theory content of geography is increasing then it is important to understand just what the nature and role of theory are in relation to geography. This is done in Chapter 3 by David Harvey who has spent some years in the study of the various modes of explanation used in geography and in other fields. Too often in the past the nature of theories, laws and hypotheses has been misunderstood. A clarification of this topic is both useful and welcome. The practising teacher may object that this is very remote from teaching a healthy but academically not very gifted class of 14-year-old students. Perhaps it is, but on the surface only, for what we teach is very much influenced by what we understand. If we are clearer about theory, we shall be more inclined to teach it or get our pupils to learn it.

Such a discussion soon leads to considerations of the aims of education. What are we really aiming at when we teach geography and geographical theory? What sort of long-term and short-term objectives do we subscribe to? Do we know whether these objectives are being achieved or not? How far can we dovetail the precise objectives of geography teaching into those of education as a whole, or is such a question meaningless? Such and other questions are considered in Chapter 4 by Trevor Bennetts who has spent some considerable time as a practising schoolmaster pondering over the objectives of geographical education. Such objectives may be transformed, however, if in the process of curriculum development, geography is no longer taught as a separate subject but becomes integrated into the teaching of the humanities. The nature and implications of such development for the teacher are considered by Michael Naish in Chapter 5.

It is the teacher's privilege to teach, but only the pupil can learn. Learning geography presents as many difficulties as teaching it. In Chapter 6 Thelma Veness examines the way in which the study of psychology can throw light on the learning of geography by school pupils. The story is taken up in detail in Chapter 7 by Herbert Sandford who concentrates on some of the perceptual difficulties facing children who are learning geography through pictures, large-scale maps and atlas maps. Perceptual difficulties lead to children misinterpreting the evidence they are given, but even if they understand the evidence it does not follow that they reason well about it. In Chapter 8 William Rhys, who has done some work on children's capacities for thinking logically about geographical data, examines some of the factors which influence children's ability to reason about problems set them in geography, and shows that for many children, certain problems cannot be fully tackled until they are 14 years old or older. The growth of understanding is linked to some extent with the growth of an adequate vocabulary to help communications between children and between teacher and pupils. In Chapter 9 Dennis Milburn examines the sort of vocabulary which children are expected to use in geography and what they make of it. He shows where some of this vocabulary is derived from, and how some misconceptions occur.

Geography gives information about peoples in other lands and as such may be responsible for the formation of the attitude of schoolchildren to foreigners. How true or false this is is examined by John Carnie (Chapter 10) who has conducted a series of experiments to elucidate the nature and source of children's attitudes to peoples of foreign origin. How far the teacher may be able to influence attitudes to foreign people is also discussed.

Two of the teacher's main problems are those of motivating his pupils and adapting his approach to the children and their particular mood at the moment of impact. These problems are considered by Gerald Hones and John White in Chapters 11 and 12, both drawing on a wealth of personal experience in the classroom and a deep intuitive understanding of children. If motivation is an issue, the use of games, discussed in Chapter 13 by Rex Walford, may be one answer, though by no means the only answer. Inevitably the teacher must consider what ideas to teach in the various branches of geography, and this is done for physical geography by Graham Stevens (Chapter 15), for urban geography by Michael Storm (Chapter 16) and for networks by Vincent Tidswell and Keith Hilton (Chapter 17); and in Chapter 18 Peter Davis looks at the sort of elementary statistical techniques that might be used in some aspects of geography. All these authors have had experience in trying their ideas out in schools, though clearly what works in one context may not work in another. To those who respond to a challenge, they have laid down a gauntlet. I deal with the question of how geography has and is being examined in Chapter 14, put examinations in their historical perspective and look critically at some of the examining techniques which are still with us at present. In looking to current experiments with objective tests and to the future, I am conscious that though American techniques of examining are more advanced than our own, few of these techniques have been applied to geography so that much work remains to be done in this field.

The changing field of geography

2 The nature of geographical knowledge

NORMAN GRAVES and TERENCE MOORE

One of the questions which any thinking student of geography sooner or later poses is: 'What is geography?' It is a question which has been asked many times, as far back as the time of Ptolemy and Eratosthenes. It is a question which has received a variety of answers, some illuminating but many more which seemed to obscure rather than to clarify the issues involved. It has been asked by the layman as well as by the professional geographer. This in itself is significant since the layman seldom asks what chemistry, physics, engineering or mathematics are. Most people believe they know what these subjects are but they are often a little hazy as to what geography is or what a geographer does. Not infrequently they may hold the naïve view that geography is nothing more than a compendium of information about the world, information in terms of simple facts about the location, size, boundaries, economics, etc. of various countries. On this view geographical knowledge is no more than the contents of a Year Book or Gazetteer. At a somewhat higher level of sophistication it is often asked whether geography is more properly an art or a science, whether it belongs with history or with physics, or perhaps with both (Graves 1971).

Why has there been this confusion as to the nature of geography, and is it possible to dispel it? Some geographers argue that it is better to get on writing geography or researching in geography, than to spend fruitless hours discussing its nature. Yet it seems doubtful whether geographers can produce new work in geography while being unaware (or only intuitively aware) of the way their work differs from or is similar to that of workers in other fields. It would seem necessary, therefore, to attempt to clarify the issues involved.

SOME RED HERRINGS

Many books which deal with the nature of geography do so by looking into the history of the subject. Sometimes this is traced back to the Greeks, sometimes only to Varenius, and more frequently no further back than the late eighteenth and early nineteenth centuries when both Alexander von Humboldt and Karl Ritter are hailed as the founders of modern geography. (Hartshorne 1939, Wooldridge and East 1956, Brock 1965, Freeman 1961.) It is argued that a discipline can best be understood in terms of its evolution, of the way its content and methods have changed over the years. Thus geography is seen as having moved from a catalogue of facts about the earth's surface to a reasoned description of the influence of physical factors on human activities and more recently to a science of spatial correlations, i.e. the study of relationships between different distributions on the earth's surface. Now, whilst such an account may be of great interest, it does not much help us to understand the nature of geography in terms of the kind of knowledge that the subject provides. If geography is no longer a catalogue of facts, if it is no longer a study of the physical factors influencing human activities, then knowing this does not help us very much to find out what geography now is as a subject. This is our first red herring. To find out what geography is, one needs to look closely and analytically at the sort of knowledge that the subject contains at the present time. That is, the subject needs to be looked at from an epistemological point of view. To this we will return later.

Another red herring is produced by writers who tell us what the purpose of geography is. These writers are not so much concerned with what geographers are doing as with what they *ought* to be doing. They are not probing the nature of the subject as it is actually studied, but saying what sort of pattern it ought to conform to. They think of geography as having a special role or a distinctive function in the scheme of knowledge and feel that any subject matter which does not conform to this role or function is *ipso facto* not geography. For example Wooldridge and East in their *Spirit and purpose of geography*, originally published in 1951, write: 'It is in bridging the gap between physical and human phenomena that geography finds its distinctive role.' They go on to explain that any division between physical and human geography is contrary to the central purpose of geography.

Now it may well be that many geographers believe that geography ought to be a subject which bridges the gap between physical and human phenomena. But to prescribe what geography ought to be or ought to do is not the same thing as describing what it is, particularly if what it is supposed to do is very different from what it in fact does. It is true that what some are prescribing today others may in practice do tomorrow. On the other hand, what some are prescribing today may never happen. To take the example of the Wooldridge and East prescription for geography (which has even earlier antecedents in Vidal de la Blache's and Mackinder's writings) it would be difficult to argue that most geographers who are producing research papers today are engaged in bridging the gap between physical and human phenomena, if by that one means that they are working on problems which involve both the physical and human aspects of geography. A glance at the contents of the current issues of the *Transactions of the Institute of British Geographers* or the *Annals of the Association of American Geographers* will quickly dispel such a notion. In general then, speculation about what geography *should* do may be a valuable contribution to the debate about the way the subject should move or evolve, but it is not a valid statement of what it actually is at the present time. Such a statement can only be produced by examining the content of current geography and fitting it into a more general plan of the various types or forms of knowledge.

GEOGRAPHY IN THE STRUCTURE OF KNOWLEDGE

In spite of the work done by philosophers, no single universally agreed theory of knowledge exists. However, the issues involved in deciding on the kind of knowledge that mathematics or physics or ethics is, have been sufficiently clarified to make it possible to clarify similar issues when dealing with geography.

It may be useful first to consider the terminology used in referring to various subjects in the curriculum. The term *subject* itself is generally used to mean merely some body of knowledge, skills or attitudes which may be taught; it does not specify anything about the *nature of the knowledge* within the subject concerned. Mathematics, art, craft, literature, home economics, accounting, telecommunications technology can all be referred to as subjects: the word can be used for any body of teachable material which it is convenient to assemble under one heading for practical teaching purposes. Thus to call geography a subject implies nothing about its nature or content.

When the word *discipline* is used, however, something more is implied. This is not to deny that the term discipline is often loosely used as a synonym for 'subject', and in that sense it has no special significance. But when someone writes of 'geography as a discipline' or the 'discipline of mathematics', he is not just referring to a convenient assemblage of facts, theories, and skills, he is also suggesting that the content of the subject is in some way logically structured – that it is built up of concepts and principles that interrelate with each other to form a complex whole which has a kind of 'order' of its own. It is, for example, usual to refer to economics and physics as disciplines, but not needlework or metalwork. It is often argued that disciplines form proper objects of university studies, while other subjects do not, and Tudor David once argued that geography should not exist in British universities since it could in no way be described as a discipline (David 1958).

The names given to individual subjects are not in themselves very significant, and some of them have changed over the centuries. The separate names for the branches of natural science, for example, have evolved as the sum total of knowledge has increased. The layman, however, recognises that there are significant differences in the content of various subjects, even within the natural sciences. Chemistry seems different from physics, which itself differs from biology. Outside the natural sciences, history seems different from geography and from economics. The problem lies in specifying the nature of these differences. Again at the common-sense level, it could be argued that chemistry is concerned with the study of the changes which occur when compounds and/or elements interact; that physics is concerned with the physical properties of material bodies when energised in one way or another; that biology is the study of living organisms; that history is the study of past events; that geography describes places; that economics is concerned with making sense of the interrelationships which result from production and trade. Whilst such descriptions are true they do not get us any nearer to describing the kind of knowledge that these subjects involve. For example, if there are real differences between chemistry and physics why do they both come under the umbrella of physical science? Again, the events of history must happen in some space or place whilst the places of geography exist and evolve through time; so is the difference between history and geography merely one of emphasis? Further, are not physics and chemistry concerned with events occurring in places through time? Is the distinction to be found in the kind of events that are studied? For instance, is the economic depression of the 1930s with its great effects on the distribution of industry and employment to be studied under history, economics, geography or sociology?

The last example seems to make it clear that the distinction between subjects cannot lie wholly in what is being studied, since the economic depression of the 1930s may be studied within all four subjects mentioned. The difference must lie somewhere else. Of course it could be argued that in the ultimate analysis there are no distinctions between various subjects, that knowledge is one and indivisible, and that all attempts to divide it into types of knowledge that are fundamentally different from each other are bound to fail. If this is true, then one could close the argument here, and say that the collection of facts, theories and skills included in geography are collected together merely for convenience. The same would be true of every other subject. Yet there is the nagging suspicion that mathematics is different from history, and geography from physics, in some fundamental way.

GEOGRAPHY IN RELATION TO THE FORMS OF KNOWLEDGE

Investigations have been made into the nature of the knowledge involved in various subjects and they have brought forward ideas about the nature of those subjects which have helped practitioners to understand their subject's position in the realm of knowledge as a whole. What Russell and Whitehead did for mathematics, Oakeshott and Collingwood have done for history. But it is only in the very recent past that any geographer has taken a truly philosophical stand and looked at geography in terms which philosophers would find acceptable (Harvey 1969). Just what philosophers have to say on this topic now needs to be looked at. Quite recently philosophers of education have concerned themselves with the theory of knowledge, as it relates to subjects in the traditional curriculum. Their conclusions in no way support the view that knowledge is indivisible, or that the differences between subjects are merely arbitrary. Hirst has put this point of view in a manner which, though it undoubtedly simplifies the issues involved, clarifies them so well that his statement cannot be ignored (Hirst 1965).

He argues that knowledge is the way in which our experience of reality is structured by our minds. To communicate this knowledge we use a system of symbols (usually language) which is public in the sense that the symbols used have common meanings and that therefore the representations of reality which are communicated have a currency beyond private experience. Thus the terms 'north, south, east and west' are generally understood symbols referring to directions which are unambiguous and accepted even in the southern hemisphere where the mid-day sun lies due north. This knowledge, however, is not undifferentiated; the human mind has structured different types of experience in fundamentally different ways. In other words, the very nature of certain experiences of reality has resulted in a characteristic formulation of that experience in symbolic terms which is distinct from the symbolic formulation of a different kind of experience. For example, the logical relationships between symbols are expressed in the languages we call mathematics and logic, but our experiences of the physical movement of bodies are expressed in terms of the symbolic language of physics. Similarly our aesthetic experiences are differently expressed from our experiences of economic life.

Each of these fundamental ways of structuring experience is called a *form of knowledge*. Each form of knowledge has its own conceptual framework and its own characteristic tests for truth. The concepts of mass, of temperature, of relative humidity, are essentially concepts in physics. These 'within-form-of-knowledge' concepts are related to one another in the logical structure of that form. In the example chosen above, the idea of relative humidity is clearly related to mass and temperature since it is defined as 'the ratio of the mass of water vapour per unit volume of the air to the mass of water vapour per unit volume of saturated air at the same temperature' (Uvarov et al. 1964). Similarly in economics the concept of national income is related to those of wages, rent and interest; in theology the concepts of sin and grace are interrelated. With some reservations it may be said that concepts peculiar to one form of knowledge cannot be used in another without making nonsense of the discourse. To take an extreme case the idea of sin has no place whatever in physics or mathematics. The tests for truth are again peculiar to the forms of knowledge concerned. In the physical sciences, the tests for truth are generally accepted to be those of testing hypotheses through experimentation, leading to the acceptance or rejection of the hypotheses. In mathematics, the test for truth lies in the degree to which a set of symbolic relationships are logically consistent with each other and with the axioms postulated. Similarly, it is argued, ethics, theology, aesthetics and the social sciences each have their own methods of testing the validity of their characteristic conclusions. The tests for truth in these fields are less straightforward and more contentious than those of mathematics or of the physical sciences.

Hirst suggests that these various forms of knowledge are historically determined and that the list is open-ended. It is possible that other forms of understanding may come to be distinguished in time. Moreover the present list does not correspond exactly with what we have loosely termed 'subjects'. Hirst lists physical science, mathematics, history, aesthetics, ethics, theology, and the human sciences as fundamental forms of knowledge in the sense that each is separate and distinct from the other. Geography does not feature in this list, nor do many other subjects such as education, medicine, engineering, architecture and so on. For these and others like them, Hirst reserves the term *field of knowledge*. He argues that for certain practical purposes (e.g. to build engines) it is necessary to bring together certain components from different forms of knowledge in order to make possible the activity concerned. In engineering the concepts and theories of physics are allied to those of mathematics and possibly to those of aesthetics in the process of designing an engine. A 'field of knowledge' is thus a looser structure than a form of knowledge; it is constituted by elements drawn from various forms, as for example, when the disciplines of psychology, sociology, and history contribute to problems in the study of the field known as 'education'.

It is possible to have reservations about this analysis of the structure of knowledge. It may be objected that the extent of the relationship between mathematics and physics, for example, makes it difficult to conceive of the latter without the former. The very concept of force is defined as the product of mass and acceleration so that though one may have a non-mathematical, experiential concept of force, its formulation in terms of the concepts of physics in fact involves a mathematical relationship. Further, the idea that each form of knowledge has its own means of testing its conclusions may appear doubtful when one considers in what ways the means of testing conclusions in social science differ fundamentally from those of testing conclusions in physical science. The testing of hypotheses would seem common to both, the only distinction being that 'probabilistic' theories are more common in the social than in the physical sciences (except at the atomic level). Again, it might be asked whether history has a series of characteristic logically interrelated concepts and whether in fact the methods of validating historical conclusions are fundamentally different from those used in science.

Despite these reservations, Hirst's ideas on forms and fields of knowledge are useful enough for it to be valuable to apply them to geography. Let us now look at geography in the light of Hirst's statement concerning the forms of knowledge. It will be remembered that a form of knowledge is one which has its own distinct concepts and characteristic tests for truth. Now it is doubtful whether geography can be said to have any concepts which are peculiar to it in the sense that they do not reduce to concepts found in other areas of study. Typical 'geographical' concepts, like 'meander', 'moraine', 'wind', 'continental shelf', 'coniferous forest', 'conurbation', 'degree of latitude', can all be reduced ultimately to concepts in, for example, physical, mathematical, biological or social sciences. There seem to be no specifically 'geographical' concepts. Nor does geography seem to have tests for truth which do not belong elsewhere. The truth or falsity of typical geographical statements would seem to be determined in the same way as those of scientific statements and factual statements in history. We may exemplify this by looking at what geographers have actually written.

A book published in 1966 under the editorship of G. H. Dury, who is a professor of geography, is entitled *Essays in geomorphology*. In Europe, geomorphology has traditionally been part of geography, whilst in North America it is considered a branch of geology, but there seems little doubt that, whether it is in practice placed under geography or under geology, the concepts and modes of verification employed are those of the physical sciences. The geomorphologist is essentially concerned with describing natural land forms and formulating theories of a scientific kind about the way in which such land forms have developed and are developing. He needs to be expert in geology and in experimental methods of investigation.

If we now look at a book entitled *Geography in religions*, also written by a professor of geography, we find that its contents are very different in character from those of the *Essays in geomorphology*. The author explains that he is considering in turn (1) the way in which environment affects the evolution of religious systems and particular religious institutions; (2) the way religious systems and institutions modify their environment; (3) the different ways whereby religious systems occupy and organise segments of earth space; (4) the geographical distribution of religions and the way religious systems spread and interact with each other (Sopher 1967). The problem now is to assign this sort of study to a form of knowledge. It seems evident that the author must have indulged in a certain amount of historical research in order to discover the facts which might lead him to make pronouncements on the possible influence of climate on religious rites. Other aspects clearly involved an understanding of various forms of land use and their relation to religious organisation. Very little use seems to be made, at least explicitly, of theoretical models which might indicate a social science approach to the subject. One must conclude, therefore, that the dominant form of knowledge in this book is that of history though clearly a knowledge of religious beliefs is essential as, well as an ability to read and interpret mapped information.

A third source of information about the nature of contemporary geography comes from a collection of essays entitled *Analytical human geography* (Ambrose 1969). It is quite clear from these essays that the authors wish to make explicit the theoretical structure of the knowledge with which they are concerned. For example, the article on 'A theory of location for cities' by Edward Ullman reviews the theoretical frameworks provided by von Thünen and by Christaller and assesses their validity in various parts of the world. In an allied article by B. J. L. Berry and W. L. Garrison called 'The functional bases of central place hierarchy', the authors show how they set out to test the validity of the concept of the hierarchy of central places in the Shohomish county of Washington State in the USA. There seems little doubt that the form of knowledge which best describes this activity is that of social science—the use of scientific method on social data.

In another article, the process of ghetto expansion in a North American town is studied by R. L. Morill by putting forward a theoretical model of such expansion and comparing it with the reality. Thus by its use of clearly defined concepts concerned with the nature of human settlement, by its testing of models or hypotheses in a scientific manner, such work may be classed with the social science form of knowledge.

Lastly, let us examine a work written in French by the professor of geography at Laval University in Quebec. It is simply called *Le Canada* (Hamelin 1969) and it is a work which would traditionally have been labelled regional geography, although it is not a regional description in the sense that each area of Canada is described in turn. The book is in five parts: Part I examines the effect of Canada's northerly position on her climate, her soils and her water surfaces; Part II looks at the physical structure of Canada, its gradual settlement and its types of settlements, its administrative divisions and lastly its regional disparities, particularly from the economic and cultural points of view. Part III is concerned with demography – the growth of the population of Canada, its ethnic origins and distribution, and the distribution of the working population among the primary, secondary and tertiary sectors of the economy; Part IV focuses on investments, production and trade; Part V concentrates on the characteristics of Canadian urban areas. This is indeed a rich offering. It looks at Canada from many different points of view. It is at one and the same time a review of the history of settlement, of the geological and meteorological conditions of the physical environment, of economic development, of cultural problems and of the basis for political divisions. It presents in effect the findings of history, of physical science, of economics, of social anthropology, and of politics. To many geographers such a book epitomises what geography should be, namely an application of the findings of various disciplines to a given area. To a philosopher looking at its content, it would undoubtedly confirm that, in terms of Hirst's analysis of forms of knowledge, geography is a field of knowledge and not a form. Its only claim to be a distinct subject may simply be that it is a subject dealing with mappable phenomena (Simons 1969).

CONCLUSION

The argument so far has been that, if we accept the idea that knowledge may be divided into discrete forms each with its characteristic conceptual structure and truth tests, then we must also accept that the geography which has so far been written does not fall neatly into any one of these forms of knowledge. It seems rather that certain parts of geography can be fairly easily classified as belonging to the physical sciences (e.g. geomorphology, climatology), other parts seem to belong to history (e.g. any aspect of geography involving mainly historical investigation, as in the *Domesday geography of eastern England*), other parts seem to belong to the social sciences (e.g. those concerned with the analysis of settlement patterns and communications). In other words, the answer to the question implicit in the title of this article is that geography involves not one sort of knowledge, but three. It could then be described, according to Hirst, as a field of knowledge, in which various forms of knowledge are brought together to tackle certain problems which cannot be solved by one form of knowledge alone. For example, it could be argued that town-planning problems are of this nature, since the planner must know not only something of the physical characteristics of the area to be planned, but something of the economic and social relationships between the town and its hinterland and within the town itself. Unfortunately not all the geography that is written is concerned with such multi-disciplinary problems, as was clear when we examined the contents of such books as *Analytical human geography* which can be classed as essentially social science. Thus one is left with the impression that the current output of geography is of a very disparate nature in terms of the type of knowledge it conveys.

Now, as we said earlier, one is not bound to accept the analysis of the structure of knowledge given above. In fact, as we have already seen, there are certain difficulties about such an analysis which are unresolved. However, most other schemes of classifying the structure of knowledge have equal if not greater disadvantages. Further, it must be remembered that the analysis of the forms of knowledge now in existence is subject to modification in the future. Three hundred years ago the social science form of knowledge did not exist as such. Economics came to maturity in the nineteenth and twentieth centuries, sociology and psychology in the twentieth century. It seems likely that much of human geography will further develop its own concepts and theory, though its methods of investigation are likely to be those of the social sciences. What also seems evident is that, in terms of research, the old alliance between physical geography and human geography is dying and much work is being done in one or the other of these fields alone. Only a minority of work is concerned with the influence of physical factors on human activity, largely because physical factors no longer loom so large in modern industrial societies. It may well be that there is no longer any useful purpose in keeping these two aspects of geography together. Physical geography has, in geomorphology and climatology, its own developing and specialised fields. Human geography is growing rapidly. Often the only links between them are the mathematics or statistics needed to handle their data. In the past the science subjects have exploded into different sub-groups as a result of the growth of various aspects of their content; it would appear likely that traditional geography will also explode. In that case physical geography might well return to the mainstream of physical science and human geography develop within the mainstream of social science.

The relevance of all this to the situation in secondary schools may seem remote; but if the analysis is essentially correct it follows that, since the various parts of geography fall under different forms of knowledge, these differences may well impose different patterns of learning. It may be argued that the physical aspects of geography should be taught in the manner of a physical science, in which experiments go hand in hand with the development of theoretical knowledge of, for example, weathering, erosion, and meteorology. Similarly it may be argued that those aspects of the subject which are essentially historical and ideographical (why did the textile industry develop in West Yorkshire and South Lancashire?) might well be taught in a manner appropriate to history, with the evaluation of historical evidence. Again human geography might be taught so as to form an introduction to the methods of social science. This is particularly important since at school level there is little evidence that geography is yet ready to split into two or more subjects. Indeed there seems to be evidence of a current trend to combine it with other forms or fields of knowledge into a group of integrated subjects or into some sort of interdisciplinary enquiry.

References

P. J. Ambrose, (1969) *Analytical human geography*, Longmans.

J. O. M. Brock, (1965) *Geography – its scope and spirit*, Charles E. Merrill.

H. C. Darby (1952), *The Domesday Geography of eastern England*, Cambridge.

T. David, (1958) 'Against geography', *Universities Quarterly*.

G. H. Dury (ed.), (1966) *Essays in geomorphology*, Heinemann.

T. W. Freeman, (1961) *A hundred years of geography*, Duckworth.

N. J. Graves, (1971) *Geography in Secondary Education*, Geographical Association.

L. E. Hamelin, (1969) *Le Canada*, Presses Universitaires de France.

R. Hartshorne, (1960) *Perspective on the nature of geography*, John Murray.

D. Harvey, (1969) *Explanation in geography*, Edward Arnold.

P. H. Hirst, (1965) 'Liberal education and the nature of knowledge', *Philosophical Analysis and Education*, ed. R. D. Archambault, Routledge.

M. Simons, (1969) 'What are geographers doing?' *Universities Quarterly*, Winter 1969.

D. E. Sopher, (1967) *Geography of religions*, Prentice-Hall.

E. B. Uvarov, D. R. Chapman and A. Isaacs, (1964) *A dictionary of science*, Penguin.

S. W. Wooldridge and W. G. East, (1956) *The spirit and purpose of geography*, Hutchinson.

3 The role of theory

DAVID HARVEY

It is perhaps best to think of a theory as a codification of experience. To write of a geographical theory is, therefore, to write of the ways in which geographers codify their knowledge in order to make that know ledgemost readily and appropriately usable in a world which is a very complicated place. In the last decade or so a considerable effort has been made by geographers to codify much of their collective experience. We have thus come to think very explicitly about such activities as model building and theory construction. Much of the so-called 'new geography' is concerned with this kind of activity. Yet it would be wrong to think of the 'new geography' as exercising an exclusive claim to this kind of activity. Geographers have always had theories of some kind, have always constructed models of the complex reality they seek to understand. What is new is the conscious exploitation of theoretical and model-based styles of thinking. The modern literature, as a result, has a rather different flavour to it compared with the traditional literature in which theories and models were implied rather than explicitly set forth.

The conscious use of theory construction and model-building techniques has yielded a mixed bag of results. On the negative side it has to be admitted that the models we have built and the theories we have set up over the past decade have not been as general or far-reaching in their coverage as we had hoped. In other words we have managed to code only a small part of the rich and varied collective experience of geographers. It is instructive to consider the reasons for this failure.

In the first place it has to be admitted that many of us who became involved in this activity were arrogant enough to suppose that we could build theories out of our own experience, or upon analogy with many of the exciting ideas emanating from the other social, biological and physical sciences. In retrospect it is easy to predict that this kind of approach would at best produce a partial theoretical structure in which much of interest would be left out. We might have spent more of our time exploring the welter of ideas and experience contained in our traditional literature, but that did not appear fashionable or *avant-garde* enough to attract serious attention.

In the second place there was a tendency to take a rather too restrictive view of what theory construction was all about. In particular, theoretical thinking became far too closely identified with a rather more specialised activity which I shall call 'mere hypothesis testing'. Hypothesis testing has a legitimate and important part to play in the development of any corpus of theory. But hypothesis testing is only part of the story. Hypotheses, even when tested and found significant against some suitably collected body of data, need to be evaluated and embedded in some overall theoretical structure if they are to make sense. Lacking such a general structure, we find that much of the hypothesis testing so characteristic of work in the 1960s has added up to not much more than a lot of bits and pieces which are hard to make sense of. It is rather like being the proud owner of several pieces of jigsaw puzzle without even being certain that all the bits come from the same puzzle.

The anxiety to hypothesis-test also led to some serious misunderstandings of the nature of normative theories. Since a normative theory is, by definition, a theory which tells us what ought to be under certain idealised circumstances, it seems hardly worthwhile trying to test it empirically when it is obvious that those idealised circumstances do not exist in reality. (It is inappropriate to try and test von Thünen's land use theory or Lösch's central place theory, and we should certainly not get disillusioned with normative theory simply because we cannot see rings of land use or hexagonal market areas wherever we look.) This does not mean that we should not seek to explore the empirical relevance of a normative theory – but this is a different matter to testing it. I shall return to this issue later on.

But there have been some important benefits from the explicit use of theories and models in geographic work. There can be no doubt that the rigour and clarity of our thinking has markedly improved over the past decade. This is not to say that we have not got into some quite fearful conceptual muddles or that we have always succeeded in communicating our ideas well. But there is a sense of progression in the quality of argument in geography in the past decade and I believe this can largely be attributed to the need to think logically and consistently when it comes to theory construction. Also, there can be no doubt that in those areas in which theoreticians do concentrate their attention they manage to generate some new and exciting perspectives on what are quite old geographical ideas. In part this excitement comes from the infusion of all kinds of new ideas from the other sciences (particularly the social sciences and biology) but in part it comes from the realisation that it really is possible to theorise explicitly about geographical problems with fruitful results. Our understanding of certain issues in geography has undoubtedly improved as a result. We are now much better equipped to handle problems in pattern analysis, locational analysis, and so on. Most recently the exploration of what may be termed the 'cognitive-behavioural' approach to geography has lent depth and stature to a very old geographic tradition. We may, at long last, be able to return to the man-environment relationship with a set of tools, many of which are derived from psychology and social psychology, that will produce some sort of solution. In these areas we have succeeded not only in coding old geographic ideas but also in reinterpreting past experience and adding interesting dimensions to it. Whatever the shortcomings of the theoretical approach to geographic problems, therefore, we can point to enough substantial achievement over the past decade to ensure that the theoretical approach will not decline in importance. Indeed, there is every indication that we will concentrate more and more on theoretical approaches in the future. It therefore behoves all geographers, of whatever ilk or stripe, to grapple with the meaning of theory in a discipline which has not a long tradition of theorising behind it.

HOW DOES A THEORY FUNCTION AS AN AID TO UNDERSTANDING?

Philosophers of science, such as Toulmin (1960, 105–6), have often likened a theory to a map. The analogy is peculiarly useful to geographers since we all, I hope, know how maps work. A map can reasonably be thought of as a codification of our knowledge and experience of a landscape. The map helps us find our way around that landscape, it helps us generalise about it (a mountainous area here, an area of dense population there) and it can be used to help us understand, in a highly simplified way, some of the basic relationships that exist within the landscape (the relationship between the communication network and the settlement pattern for example). The map is also a form of communication in which the discoveries and experiences of the map-maker are put together in such a way that a person can learn much about a landscape even though he has never been there. As soon as we look at a map we generate certain expectations in our own minds about what the landscape looks like. We may be wrong, of course, but that is because we are unable to interpret the map correctly.

We can make exactly the same observations about theory. The theoretician will try to construct a theory which will help us find our way around among a complicated set of relationships. The theory will also generalise and it will also help us understand some of the basic relationships which exist between phenomena. A theory is also subject to misinterpretation unless we are very careful.

It is important to note one other point. A map does not portray everything. Nobody would expect the map-maker to record every detail in the landscape and nobody would criticise the map-maker for being selective (although he might be criticised for selecting the wrong things or being inconsistent in his selection). In the same way it would be invidious to criticise the theoretician for not being able to capture the total complexity of reality in his theory. Those geographers who have been excessively critical of theory for this reason would do well to consider how valid that sort of criticism would also be of the map. Maps and theories are of necessity selective portrayals and generalisations of a much richer and more complex reality. Without a map or a theory, however, it can prove very difficult indeed finding one's way around. It is all too easy to get lost in too much richness or complexity, and theories and maps help us navigate through very complicated terrain with much greater ease.

Both maps and theories, then, function as:

1 efficient storage devices for information collected over many years by many different people;
2 general descriptions of what a certain area of 'reality' looks like;
3 a basis for generating expectations about what will happen if we go into a certain area – more specifically we may use the map and the theory to deal with applied problems such as navigating (in the case of the map) or predicting (with the aid of a theory);
4 a basis for thinking about more complicated relationships. These more complicated relationships may be 'higher order' relationships such as some of the generalisations suggested by looking at map patterns, or they may simply be of the sort in which we use the map or the theory as a base from which to explore a given territory for more intricate variation.

HOW CAN WE BUILD THEORY?

It is useful to pursue the map analogy. To construct a map we must consistently follow some set of rules. These rules can differ depending upon the kind of map we have in mind. The rules we follow for constructing a dot map are different from those followed in constructing a choropleth map, and these in turn are different from those used to construct an isopleth map. All of these are different from the rules used in constructing an ordnance survey map at 6″ to the mile and the rules for constructing ordnance survey maps will change according to the scale of the map. So we can expect theory construction to follow different rules depending upon the kind of theory we want to construct. In fact there are as many different types of theory as there are types of map and each kind of theory has its own peculiar rules of construction. An early mistake of theoretical geographers was to think of theory building as a far more monolithic operation than it really is. There is not space here to consider all these different kinds of theory, but it is instructive to consider, as a starting point, that particular kind of theory which we call a scientific theory.

A scientific theory is a theory which is built up in a certain way. To start with we impose on it the condition that it must be internally consistent. It is also usual for a scientific theory to be built up by the deduction of a large number of statements from a few primitive statements. The similarity to map construction of a certain type is fairly obvious. The surveyor will seek to make the positioning of objects with respect to each other consistent (in terms of distances and angles) and he will also build up a total picture on the basis of deductions from a few simple statements. For example, only one base line is necessary for a trigonometric survey of the whole of the British Isles – after the observation of angles all other lengths can be calculated from the laws of trigonometry. By deductive laws of inference the theoretician will likewise be able to deduce how all kinds of phenomena will relate to each other given a few basic relationships.

The biggest problem in scientific theory, however, lies in what is known as the 'verification–falsification' problem. How can we tell whether a theory is true of false? We know that the theory is true in the sense that it is internally consistent, but how can we tell if it is truly representative of the landscape we are attempting to chart? Here the surveyor has a distinct advantage, for he is all the time working very closely with the reality he is seeking to represent. Most scientific theorists insist that at least some of the statements contained in a theoretical structure must be closely attached to real world observation. Herein lies the significance of hypothesis testing, for on the basis of the theory we can set up hypotheses which, by the application of suitable testing procedures, can be checked against the reality the theory is supposed to apply to. If repeated testing shows these hypotheses to be always true (or if the occasions when they are not found true can reasonably be regarded as aberrations) then we often speak of the theory as a 'true' theory. There are many theories in the natural sciences which are true in this sense. There are not too many such theories in the social sciences; but in both the natural and social sciences there is considerable argument as to whether these rules for verification are entirely appropriate. In fact there is no general agreement as to what is meant by a 'true' theory. To demonstrate some of the problems involved it is useful to contrast the empirical kind of scientific theory in which the hypotheses are regarded as certainly true with the probabilistic and normative theories.

A probabilistic theory will be similar to the kind of theory we have been examining in that it must be consistent and coherent and the statements made in it must be linked together in some logically water-tight manner. But typically the hypotheses in a probabilistic theory have the form '*x* will probably occur' or, more specifically, that there is 'a *p* per cent chance of *x* occurring'. At first sight it may seem difficult to liken this kind of theory to a map. But there are many statements on a map which have this form. Consider a map showing where the watercourses are. After a very dry summer we may come to a point recorded on the map as a stream crossing only to find that there is no stream running. The bournes along the chalk downs sometimes run and they sometimes don't. So there are many features on an ordinary map to which we may attach a certain chance as to whether they are there or not at any one particular time. A much better analogy, however, would be the kind of map on which we would record 'areas subject to earthquake damage' or 'areas subject to hurricanes and typhoons'. If we go to the areas marked on the map we will not necessarily experience an earthquake or a typhoon, and we would not say the map was wrong because we did not have these experiences when we went to such places. These maps tell us that there is a greater probability of having such an experience in some areas than there is in others. Probabilistic theories are of this type and it is, consequently, rather difficult to check them against reality without collecting a lot of information to determine what the probabilities are. There are quite a few probabilistic theories now in use in both physical and human geography. In human geography, for example, we make statements such as 'the further apart people live the less likely they are to communicate with each other'. We can accept a statement of this type and not be surprised if some people who live very far away from each other do communicate with each other in the same way that we can accept the map of earthquake susceptibility without being too surprised if an area of very low probability (such as England) occasionally gets an earthquake.

A normative theory should be logically correct in the sense that all of its statements should be consistent with each other. But the basis for a normative theory does not lie so much in the reality we are seeking to understand as in our own imagination. In normative location theory, we set up certain goals or objectives (for example, we assume that everyone is trying to maximise their profits or we assume that the location pattern is going to be the most efficient one possible) and then we determine what the landscape will look like under these conditions. Weber, Lösch, von Thünen, and most of the other location theorists did just this. It is rather like designing a completely fictitious map. The map looks consistent and coherent but what relationship do fictitious maps of this sort have to the real world? The answer to this can best be sought by considering how such fictitious maps may be used.

Consider a map put out by the local planning office. There are some features on the map that you will recognise. But there are others which you will not because they are not yet built. We do not criticise such maps when we look at them as 'wrong' because the features they portray are not there in reality. The planner has imagined what reality will look like if his plan comes true. But there are certain limits to what we will accept from the planner. If the plan contained only houses and streets, and no parks, schools, shops or industry, we would quickly say the plan was unrealistic. What we are doing here is qualifying our imagination by our understanding of what is reasonable or unreasonable.

Let us take the analogy one stage further. Suppose now we are looking at the map of a completely new town – Milton Keynes for example. We cannot recognise anything at all in the existing landscape and so the plan has no relationship to existing reality. Yet we do not dismiss the plan out of hand as 'unrealistic' (although we may find grounds later on for doing so because it does not conform to our notions as to what a town should be like). In the same way that we would not dismiss such a plan as 'untrue' because it did not represent something which exists, so we would be foolish to dismiss normative theories because they describe things which do not exist. In fact some normative theories come close to describing events realistically. This happens when the conditions we assume in the theory are nearly met in a real-life situation. If there is strong competition for land in a city, for example, we might find the von Thünen model coming close to replicating what actually happens. In this case we can say that the normative theory has empirical relevance.

Normative theories are also useful to us in the same way that the planner's maps are – they provide us with a way of thinking about improvements in the future. Geographers have long been interested in problems of planning – it is in fact one of the main applications of their skills. It follows from this that geographers are bound to be interested in normative theory because this kind of theory is very useful for planning efficient patterns of land use, efficient lay-outs for transportation networks, and so on.

We have many different maps for many different purposes. It is useful to think about theories in the same way. When we evaluate the utility of a map or a theory we have to consider the purpose for which the map or theory is constructed. If we want to navigate from one place to another we would never use the planner's future map and we would likewise be foolish to use a normative theory to predict what will happen. If we want to plan for the future, or improve our efficiency, then the planner's future map and the theoretician's normative theory become indispensable. Geographers have not always recognised these differences – in the 1960s we wasted a lot of time trying to test essentially normative theories against a reality which obviously was not designed in a normative way. This was a mistake and we are still suffering from its consequences. Furthermore, it should be clear that there is no unique set of rules for building a theory beyond the very general rule that it should be internally consistent and coherent and that it should be built up according to certain rules of logic. But within these general constraints (and the cartographic analogy should be obvious here) it is possible to build all kinds of theories in all kinds of different ways for all kinds of different purposes.

HOW CAN WE TEACH THEORIES?

The art of interpreting and using maps is not easily acquired. It is a long, painstaking process in which the student (usually from a very early age) begins to abstract from his environment and to develop certain cognitive maps of it. The geography teacher is specifically concerned with developing this skill in such a way that the student can relate easily from the map to the reality he is seeking to understand.

The process is relatively simple with ordnance survey maps in that a physical exploration of a landscape can go hand in hand with the development of map-reading skills. It is more complicated when it comes to getting people to understand choropleth or isopleth maps and the various other kinds of 'representational' map in which we make heavy use of abstract symbols to say something about the characteristics of various parts of the country or of the world. It is not too difficult to have experience of contours, but it is rather more difficult to get direct experience of isopleths of population density on a world-wide scale. There are certain kinds of maps which we can never relate to 'reality' in any direct experiential sense. Part of the art of teaching cartography is, in fact, to get students to the point where they can 'read' a map and understand its implications *without* having to refer back to some direct map-reality experience.

The same sort of process has to go on in teaching theory. It is just as laborious and just as difficult. Teaching theory is not easy and we have scarcely understood many of the educational difficulties involved. Part of the problem here is, of course, that theories have been developed mainly by academic geographers working in the universities and, naturally enough, these geographers have little knowledge of the problems of the school teacher or the educationalist. It has always seemed to me to be the role of the educational theorist and the teaching-college geographer to grapple with this problem in all of its complexity. Unfortunately there has been some resistance among these groups to the notion of theoretical geography and we have not, therefore, progressed as much as we might.

Perhaps the safest place to start with the teaching of theory is to concentrate on those kinds of statement contained in theory which a student can gain direct experience of. Consider the statement that 'the further apart people are the less likely they are to communicate with each other'. We can gain experience of this by getting pupils to record who they have communicated with that day and who their parents have communicated with and plot the results (remember this is a probabilistic statement). The inverse distance law is also a good one to begin with. Find out how far the children travel to get to school, or how far their parents travel to go to work or to shop for different kinds of goods. In this way statements contained in theories will begin to make sense.

It is also important to get the pupil to think in terms of logical connections. If, for example, people travel on average half a mile to buy their groceries but they travel four miles to buy clothes, how far apart in a city would you expect to find clothes stores as compared with grocery stores? When you do this kind of thing you are beginning to use a theoretical style of thought to generate expectations. You would expect grocery stores to be scattered and not so far apart as you would expect clothing stores. Is this in fact the case? It should be possible to go out into a city and find out. If it is not the case, then why not? In the same way it should be possible to give a student a grasp of the intuitive sense of the von Thünen land use theory. This theory predicts that under conditions of strict competition (and overall economic efficiency) we will find that the nearer we get to the centre of a city-the higher will be the density of population (in residential areas), the greater will be the cost of land per acre, the higher the buildings will tend to be (because by building upwards you save land costs), and the more we will find 'space-intensive' land uses and the less we will find 'space-extensive' land uses. These predictions can easily be checked and the empirical relevance (though not the truth) of the von Thünen theory can quickly be demonstrated (just try looking for space-extensive uses, such as petrol stations, in the centre of any large city!) Ultimately, of course, we have to wean the student away from a condition in which he always seeks to relate a theoretical statement to some immediate perceptual experience and get the student to understand the theoretical structures themselves (in much the same way that we hope the student will understand the map directly and not always need to refer back to perceptual experience).

The problems of teaching geographic theory are not likely to be resolved easily, but they are much the same as those involved in teaching an understanding of the map. With careful thought they are likewise not impossible of effective resolution.

CAN THEORY HELP US UNDERSTAND BETTER WHAT GEOGRAPHY IS ABOUT?

If a theory is a codification of experience and geographical theory is a codification of the geographical experience, then we can expect that a careful assessment of the nature of geographical theory will provide us with many insights concerning the nature of geography. As I remarked in the introduction to this essay, however, we have not yet developed geographical theory to a sufficient extent for it to capture many important aspects of the geographical experience. It is therefore too early to speak with any certainty; but there are some interesting possibilities.

In human geography, for example, many of the theories developed have a similar structure. They attempt to relate a set of social processes to a spatial form. In location theory, for example, the usual structure is to attempt to derive what the spatial form ought to be given certain assumptions about the nature of the social process (e.g. optimising behaviour on the part of individuals). These are normative theories, of course. The probabilistic theories have a similar kind of structure to them. But it is also possible to think in the other direction. We can show how a particular spatial form (the physical lay-out of a city or the shape of a surface) can affect social processes (such as communication, transport flows, movements in the population, and the like). The gradual exploration of this notion of the interaction between spatial form and social process as a focus for geographic thought has resulted in the emergence of some fascinating ideas. It is clear, for example, that space can be manipulated to accomplish some social purpose – the very spatial lay-out of a classroom has much to say about the nature of the teacher-student relationship (seminars always go better around circular or octagonal tables, preferably in a room which is small enough so that no one can escape from direct interaction). The spatial lay-out of a city has much to say about the class structure in a society and often spatial segregation replaces social controls over social mobility. In the United States and Britain the tacit rules of social class distinction are breaking down and being replaced by a society which manages to accomplish much the same thing by a pattern of unequal spatial segregation (a process which educational policy has to battle with as the Plowden report has recently indicated). The relationship between social process and spatial form provides one fascinating focus for geographic thought. The fact that we think about this kind of thing very explicitly now is a tribute to the provocativeness of theoretical thinking.

It would be erroneous to suppose, however, that this is the only focus for geographic thought. Some of the work which has recently developed in the 'cognitive-behavioural' approach to geography is directing our attention to another focus. The central concept of this approach is what is called the 'cognitive map' or 'mental map' in which we seek to discover how people are structuring their knowledge of their physical and spatial environment. If we can find this out we are then in a much better position to understand how it is that people behave in their environment in the way that they do. This question is obviously very much intertwined with the sorts of questions which psychologists typically ask. Its geographical significance comes, however, when we seek to apply this understanding to explaining how it is that certain geographical patterns arise. Again, I come back to the notion that geography is essentially concerned with understanding how a particular landscape pattern comes about, but in order to answer this question we need a good deal of information on how people reach decisions about where to put roads, railways, houses, industrial plant, and so on. It is therefore hardly surprising to find that an important focus for geographical work is what has been called 'the decision process in its spatial context'.

Preliminary work on the nature of 'cognitive maps' indicates, however, that these maps are not formed independently of the environment in which the decision-maker gains his experience. In other words, man is influenced by his natural, social, and cultural environment, and the cognitive map he develops as a result affects the decisions which in turn mould that environment into something different. This process is extremely important in learning, and it has important implications. There can be no question that the cognitive maps of children raised exclusively in an inner city area are substantially different from those of children raised exclusively in rural areas. The man-environment relation as it enters into the learning process is at the very heart of our own cultural dynamic. Here, again, is a fascinating focus for geographic thinking and one that seems bound to grow and develop in the future.

Thinking theoretically about geography has also done much to clarify our relationships to other disciplines. We are all interdisciplinarians now, to some degree or other, but geography has a long tradition of attempting to synthesise the thinking of other disciplines in terms of space or place. Our theory does not deny this role but it does give it a particular flavour. We are not synthesisers of knowledge in all of its complexity, but we do quite consciously take ideas and concepts and theories from other disciplines and seek to examine their spatial or regional implications. In this sense, most of the theory which we have, derives from the physical, social, or biological sciences. It is given its distinctive flavour by the way in which we use it to understand spaces and places, and the way in which we see particular spatial forms or particular local environments modifying the basic forces which other disciplines study.

This role places quite a burden on us. It means that we really have to strive hard to understand psychology, economics, sociology, physics, chemistry, and biology, and the sheer necessity for specialisation is bound to force many of us to concentrate on just one aspect of this vast programme. We can anticipate a new breed of geographers each with a part training in some other discipline and each specialising in one aspect of our grand theoretical design. There can be no question that geography as a discipline always has had pretentions to grandeur in synthesis. The trouble is that it has never really developed the tools to bring this about. Now, however, there are signs that we are tooling up in the right way. And one of these signs is a growing awareness that theory has much to offer us, both in the way of efficient understanding and in the way of provoking us to new dimensions of thinking about some very old and intriguing geographical problems.

References

(The following are selected mainly for their theoretical content, but I have also included some references which review recent developments in geography.)

R. Ambler, J. Adams and P. Gould, (1971) *Spatial organization: the geographer's view of the world*, Prentice-Hall.

R. J. Chorley and P. Haggett (eds.), (1967) *Models in geography*, Methuen.

R. U. Cooke and J. H. Johnson (eds.), (1969) *Trends in geography*, Pergamon.

R. Downs and D. Stea, (forthcoming) *Cognitive mapping: images of spatial environments*, Aldine.

P. Haggett, (1965) *Locational analysis in human geography*, Edward Arnold.

D. Harvey, (1969) *Explanation in geography*, Edward Arnold.

R. L. Morrill, (1969) *The spatial organization of society*, Wadsworth.

E. J. Taaffe (ed.), (1969) *Geography*, Prentice-Hall.

S. Toulmin, (1960) *The philosophy of science*, Harper Torchbooks.

4 Objectives for the teacher

TREVOR BENNETTS

The teaching of geography in schools is rapidly changing in character, and the likelihood is that it will change even more in the near future. We are in the midst of secondary school reorganisation, we are in a period of intensive reappraisal of the curriculum and we see the parent discipline moving rapidly towards new horizons. The combination can be very stimulating, but it can also be extremely confusing. The individual teacher may be disturbed by the pace of change, by the problem of getting help and even by uncertainty about the purpose of it all. Whilst there has been considerable discussion about subject matter and teaching methods, there has been comparatively little discussion in the current literature about the educational aims involved in teaching geography in schools.

Before considering some aims that may be appropriate for geography today, it is worthwhile first considering why we should be concerned with educational aims and useful ways of describing them. Professor R. S. Peters has pointed out that 'to ask questions about aims in education is . . . a way of getting people to get clear about and focus their attention on what is worth while achieving' (Peters 1966). When we select our aims for a school curriculum we are making value judgments. Our current failure to describe and analyse our aims adequately exposes us to a number of risks:

1 That we may be unaware of the range of possible educational aims, even within the framework of our own subject, and therefore unknowingly restrict the opportunities we make available to our students;
2 That we have no sound base from which to design a curriculum, for without clear objectives we have no valid criteria by which to select subject matter and teaching methods;
3 That we have no rational way of evaluating our students' achievements, for until we specify our objectives we cannot set about designing relevant tests.

4 That we confuse the syllabus content with educational objectives.

The last of these is more prevalent today than we like to admit. Perhaps one reason why there has been so little discussion of aims is that we have not learned how to describe them in a helpful manner, and this has discouraged us from thinking much about them. Statements of aims are often vague, and either seem completely divorced from what takes place in the classroom or give the impression of being superficial attempts to justify existing practices. It may help if we recognise that statements about aims can serve different purposes:

1 They may indicate the direction in which we wish to move. This requires a general statement of aims that provides a broad guideline or a necessary point of reference for curriculum planning (e.g. students should learn to think like geographers).
2 They may provide a more specific guide that helps us to select appropriate lesson content and teaching methods (e.g. students should be introduced to the concept of time-distance and its relevance for commuting).
3 They may describe the changes in behaviour – in terms of knowledge, understanding, attitudes, skills, etc. – that we expect as a result of the educational activities planned, and thus provide a detailed checklist against which we can evaluate progress (e.g. given a suitable base map for a city and information on travel time at peak hours, students should be able to carry out a simple map transformation, and examine the relevance of the map produced to the pattern of suburban development).

Let us consider the problem of identifying the general goals that geography teachers are concerned with. This at least would provide an indication of the range of our interests and would make a useful starting point for analysis. Geographers have in fact proposed a great variety of aims, and have made many claims for their subject, and we could start by trying to divide these into groups. One way is to recognise a difference in emphasis between those statements that focus on the students, those that focus on the needs of society, and those that focus on the parent discipline. In the first two cases the subject is regarded as a suitable medium for educational objectives that are derived from sources outside the discipline itself; in the third case the parent discipline is regarded as the source of the educational objectives.

STUDENT-CENTRED AIMS

We can group here all those statements of aims that emphasise the educational outcomes as providing something that is personally useful or satisfying to the student. Those that have been described as being of direct utility have usually been related to employment, leisure and the better understanding of current affairs. If we disregard entry qualifications, most of the geography taught in schools has little direct relevance to employment, and as we do not usually know what occupations our students will take up, it is hard to see how this could be otherwise (Graves 1971). The aims associated with the student's enjoyment of leisure and understanding of current affairs have often been vaguely expressed, and appear to have had little influence on school curricula. If we want to make some contribution to such aims, it probably helps if we specify the aims more clearly and then plan our work accordingly. When we take a group of students for fieldwork in the Lake District, do we plan to provide opportunities for the students to be introduced to the pleasures of fell walking, or is this just a possible spin-off effect, with which we are not overmuch concerned? It is certainly not an inevitable spin-off, as many a student with aching limbs and blistered feet would testify. Do we try to show the relevance of geography to the understanding of particular news items, or do we simply assume that a study of geography must lead to the collection of a vast store of relevant information that will inevitably shed light on current affairs?

Most of the student-centred aims relate to the acquisition of skills, particularly cognitive skills. This is very important, for we are surely concerned with skills that we believe are of value and have application outside the classroom. But again we should spell out clearly the skills we are aiming at. We must beware of thinking in terms of general abilities (Hirst 1965; Bloom 1956). It is one thing to write of the integrative role of regional geography, another thing to assume that the experience of studying regional geography teaches the student to handle complex situations, integrate information, maintain a total view, analyse in a rational manner and make balanced judgments. If we pitch our claims at a more realistic level, we might achieve more. The skills that are acquired will be limited by what we have to offer within the subject.

SOCIETY-CENTRED AIMS

Most attempts to describe social aims in geography have focused on the idea of citizenship, and the contribution geography can make to our understanding of the functioning of a community and the close links between different communities. Although most statements emphasise cognitive aims, others involve attitudes. In particular, it has been claimed that a study of geography can further a sense of responsibility towards one's own community and sympathy towards others. But thinking about citizenship in 'them-and-us' terms is not always helpful. The spatial scale at which we identify responsibilities and attitudes is relevant. The 'us' part can be interpreted in local, regional, national, and even world terms, and these can be in fierce conflict. Assuming that our teaching can influence such attitudes, it is conceivable that we might, unwittingly, strengthen rather than weaken the 'them-and-us' view.

The belief that we do influence social attitudes by studying geography is anyway based more on faith than on serious evaluation. We have been content to state our social aims at a high level of generality and have usually avoided the difficult task of translating these aims into behavioural objectives. Phrases such as 'loyalty to place' and 'world citizenship' are of little value unless we specify more fully what we mean by them. Once again we need to be very much clearer about the objectives we are after, and we need to investigate carefully how these can be achieved. We know very little about the type of learning experiences required to bring about changes in attitudes, and the ethical implications are so important that, if aims of this type are to be given a high priority, they should be made explicit.

It is perhaps not surprising that in recent years geographers have tended to pay less lip service to vague notions about citizenship, and more attention to human problems that research geographers study. This approach has a number of attractions:

Motivation Television has made many children more aware of regional, national and international problems. They may recognise that some of these problems are relevant to their own lives and that, in any case, such problems are intrinsically interesting.

Teaching methods Focusing on specific problem-orientated themes that are newsworthy encourages an inquiry-mode of teaching. At the same time it calls for careful selection of data and methods, and careful structuring of ideas.

Source materials The post-war period has seen an enormous growth in the importance of applied geography, and many geographers have acted as planning consultants or joined the planning profession. In making their contribution, geographers have produced a wealth of information and ideas that can be used in schools.

What are the human problems that geographers study? They are certainly extremely varied, but we can recognise a lively concern for:

1 The well being of the human population – the population explosion and the problems of feeding the world's rapidly growing population; contrasts in prosperity and opportunity revealed at various scales – developed and underdeveloped countries, regional growth and decay, rich and poor neighbourhoods; contrasts in economic and political power; conflicts between peoples – economic, political and racial tensions;
2 The quality of the environment – coping with harsh natural environments that are marginal for settlement; helping areas that are vulnerable to periodic disasters; improving inadequate man-created environments, such as those suffering from overcrowding, pollution and decay; protecting high-quality environments;
3 The environment interpreted in resource terms – the adequacy of resources to support the requirements of the population; pressure on resources, and problems associated with the development, waste, destruction and conservation of resources;
4 Alternative ways of using and organising space – optimum or most acceptable locations and distributions; conflicting land use demands; communication systems; the political organisation of space;
5 Technology and man's ability to improve or damage the environment – the value of 'resource converting' and 'space adjusting' techniques (Ackerman 1958); man's growing ability to pollute and destroy;
6 Change and the problems associated with it.

These are not narrow, academic problems but matters of great public concern. They are complex problems that require the attention of scholars from many disciplines, and are obviously suitable for integrated studies. But they could also form the themes for a course in geography. The general educational aim might then be stated in terms of introducing students to the sort of human problems that geographers study, to the methods of study that they use, and to the ideas that they have developed in their search for understanding. We are turning to the discipline as a possible source of educational objectives.

METHODS OF INQUIRY IN GEOGRAPHY

We may now begin to ask, rather more searchingly, what are the methods of inquiry that are most characteristic of the discipline? What sort of questions do we ask and what sort of answers are we looking for? How do we go about acquiring information and how do we evaluate the information we find? What techniques do we use to collect, measure and describe data, and how do we set about analysing it? Do these techniques involve skills that have wide applicability?

We must at this stage recognise the considerable differences between the regional viewpoint of geography and the more scientific viewpoints. It is the regional viewpoint that has the literary tradition, and the attempt to describe the personality of a place may well be a form of art. We must consider whether we are aiming at the students acquiring an appreciation of this art and having the opportunity to practise it themselves. It is certainly a formidable challenge. But the last ten years have seen a marked swing away from the regional viewpoint of geography and towards a more scientific approach. Can geographers now support the claim that their subject is a useful introduction to scientific method? Neither text books nor external examinations suggest that a scientific approach is widely practised in school geography. Although geography teachers have frequently been exhorted to adopt a scientific approach and make use of scientific methods, they have, until recently, been given little guidance as to what might be involved.

The geographer's interpretation of science was roughly as follows. The characteristic feature was the method, which consisted first of assembling all the relevant information and then analysing it. Whenever possible, information should be obtained by direct observation, and a high value was placed on accuracy and detail. Analysis was seen mainly in terms of mapping the data and seeking correlations, but the reality we studied was so complex that we would often have to be content with detailed and accurate description rather than explanation. Thus accuracy and detail almost became ends in themselves. Geographers had accepted a stunted form of the inductive model of science. The model did not encourage us to question what information was relevant, and it supported our simple faith in the 'primacy of facts' and the 'evidence of the senses' (Medawar 1969).

More recently, geographers have gained a deeper understanding of what is involved in a scientific approach (Ackerman 1963, Davies 1966, Campbell and Wood 1969, Harvey 1969) and we should be more aware of some of those characteristics of science that we have neglected:

1 Science is problem-orientated, and scientific inquiry begins with questions, with the recognition of unsolved problems to be investigated. The questions that we ask are likely to be related to the ideas that most interest us, and therefore the questions are likely to be within the framework provided by the conceptual structure of our discipline.
2 Science involves a search for general explanations, and focuses our attention on regularities and patterns.
3 A scientific mode of inquiry involves the formulation and testing of hypotheses, and the construction of a body of theory. Careful observation and description do not in themselves produce scientific knowledge. This form of knowledge 'is not arrived at by applying some inductive inference procedure to antecedently collected data, but rather . . . by inventing hypotheses and tentative answers to a problem under study, and then subjecting these to empirical test' (Hempel 1966). It follows that hypotheses must be formulated in a way that makes testing possible. It also follows that intuition and imagination play an important part in scientific discovery.

If school geography is to be a useful introduction to scientific method, we must set out to stimulate our students to ask searching questions, we must teach them appropriate methods of analysing the various types of data that we handle, and we must encourage them to formulate hypotheses and then to test them rigorously. The evaluation process is vitally important. Students will not necessarily have an understanding of the scientific mode of inquiry if they are merely instructed how to carry out a number of techniques of analysis. They need to be aware of the purpose of the inquiry and the limitations of the methods used and the conclusions arrived at. This is particularly relevant to the increased application of mathematical techniques in school geography. Mathematics provides means by which geographers can produce more precise descriptions and clearer hypothetical statements, and means of evaluating those statements. The techniques are means to an end, and will only be of value if students understand why they are being used, and what they can and cannot achieve. We need to know which techniques can be grasped by students of a particular age, experience and ability, and the best means of introducing these techniques. This will require careful planning, including cooperation with mathematics colleagues, and empirical testing in the classroom. The prospects are exciting, but there is a lot of work to be done before we can claim that school geography is contributing much to the numeracy of our students. Nevertheless, if we are aiming to show students how geographers investigate certain types of problems, we can hardly omit mathemetics, and we should therefore recognise that we can contribute to our students' grasp of mathematical skills.

The scientific mode of inquiry also has relevance for fieldwork. Work in the field can serve various purposes and take various forms, but as teachers become more interested in a scientific approach the guided tour is likely to become less prominent, and, at least in part, to be replaced by the purposeful collection of data to test general ideas that the students are investigating (Everson 1969). The work in the field may also be used to identify new problems that lead to further investigations. In this way, the landscape is being used as a laboratory, and the students are engaged in the process of discovery and in the scientific pursuit of useful and valid generalisations.

Whereas we may think of a scientific approach, as described above, as a comparatively recent development in geography, we are likely to regard the use of maps and diagrams as highly traditional. Professor Balchin has recently suggested that one of the basic skills of the complete geographer is graphicacy, a skill which he equates with literacy and numeracy (Balchin 1970). Here again we must consider whether we are training students in skills that have application beyond the immediate tasks set in geography lessons. Do we convince our students of the value of using graphic means to describe and analyse data and to sort out ideas? We have perhaps tended to use maps and diagrams as a means of communicating information, and particularly as a means of summarising conclusions, rather than drawing attention to their value as analytical tools. In this respect we under-use Ordnance Survey maps and Land Utilisation maps. We expect our students to identify map symbols, to locate places by means of a grid reference, and to measure distances, directions and gradients. But when it comes to analysing location and distribution patterns, whether it be of relief, drainage, land-use, settlements or communications, we operate at a comparatively simple level and rely on the use of rather vague descriptive terms. Even worse, we encourage our students to see correlations that are more apparent than real, and we encourage them to believe that they can 'explain' locations and distributions from what is often totally inadequate information (Wallwork 1967). We might do better if we defined our objectives in terms of our students' understanding of the value and limitations of maps as sources of information, and the value and limitations of the analytical techniques we use.

One important class of diagrams that deserves fuller recognition in schools are the diagrams that describe relationships and ideas. Research geographers are adept at producing sophisticated flow diagrams to describe their conceptual models, and many of us are becoming more aware of the value of diagrams as an aid to thinking. We resort to drawing little boxes and lines as much to clarify our own minds as to communicate our ideas to others. This form of graphicacy is a skill of wide applicability and deserves more attention than it has so far received.

GEOGRAPHICAL CONCEPTS

I have left until last the most important reason for regarding a discipline as a source of educational objectives, and this is that a discipline is productive of valuable ideas that further our understanding of reality. Disciplines are highly selective in what they study. The ideas that they develop and the methods of inquiry that they employ merely enable them to interpret some aspects of reality. If we wish to show our students what geography has to offer, in terms of the type of understanding it has achieved, we must identify the organising concepts and principles that summarise geographers' current thinking. Bruner has emphasised that these basic ideas are fundamental to the process of learning. 'The teaching and learning of structure, rather than simply the mastery of facts and techniques, is at the centre of the classic problem of transfer. . . . If earlier learning is to render later learning easier, it must do so by providing a "general picture" in terms of which the relations between things encountered earlier and later are made as clear as possible' (Bruner 1960). However, he also notes that 'much too little is known about how to teach fundamental structure effectively or how to provide learning conditions that foster it'.

It would help if we could describe the conceptual structure of geography. Where theory is well developed, knowledge is more fully integrated and it is easier to identify the key concepts, but geography has been notably weak in the development of theory. The attempts to outline different viewpoints in geography (Pattison 1964, Haggett 1965, Ackerman 1965, Harvey 1969) suggest that we might try to describe several structures and clarify what each has to offer. The danger in a period of rapid change is that we describe structures that are already out of date.

What is clear is that the spatial viewpoint has emerged as the main focus of geographical research, and it has been highly productive of general ideas. Use has been made of concepts derived from geometry and from the behavioural sciences, and these have been developed in the attempt to describe spatial patterns and to identify the processes that produce these patterns and produce change in space. Although geographers are interested in a large number of activities associated with man's use of earth space – ranging from work, leisure, settlement and communications to social, economic and political organisation – spatial concepts have been developed that have relevance across a wide field of interest. Whatever the activity, ideas of relative location, spatial distribution, spatial interaction, distance, nodality, accessibility, network, interaction field and spatial system are likely to be of value, and the list can easily be added to. Similarly we may think of environment, resource and conservation as high-level concepts with wide applicability. Geographers may now place less emphasis on man-land relationships, but they have not lost their interest in the environment. The decline in interest in 'natural environment' is more than balanced by the growth of interest in what has been described as 'behavioural environment' (Kirk 1963). Perhaps one of the most significant developments has been the attempt to combine the man-environment and spatial viewpoints in a systems framework (Berry 1964). The interpretation of nodal regions as open systems is another example of the influence of systems analysis on thinking within the discipline. But this is looking at regions from the spatial viewpoint. The traditional regional viewpoint, with its emphasis on the unique character, or personality, of places, has not been particularly productive of general ideas.

I have done no more here than suggest a limited number of concepts that are particularly important in geographical thinking. If our aim is to further our students' understanding of geography, such concepts are highly relevant. But the teacher who is writing a syllabus must translate general aims into specific objectives. He may be concerned with themes such as settlement patterns, industrial location, agriculture or problems of underdevelopment. Understanding will involve not merely the high-level concepts that bridge the themes, but also lower-level concepts that have narrower applicability. If the teacher rates general ideas higher than factual detail, he must set about specifying what these ideas are and he will then be in a position to select relevant lesson content and teaching methods. Let me suggest a number of principles that might be appropriate for the study of agricultural geography in the junior part of a secondary school:

1 Farming is the production of food and materials by the growing of crops and management of animals. It is therefore dependent upon biological processes.
2 The crops and animals have their own inherent characteristics – they have particular requirements and their products have particular qualities.
3 Plant growth requires warmth, moisture, mineral nutrients (derived from the soil) and space. Animals also have physical requirements including adequate water, fodder and healthy living conditions. The potential output of a farm is therefore strongly affected by environmental conditions, such as weather, soil and slope.
4 The variable character of weather introduces an element of uncertainty into farming.
5 The soil is not an inexhaustible resource.
6 Many farming practices have been devised to enable the farmer to take better advantage of weather conditions and to maintain or even improve soil fertility.
7 The profit made by a farmer depends on the price he obtains for his products and the cost of producing them.
8 The farmer contributes various inputs to his enterprise – e.g. skill, labour, machinery, fertilisers, seed and animals – all of which aid production but at the same time contribute to costs.
9 Farming can be intensive (a high level of inputs and outputs per hectare) or extensive (a low level of inputs and outputs per hectare). The former is often practised where land is expensive and the latter where land is cheap.
10 The functioning of a farm is influenced by its accessibility to external sources and markets, and by the accessibility of its various parts.
11 The pattern of accessibility within a farm is mainly a product of the size and shape of the farm, the location of the farmstead, the route network, and the land-use pattern.
12 The more accessible land tends to be farmed more intensively than the less accessible.

Most geography teachers would probably wish to modify such a list. They might question the value of some of the generalisations and they would almost certainly point out omissions. Deciding on educational objectives involves value judgments. What is important is that we try to specify what these values are. By this means we can clarify our own views and stimulate useful discussion.

This approach can be extended to the whole of the syllabus. We must clarify our aims if we are to plan educational programmes in a rational manner, and we must give careful thought to the task of translating general aims into much more specific objectives. The parent discipline, being productive of useful ideas and useful methods of inquiry, is a valuable source of educational objectives. It is vital that we measure its contribution in these terms and not in terms of some undefined set of basic facts.

References

A. E. Ackerman, (1958) *Geography as a fundamental research discipline*, Research Paper no. 53, University of Chicago.

(1963) 'Where is a research frontier?' AAAG, vol. 53, no. 4.

(1965) Chairman, *The science of geography*, Report of the *ad hoc* committee on geography, Earth Science Division, National Academy of Sciences, National Research Council, publication 1277.

W. G. V. Balchin, (1970) *Geography: an outline for intending students*, Routledge.

B. J. L. Berry, (1964) 'Approaches to regional analysis: a synthesis', AAAG, vol. 54, no. 1.

B. S. Bloom (ed.), (1956) *Taxonomy of educational objectives: Handbook 1 – The cognitive domain*, Longmans.

J. S. Bruner, (1960) *The process of education*, Vintage Books.

W. J. Campbell and P. A. Wood, (1969) 'Quantification and the development of theory in human geography' in R. U. Cooke and J. H. Johnson (eds.) *Trends in geography*, Pergamon.

W. K. D. Davies, (1966) 'Theory, science and geography', *Tijdschrift voor Economische en Sociale Geografie* 57, reprinted in P. J. Ambrose (ed.) *Analytical human geography*, Longmans.

J. Everson, (1969) 'Some aspects of teaching geography through fieldwork', *Geography*, vol. 54, part 1.

N. J. Graves, (1971) 'Problems in the specification of the objectives of geo-

graphical education', unpublished paper presented at the symposium on Geography in Education, IBG Conference, January 1971.
P. Haggett, (1965) *Locational analysis in human geography*, Edward Arnold.
D. Harvey, (1969) *Explanation in geography*, Edward Arnold.
C. G. Hempel, (1966) *The philosophy of natural science*, Prentice-Hall.
P. H. Hirst, (1965) 'Liberal education and the nature of knowledge' in R. D. Archambault (ed.) *Philosophical analysis and education*, Routledge.
W. Kirk, (1963) 'Problems of geography', *Geography*, vol. 48, part 4.
P. Medawar, (1969) *Induction and intuition in scientific thought*, Methuen.
W. D. Pattison, (1964) 'The four traditions of geography', *Journal of Geography*, vol. 63, no. 5.
R. S. Peters, (1966) *Ethics and education*, Allen & Unwin.
K. L. Wallwork, (1967) 'Map interpretation and industrial location: the example of alkali manufacture in Lancastria', *Geography*, vol. 52, part 2.

5 Geography in the integrated curriculum

MICHAEL NAISH

'Geography now holds an undisputed place in the curriculum of virtually every secondary school in Britain.' These are the opening words of the 1967 edition of the IAAM book *The teaching of geography in secondary schools*, and those geographers who felt secure in this assumption, together with those who had helped towards the establishment of such a position, may have felt severe misgivings as the idea of integrating subjects by such means as inter-disciplinary enquiry began to take root. G. B. G. Bull expressed the feelings of many when he wrote 'The pilgrim's progress of the geography teacher in quest of due appreciation of his subject's educational value is from time to time troubled by the emergence from roadside undergrowth of phantoms tempting him to stray from the upward and uphill path. . . . Lately a new seducer has emerged, in the shape of Inter-Disciplinary Enquiry or the Humanities programme centred around topics or areas of enquiry' (Bull 1968). There may well be misgivings about the possibility of geography losing its identity in what might at first sight appear to be the amorphous non-discipline of integrated studies.

There is no doubt that geographers, together with other subject specialists, are faced with problems in this period of experimentation with the school curriculum. The problems are concerned with the future role of geography in schools, both in the context of the integrated curriculum and also in that of the rapid developments taking place within the subject. The two contexts are very much interconnected since in most of the recently published ideas about integration, geography is included in the humanities, while in much of the writing about methodological developments within the subject, the increasingly scientific nature of geography is stressed (Naish 1970). The equivocal position of geography between the arts and the sciences may be considered by some teachers to be ample justification for its importance as a synthesising discipline in any scheme for integration of subjects.

The purpose of this chapter is to consider the position of geography in the integrated curriculum, and the chapter falls into four main sections. The first is an attempt to define what is meant by 'the integrated curriculum'. Secondly, the theoretical basis of the integrated curriculum is considered, and this leads, thirdly, to a consideration of certain questions about such a curriculum. In the fourth and final section, the part to be played by the teacher of geography is discussed.

DEFINING THE INTEGRATED CURRICULUM

To answer the question 'What is the integrated curriculum?' we need to consider certain aspects of the historical development of school curricula which have their origin in the thinking of Rousseau and Dewey, and in particular in the idea of child-centred education. Early examples of integration based on core curricula were to be found in the USA in the late nineteenth century. D. Lawton (1969) describes such an attempt based on the core of history, literature and the Bible, with subordinate subjects such as science, mathematics and the fine arts fitting in where they could. He attributes the failure of this and other early schemes to faulty theory such as the idea of 'the unity of knowledge' or the belief, held by some at the time, that 'each child repeats the phases of development of his race'.

The second phase in the history of attempts at integration of subjects is that of the social studies movement of the late 1940s and early 1950s, which took place particularly in the new secondary modern schools created as a result of the 1944 Act. This again was linked with the theory that the curriculum should be based on a core, which in this case was commonly made up of history, geography and civics, known collectively as social studies (Cannon 1964). By basing the work on this core, teachers were, it was thought, enabled to work from the interests of the children, and slot in other subjects where they might seem appropriate. While committed and enthusiastic teachers achieved some success in this, most schemes failed for a variety of reasons which may be summarised as follows:

1. According to Lawton (1969), a basic cause of failure was to make one form of knowledge dominant over all others.
2. This was, as N. J. Graves (1968) points out, the period of rapid expansion in the universities and colleges, which produced an increasing number of subject specialists who were naturally more interested in teaching their specialisms.

3 The subject associations were opposed to the whole idea of integration. This is amply documented in the case of geography, by a pamphlet produced by the Education Committee of the Royal Geographical Society in 1950, which set out to defend geography against possible take-over, and by an article in the Society's Journal in 1955, which reaffirmed faith in geography as a discipline whose nature involved accurate observation and recording followed by analysis and interpretation.
4 There was a lack of materials and resources.
5 The desire to enter pupils for O-level subject examinations became dominant.

The most recent phase in the history of attempts to establish integrated studies in schools is connected with the rapidly expanding interest in curricular development, which began in the USA in the late 1950s after Russia's early successes in the space race, and which burgeoned in the United Kingdom in the second half of the last decade. Lawton (1969) sees three reasons for this important recent development. These are:

1 *Economic pressure*, producing a demand for scientists and technologists, the need for flexibility and adaptability, and for the better understanding of principles rather than the conning by rote of lists of facts.
2 *Ideological pressure*, as society changes from an élitist towards an egalitarian structure.
3 *Growth of rationality*, as transition takes place from a mainly religious society towards a more secular one.

In addition there is the pressure exerted by the need to consider the sort of planning required to cope with the raising of the school leaving age.

Integration is seen by some as one approach to curricular development, and it is possible to trace the growth of this approach through publications such as *Society and the young school leaver* (Schools Council 1967) and *Young lives at stake* (James 1968). The first describes attempts at integrating subjects in schools by studying various topics or themes from the points of view of several subjects, while the second recounts the work of the Curriculum Laboratory of Goldsmiths' College in the University of London from 1965. Both publications are very much concerned with the raising of the school leaving age, and indeed it was this same problem which originated the work of Stenhouse (1968) and his team in the Humanities Curriculum Project of the Schools Council.

What, then, is the present position? It is difficult to assess since there is not only a variety of approach to the integrated curriculum, but also confusion of terminology. However, it is possible to isolate four main trends:

1 Social studies. In some secondary modern and comprehensive schools the remnants of the post-war social studies schemes are still to be found, where geography is commonly combined with history and civics. There is also increasing interest in the inclusion of the social sciences in the curriculum, although at present the social sciences are a neglected field of study in schools (Lawton et al, 1971).
2 The pre-disciplinary approach found in primary schools, where the subjects are studied in embryo form (Geographical Association 1970).
3 The inter-disciplinary approach, where subjects are studied in parallel, so that interrelationships may be stressed, and differences preserved rather than blurred. The study may or may not be topic-based.
4 The multi-disciplinary approach, where material is 'fused' around topics or ideas in a project approach in an attempt to 'integrate', or in the Chambers (1965) definition, 'to make up as a whole'. The Schools Council Humanities Project is a good example of this, since although ideas, methods and concepts from a variety of subjects are of necessity employed, there is not necessarily any attempt to make clear the distinctions between these contributions.

This classification probably falls short of providing a full description of the sort of developments taking place in those schools which are experimenting with integration. To help fill in some detail, it is necessary to look briefly at actual examples of school experiments and of the various Schools Council Projects.

Three schools in the London area will serve to illustrate the variety of approach which is possible. Walworth School, in south-west London, runs a World Studies course in the first three years for all children, where geography, history and English are combined in order to consider the idea that 'the world can only be understood by the study of Man struggling to overcome the problems set him by his environment'. Readers can find a more detailed description of this scheme in the Bulletin of the University of London Institute of Education (Hogan *et al.* 1969). Thomas Bennett School, Crawley, has a humanities programme in the fourth and fifth years, which aims to integrate history, geography and the social sciences. The course works towards GCE and CSE Mode 3 examinations in each of these subjects at the end of the fifth year, catering for the whole ability range. At Sheredes School, Hoddesdon, an integrated humanities course involving English, history, geography and religious education is being built up with each intake. This was started with the first year of September 1969, with which the school opened. A syllabus has been designed for a five-year course, not only to provide scope for work in interrelated areas, but also to enable study to be made in depth within the specialist disciplines. The course will lead to GCE O-level or CSE Mode 3 examinations, and it is hoped that 20%–25% of the marks will be awarded for individual studies in the separate subjects. Themes for study range from 'How man survives' in the first year, to 'Urbanisation' in a study of 'The twentieth-century world' in the fourth and fifth years.

These three examples are inadequate to show the great variety of approach to integration which is possible. It is to be found in methods of working as well as in ways of organisation. Some schools may retain streamed classes while some may work unstreamed. Some continue to work in rows of desks with little movement or flexibility. Others abandon the traditional lay-out of the classroom, and make more use of 'work spaces'. Some schools may be fortunate enough to have the services of a well-stocked resources centre with classrooms as work spaces clustered around it. The future architecture of schools seems likely to be based on the need for this sort of arrangement. Some attempt class teaching, while others prefer to work in terms of group or individual assignments, requiring the children to work through a programme of tasks. The groups involved in this sort of study may be rigidly restricted in numbers and personnel, or may be quite flexible.

For some schools, team teaching is an essential concomitant of integrated studies, where the whole year-group will meet at the start of a new session of study to hear a lecture which is intended to incite interest and spark off ideas. The children are then broken up into groups for follow-up work. This may take the form of class teaching, or may be based on group or individual assignments. In some cases the children may be responsible for their own choice of follow-up studies, while in others they will have work assigned to them. The period of study is concluded by some kind of summing-up, which might include an exhibition of work (Shaplin *et al.* 1964). This form of approach has obvious incidental benefits such as the necessity for teachers to collaborate in planning, and the possible breakdown of the one-teacher/one-class situation. All this inevitably involves the teachers in a fundamental change of role, and there are important implications for teacher training, and in particular for in-service training.

While it is possible to indicate this variety of approach, it is more difficult to assess the extent of these developments in schools. The impression is that at present they are not very widespread, but that as the results of the various Schools Council Projects are published and disseminated, so more schools may wish to experiment. The Environmental Studies 5–13 Project was set up in 1967 and began to publish a number of guides in 1971. Guides such as *Starting with Maps* and *Starting with Rocks* have clear geographical connotations. The approach being considered by the Project is one involving children actively in observation, recording and interpretation, an approach well known to geographers and one which, in the words of the Project's handout, 'cannot be made on the basis of rigidly differentiated subjects. On the other hand it is incorrect to think that the approach is antagonistic to the pattern of subject-divisions so long as these are not insisted on at too early a point in the child's development' (Schools Council 1970).

A second project of direct interest to geographers is the Development Project in History, Geography and Social Sciences in the Middle Years of Schooling (8–13) which the Schools Council has set up to run from April 1971 until April 1974. The researchers will certainly wish to consider the role and interrelation of the three subject disciplines, although there is no reason to assume that the conclusions will show that these three disciplines necessarily form a self-contained area of the curriculum. The two Geography Projects considering geography for 14 to 16 year olds will also presumably need to consider the relationship of geography with other subjects, and there is some geographical content in the packs of materials produced by the Schools Council Integrated Studies Project based at the Institute of Education of the University of Keele, which has been working since 1967 on problems of the relatedness of the disciplines and the wider collaboration of teachers. Mention has already been made of the Humanities Curriculum Project directed by L. Stenhouse, and of the Social Studies Project at the University of London Institute of Education. Other Schools Council projects interested in the idea of integration are the General Studies Project (15–18) and the investigation into the Whole Curriculum for the Middle Years of Schooling (8–13).

To sum up this section, it is possible only to reiterate that there is little information available as to how widespread attempts at producing integrated curricula are at present in schools. There is confusion of terminology and a great variety of approach. Experimentation is likely to increase as the results of the various projects are published. The most important stage, that of evaluation, is yet to come.

THE THEORETICAL BASIS OF INTEGRATION

Lawton (1969) has suggested that faulty theory was the cause of the failure of the late-nineteenth-century attempts at integrating subjects. It is clearly necessary for geography teachers to know something of the theoretical basis of the present revived interest in the possibility of integration.

One of the basic ideas may be traced to the thinking of Rousseau and later of Dewey. This is the notion of child-centred education, that children are not little men and little women, but creatures quite different in physical make-up and psychology from adults, with different interests and different abilities. Studies of child-development and of cognitive development are clearly of great importance here. School work should, so the theory proceeds, be relevant to the needs and interests of the child, and this is the key to motivation. This is reflected in some integrated schemes by the tendency to begin work on a topic through study of the local area and then to proceed concentrically to the study of other more remote areas. A second idea to follow from the adoption of a child-centred approach is that children are encouraged to enter into the business of decision-making (James 1968). They are thus encouraged to take more responsibility for their own progress, and may be helped towards coping with problems of decision-making in adult life. A further expectation is that children will be able to display 'natural curiosity' and be engaged in 'spontaneous enquiry' (Pring 1970).

A second main strand which some add to the theoretical argument is the idea of the unity of knowledge, in spite of the fact that this has been held responsible for the failure of some early attempts at integration. The argument is supported by Hogan et al. (1969) when they write 'We felt that the only content capable of embracing the needs of all three subjects and of stressing the unity of ALL (sic) knowledge was the study of a whole society.' Others argue that subjects are the creation of the adult mind, and that they are imposed extrinsically on children. Children do not see life in terms of subjects, runs the argument, and themes or topics can be made to seem more relevant than subjects, which exert a constraining influence, show only a narrow view, and restrict divergence and creativity in thinking. Working on the basis of themes or topics also makes room for the inclusion of subjects which at present do not have an established place in the school curriculum, subjects such as sociology, anthropology, psychology and economics.

A third main theoretical consideration which is often argued is that integration of subjects may contribute towards a more intelligent approach to learning. By working in more flexible groups without the restriction of the forty-minute period, and with the advantages of team teaching, it is claimed that all the disadvantages of class teaching will disappear. These disadvantages are seen to be the rigid guiding hand of the class teacher, allowing little room for decision-making on the part of the children, and the expectation that all children will produce the same standard of performance within a certain narrow range. If integration means a change in organisation of the teaching routine, then there will be great advantages in working in fluid groups with access to a wide range of resources and sources, and with the timetable in blocks. In this way children no longer spend wasted time in moving from one room, teacher and subject to another, and in having to adjust to each change as the working day proceeds. Some see a need for collaborative learning, that is group learning, at a time when family relationships may be breaking down, when there is a need for better communication, and when entry into the sphere of adult work is being further delayed. But individual learning retains its importance and is enhanced by greater freedom than in the class teaching situation. Learning is based on enquiry, and there is the opportunity to study a topic in depth. For some, integration of subjects treated by team-teaching methods may be a pragmatic approach to solving the problems of control in large schools.

In all this, some people recognise the extension into the secondary sphere of the best methods tried in primary schools, in particular in the greater emphasis on ways of learning. Basic in this is the feeling that it is more important to concentrate on the learning of skills and principles than it is to learn strings of facts which may be forgotten quickly. In primary schools the concentration will be on the skills of reading and writing and the use of language and number. In secondary schools, perhaps the aim will be to instil the problem-solving approach of posing and testing hypotheses in the light of the available evidence (Pring 1970, Everson 1969). Lawton argues that this learning of skills and principles ought to be based on a common culture for all children, since it is necessary to insist on a basic minimum understanding if there is to be equality of opportunity. He proposes a curriculum based on the five cores of mathematics, the sciences, the humanities, including geography, the expressive arts, and moral education. He sees the advantage of a 'cooperative approach to the curriculum' as helping children to apply knowledge of a subject or discipline to the problem of life outside the school, that is 'to combine one kind of knowledge with other disciplines' (Lawton 1969).

These, then, are some of the theoretical arguments posed in favour of integration, and it will be appreciated that the theory is based on a mixture of sociological, psychological and philosophical considerations. The sociological ideas are those concerned with the needs of children as members of society, the psychological with the theory of learning, and the philosophical with the nature of knowledge. These ideas have been presented in the form of arguments such as might be put forward by supporters of integration, but clearly there are a number of important questions which need to be asked.

IMPORTANT QUESTIONS

Experimentation is vital in schools if education is to have any relevance in a rapidly changing world, and there has been a notable lack of experimentation in the past. But as important as experimentation is evaluation. We need to try to be objective about everything that we do in schools if we are to make reasoned judgments about curriculum development. The questions that follow might be those that an evaluator would need to consider, or they might be the sort of questions that teachers considering the possibility of curriculum integration could ask.

1 *What is the justification for the idea of the unity of knowledge?* Those who argue for the unity of knowledge need to consider the epistemological implications of their argument. Hirst's (1965) work is basic here, for he postulates a number of forms of knowledge, each with a distinctive association of concepts and methods of procedure, as well as distinctive methods of testing its findings against experience. To accept Hirst's theory of knowledge is to deny the unity of all knowledge, and

it is difficult to argue against his fundamental thesis, although certain of the details may be open to question (Graves & Simons 1966). Pring (1970) makes the point of this question well when he writes 'No enquiry can take place except within a particular system of thought, and this involves recognising the implicit rules of procedure built into the acceptance of *this* system rather than another.' This leads naturally to the second question.

2 *How can we ensure that structure and purpose can be retained in integrated study?* It is clear that in any enquiry, at any moment in time, the study will necessarily be of a particular sort, using certain appropriate methods. This would imply that the character of subject disciplines ought to be maintained and made clear to the learner. Integration should, as Lawton (1969) suggests, preserve the differences between subjects and at the same time demonstrate their connectedness. There are few geographers who have not wished at some time that the curriculum could be so planned that, for example, work on weathering might coincide with an appropriately related piece of work in chemistry, or the meteorological side of climatology with the relevant topics in physics and mathematics. Similar links in human geography may be imagined.

Structure seems to be vital if uncoordinated mish-mash is to be avoided, and clear objectives in the work will help to maintain this structure. Aims which are achievable and which can be verified by testing are as necessary in integrated study as in any other approach, and both long-term and short-term aims need to be considered. Bruner (1960) stressed the need for structure in our teaching, and here he is referring to the conceptual make-up of the material we are to teach. This brings us on to the next question.

3 *How can we be sure that we are best aiding conceptual learning by means of integrated studies?* Through the work of Piaget, Bruner and others, we are now on the way towards a better understanding of how conceptual learning takes place, and in geography, research by Lunnon (1969) and by Rhys (1966) has shown that it may be possible to organise geographical concepts in such a way as to aid understanding and learning, and to help children explore the realms of logico-deductive thinking involved in Piaget's stage of formal operations. We know enough of the process of concept attainment to suggest that children extend their understanding of a concept by constant revisiting of the basic idea and by the feeding in of scraps of experience derived from repeated experience of working with varied exemplars of the concept

in a variety of different situations. The question is whether this revisiting, consolidation and repetition of experience is possible when a subject discipline crops up irregularly and infrequently in an integrated studies programme. It is possible to take this a step further and ask the fourth question.

4 *Are the basic concepts of the individual disciplines adequately taught in the integrated situation?* This is closely linked with the last question, and it is one which concerned Graves in his paper for the Education Committee of the Royal Geographical Society in 1968. He put the question rather differently, asking 'Are the contents of courses conceived within an IDE scheme as worthwhile educationally as the contents of the separate courses which might otherwise be taught?' This remains difficult to answer since there has as yet been little evaluation of integrated schemes; but as Graves wrote, 'developing a worthwhile course on IDE lines must be an extraordinarily difficult task, since the topics chosen must not only enable the dovetailing of various disciplines in some coherent pattern, but each succeeding topic chosen must build upon the previous topic in such a way that principles and concepts learnt are gradually enriched and developed. This is no mean task within one subject; designing a scheme to cover many subjects centred around a topic is a job of enormous complexity.' It is obviously doubtful whether an integrated course could cover the content which a geographer might hope to cover in a subject-based curriculum given the same time.

The next question concerns children learning, and asks:

5 *How can we be sure that integrated study places children in the optimum learning situation?* One of the basic requirements for learning is that the learner needs to be able to recognise the form of what he has to learn. He must first understand what is to be learned, be it concept, principle or skill. He must then be able to break it down and classify it into parts. He then learns a part at a time, and gradually pieces the parts together to make a coherent whole. If this is the case, then the logic of a subject approach becomes clear, since the very existence of subjects helps in this process of breaking down, separating, classifying and simplifying. We need, therefore, to ensure that this process is not obscured in the integrated situation. It is essential that children shall not be faced with even greater chaos than might be involved in the timetabled-subject approach. Are children capable of integrating subjects in the study of a theme, of seeing relationships between subjects, let alone of extracting an ultimate understanding of disciplines

from an inter-disciplinary approach? It is necessary to consider whether all children are able to respond well to flexible grouping and individual work, or whether some are lost in a bewildering whirl of exciting but meaningless flux. Clearly the organisation must be such that this is unlikely to be the case.

But we need to consider teachers as well as children, and the next question seems important enough to be asked.

6 *How do teachers cope with working in an integrated studies scheme?* One has only to read the description of the Walworth School World Studies scheme to see that working an integrated studies course can be very demanding on teachers, but then so is any other approach to teaching if entered into with spirit. One possible danger is that the problem of teacher participation in the running of a large school might be made more acute. It is not uncommon for junior members of staff to feel less than fully committed since they are not involved in decision-making. It is to be hoped that experiment with the integrated approach will not make the hierarchical staff structure of such schools worse through the appointment of such dignitaries as Directors of Studies, or Team Leaders without due consideration for the effect on staff morale. As Bull (1968) points out, the situation is worse still when the Director of Studies is not one of the subject specialists.

The final question is possibly the most important.

7 *Are we sure that the benefits which may incidentally accrue from the integrated approach cannot also be achieved in a subject-based curriculum?* It seems a possibility that many of the theoretical ideas discussed earlier could lead to beneficial practice. More flexible timetabling, fluid grouping, well-stocked resource centres, adaptable architecture, involvement of the children in decision-making where their own progress is concerned, team-teaching within subjects and adoption of the enquiry approach such as has been common practice with many geographers for many years, are all possible and may be desirable, but it is not obligatory to introduce integrated studies in order to achieve these benefits.

CONCLUSION

The point of these questions has been to put forward some of the arguments that might be used to counter the theoretical arguments in favour of integration stated earlier, in order to achieve some sort of balance in this discussion of a controversial topic. It is clear that none of the questions was designed to query the idea of integration *within* subjects, since it is assumed that most geographers would agree that this internal integration is worth aiming for. In any curriculum we should wish to attempt to integrate one idea with another, one topic with the next, and one year's work with the last (Lawton 1967).

As with other controversial areas of discussion in education, a balanced view may be the most appropriate. Certainly there is a case for showing the relationship between subjects. No thinking teacher would wish to consider his subject in sterile isolation. There is also a case for following inter-disciplinary approaches at certain stages in the curriculum. Different people will have different views on this, but it seems reasonable to suggest that work will be mainly 'pre-disciplinary' in the primary school, and that during the transition period of the first years in secondary or middle school some of the work could well be of an integrated nature, provided that it is possible to teach the basic skills of the subjects involved and that the contribution of each subject is made clear. In the sixth form the opportunity is presented by the need to develop viable general studies courses (Schools Council 1969). Problems such as that of race relations, which, as Pring suggests, cannot be raised within any one cognitive structure, could be approached by means of inter-disciplinary enquiry, as could concepts such as 'power', which are 'complex in meaning, are central to our thinking in the different disciplines of thought, need close scrutiny in themselves, and thereby offer fresh ways of entering into different areas of knowledge'. The integrated approach might also be more appropriate for those who need some alternative to longer-established methods, particularly for young school leavers. As Graves (1968) suggested, 'The specific curriculum experiment involving "integrated teaching" might succeed with weaker pupils where traditional class teaching has failed.' Others argue that this would simply serve to fossilise the differences between the 'academically able child' and 'the Newsom pupil' (Bull 1968).

Much depends on the circumstances of the individual school. School policy as regards streaming, the nature of the school's catchment area, the degree of support to be expected from parents are obviously points to be considered in the organisation of the curriculum, as well as the degree of commitment of the staff and the availability of finance for the establishment of a resource centre. As Bull put it, 'In some situations geographical education will be better furthered by IDE, in others through teaching geography as a specialist subject. Sometimes the method of exploring a topic in its various aspects and in depth will prove rewarding; at other times the exploration of the principles and skills of individual disciplines will yield the better results.'

Finally, what might be the responsibilities of the geographer in the integrated situation? Many of the suggestions which follow have already been hinted at in the theoretical discussion earlier in the chapter, but it may be useful to draw them together here and attempt to offer some practical advice.

It seems vital to ensure that a specialist geographer is included in both the planning and the execution stages of an integrated course if the whittling away of the essential geographical content of the curriculum is to be guarded against. It is all too clear that without the aid of trained geographers in planning such courses, the popular quiz-programme conception of geography is too easily accepted, and the geographical content is restricted at worst to simply showing the position of a place to be studied on the globe.

Presumably the professional teacher of geography will have certain aims and objectives. He will have considered with care which particular geographical concepts his pupils should be familiar with, and which skills they should have practised by a certain stage in their studies. He will also have considered the possibility of planning the pupils' acquaintance with these concepts and skills in a developmental order so that learning is built up step by step, and consolidation of earlier work is possible.

Clearly, if he is involved in an integrated course of study, the geographer, and other subject specialists for that matter, will wish to ensure that these essential features of their fields of study do not disappear. It would seem to be a useful piece of practical advice, then, to suggest that teachers might draw up a list of what they consider to be those geographical skills and concepts which form a vital part of the school curriculum. This list might be drawn up in the form of a table with concepts and skills listed along the horizontal axis, and age of the children on the vertical. In a detailed table of this sort it is also possible to include notes on the source materials and teaching aids available for teaching a particular item to a particular age or ability group.

The whole point of preparing a document of this kind is that it will clearly help the teacher to know what it is he wants to teach and how he is going to involve the children (or students) in the learning of it. The geographer who has considered these problems will be in a position to contribute constructively to the planning of an integrated course.

The Geographical Association Memorandum to the Central Advisory Council for Education was quite clear on this last point: 'If unifying schemes of work are envisaged outside the normal subjects on the timetable, then we submit that the geographer is usually the person best qualified to supervise and integrate this work' (Geographical Association 1962). It has often been claimed that the core of geography is the synthesis of contributions from many different fields of study, and it may be that geography has an important part to play in helping children to envisage the whole picture rather than a number of separate parts. Consider, for example, the possibility of using geography as the starting point and unifying matrix in an integrated course involving, say, history, geography, social science and English. Even if the title of one of the topics in the course sounded as ungeographical as 'Life in Industrial Society', it would be possible to select an industrial area, such as South Lancashire and North Cheshire, and begin with a study describing the present-day geography of the area. The skills of map and picture interpretation and statistical analysis could well be involved in this, since in the main the study would be based on source materials of this nature rather than text-book descriptions. The sociological implications of a densely populated industrial area would also be considered in this first stage.

The second stage of the study would be an attempt at explanation of the present-day picture. This would certainly involve further geographical study in which the importance of such diverse factors as geology and the influence of economic considerations on location of industry would be discussed. The historical element would also be strong, since the area provides such an obvious case study for the economic and industrial developments of the eighteenth and nineteenth centuries, and the rapid changes which have taken place since the early 1940s. The history of the Trade Union movement would also be relevant, particularly if local examples could be used.

In English there would be opportunities for studies such as the analysis of contemporary newspaper cuttings. For able children this could lead to a consideration of what constitutes journalistic style, while at the same time it would help to fill out the description of the area with up-to-date information. There would also be opportunities to study the work of writers such as George Orwell, while photographs of the more congested areas, or reproductions of Lowry's paintings, might be the starting point for original writing.

In the final stages the study could return to maps in an attempt to show the interrelationship of the various factors which have been involved in the evolution of this area. It is clear that this idea for the study of a topic would make it possible for children to consider important concepts and to practise certain basic skills in each of the fields of study involved.

The reader will be aware that this is simply an outline of only one possible topic for study, and that to construct a whole year's course along these lines is a far more complex business. In any integrated scheme, the geographer would presumably wish to attempt to ensure that learning sequences are planned in accordance with established pedagogic principles and research findings. The topics and themes selected must be genuinely relevant, useful and fruitful rather than trivial and ephemeral. It is clear, too, that the geographer has a responsibility for considering new developments within the subject, which may be at least as important as thinking about relationships with other subjects. This could well affect decisions about integration, since it may be that geography has more affinity with the sciences than with the arts. The geographer will also wish to try to make sure that evaluation of the work is thorough and objective, and that any necessary follow-up action is taken promptly and made effective. Perhaps above all, he should strive to preserve that sense of balance which is so vital in a period of rapid change.

References

J. S. Bruner, (1960) *The process of education*, chapter 2, Vintage Books.

G. B. G. Bull, (1968) 'Inter-disciplinary enquiry: a geography teacher's assessment', *Geography*, vol. 53.

C. Cannon ,(1964) 'social studies in secondary schools', *Educational Review*, vol. 17.

Chambers' Twentieth Century Dictionary, (1965).

Education Committee of the Royal Geographical Society, (1950) *Geography and Social Studies in Schools*, RGS, revised 1954.

(1955) 'Geography and Education', *Geographical Journal*, vol. 121.

J. Everson, (1969) 'Some aspects of teaching geography through fieldwork', *Geography*, vol. 54.

Geographical Association, (1962) 'Memorandum submitted to the Central Advisory Council for Education, November 1961', *Geography*, vol. 47.
(1970) *Geography in the primary school*, GA.

N. J. Graves and M. Simons, (1966) 'Geography and Philosophy', *University of London Institute of Education Bulletin*, no. 9.

N. J. Graves, (1968) 'Geography, social science and interdisciplinary enquiry', *Geographical Journal*, Vol. 134.

P. H. Hirst, (1965) 'Liberal education and the nature of knowledge', *Philosophical Analysis and Education*, R. D. Archambault (ed.), Routledge.

D. F. Hogan, P. S. Hore and M. Tucker, (1969) 'Integrated studies at Walworth School: a pragmatic approach by English, history and geography', *University of London Institute of Education Bulletin*, no. 19.

IAAM, (1967) *The teaching of geography in secondary schools*, Cambridge University Press.

C. James, (1968) *Young lives at stake*, Collins.

D. Lawton, (1967) 'Social studies and the social sciences', *Ideas*, no. 4, Curriculum Laboratory of Goldsmith's College, University of London.
(1969) 'The idea of an integrated curriculum', *University of London Institute of Education Bulletin*, no. 19.

D. Lawton, J. Campbell and V. Burkitt, (1971) *Social Studies, 8–13*, Schools Council Working Paper No. 39, Evans/Methuen.

A. J. Lunnon, (1969) *The understanding of certain geographical concepts by primary school children*, (unpublished), M.Ed., Birmingham.

M. C. Naish, (1970) 'New curriculum developments in geography', *New Era*, vol. 51, no. 8.

R. A. Pring, (1970) 'Curriculum integration', *University of London Institute of Education Bulletin*, no. 20.

W. T. Rhys, (1966) *The development of logical thinking in the adolescent with reference to the teaching of geography in secondary schools*, M.Ed., Birmingham.

Schools Council, (1967) *Society and the young school leaver*, Working Paper no. 11, HMSO.
(1969) *General Studies 16–18*, Working Paper No. 25, Evans/Methuen.
(1970) 'Project on environmental studies', Cartrefle College of Education brochure.

J. T. Shaplin and H. F. Olds (eds.), (1964) *Team teaching*, Harper & Row.

L. Stenhouse, (1968) 'Humanities curriculum project', *Journal of Curriculum Studies*, vol. 1, no. 1.

Problems of learning and teaching

6 The contribution of psychology

THELMA VENESS

A curriculum subject like geography can be viewed from at least two perspectives. The first perspective is the one that probably gives it the most obvious reason for being in the curriculum: that it represents the systematic and coherent exposition of a body of knowledge which has intrinsic value and is part of the equipment of an educated man. Psychological analysis would tend, however, to be interested in the second perspective, namely the kinds of tasks involved in learning the subject. The supposition here is that, if the principles of transfer of training are correctly applied, the teaching of geography will to some extent transfer to other kinds of intellectual activity in which the pupil may be engaged; and that the learning of geography should provide some of the intellectual satisfactions that come from exercising relevant skills.

Had educational psychologists managed to complete the task, which seemed to be spurring them on at one time, of drawing up a list of separate and independent abilities, then one could have ventured on the enterprise of analysing what actually goes on in the learning of a curriculum subject in terms of the specific abilities it taps, the discrete intellectual skills it involves, the different kinds of creative experience it offers. If such a tally had been possible, geography might well have come out rather high in the league table in terms of the different kinds of mental jerks that are involved. Geography of course, cannot claim to offer all forms of intellectual experience: any discipline has its own limitations. For example, creativity and aesthetic sensibility are better served by other curriculum experiences: the way geographers conceive their subject at the moment does not give much premium to inventing one's own world (though if geographers follow applied scientists into the futurology business, even that enterprise may become legitimate in the geography laboratory).

At the higher education level, geography still tends to be regarded as both a science, an art and a social science, which in itself indicates the range of intellectual experience available within geography. Psychology presents the same hybrid appearance to the tidy-minded. Possibly geographers have not until now drawn much from the study of psychology, but certainly some well-known psychologists have strayed, often via ethnology, into geographical spheres. The prime example of this is Sir Francis Galton, author of that fertile book *Inquiries into human faculty* (1883), who constructed the first weather-maps printed by *The Times*, and coined the term 'anti-cyclone'. (His curiosity afforded some interesting topological dilemmas. On one occasion when in Africa, he became fascinated with the unusual contours of Hottentot women, and wished to record the particular angle of slope involved. Victorian delicacy, however, would not permit him to take direct measurements. He solved this dilemma by having recourse to a theodolite.) This chapter reviews some of the ways in which psychologists have investigated the kind of intellectual skills used in geography.

CONCEPTS

Piaget's work on children's scientific and mathematical concepts has had an impact on several curriculum subjects, reminding us that where the systematic unfolding of a coherent discipline makes assumptions about the mastery of basic concepts, then this is better left to the secondary school years. The work of Bruner, and people building on Piagetian foundations, has nevertheless given pointers to the way in which planned exposure to the most fundamental concepts in the junior years helps later understanding of more sophisticated ideas.

Much of Piaget's earlier work comprised a documentation of children's notions of physical reality, including weather and natural features of the environment. In *The child's conception of the world* Piaget lists three main types of misconception: realism, the tendency to see a psychological event, such as a dream, as having the same kind of reality as a physical object; animism, the tendency to see physical objects as if endowed with consciousness and will; and artificialism, in which natural phenomena are seen as products of human creation, as being made by man to serve the purposes of man:

> The first stage is magical: we make the clouds move by walking. The clouds obey us at a distance. The average age of this stage is 5. The second stage is both artificialist and animistic. Clouds move because God or men make them move. The average age of this stage is 6. During a third stage, of which the average age is 7, clouds are supposed to move by themselves, though the child says nothing definite as to

how this movement is effected. But in addition to this, the movement is conditioned by moral and physical causes, which shows that the artificialism has simply been transferred to the objects. It is the sun, the moon, etc., that make the clouds move along; only, the heavenly bodies determine these movements, not as a physical cause determines its effects, but rather as one man compels another by commanding him, with or without the addition of physical force. During this third stage, the child says nothing definite about the 'how' of the cloud's spontaneous movement, but it is obvious that he has at the back of his mind a motor schema which prepares the way for the explanation which comes during the fourth stage. For according to the children of the fourth stage, the wind pushes the clouds, but the wind has itself come out of the clouds. The average age of this stage is 8. When, finally, the fifth stage is reached (average age 9), a correct explanation is found.

One can of course take the view that these are merely childish thoughts to be rectified by good instruction. It is more important to see them as exemplifying the human endeavour to make sense of the flux of events and as a grasping out for notions of cause and effect – a very great asset for the geography teacher. The child makes the best sense it can of reality and this will often be in its own image. With many geographical phenomena the dice are loaded against the child. Actual commerce with such things as wind and tide cannot be achieved by simple handling and pictorial representation. Some of these concepts are in fact very tough even for an intelligent fifth-former to grasp when they are set in the causal networks of the discipline. The grown-up story of what a wind is all about is quite unlike what the child can experience (a wind on his face or catching his kite) and it demands from him an understanding of a number of high-level abstractions. The geography teacher has distinct limitations to the possibility of generating geographical knowledge from discovery alone. To quote Plowden (Central Advisory Council for Education 1967) on a similar point: 'A key problem to the teaching of geography is to balance the knowledge which can be learned by children through their own senses with knowledge about distant places.' The necessity to start from the child's own experience suggests that as far as possible the concept of space, time and cause implied in learning geography should be brought nearer home, as in the study of local geography.

PERSPECTIVE

Projects involving maps, and questionnaires about the local area, formed the bases of an enquiry by J. D. McAulay (1966) into second grade children's growth in understanding geographical relationships. The children were given such problems as to locate their houses from the school playground, identify some hills that were visible, work out the reasons for there being a tunnel and a bridge on the journey into town. The investigator reports an expansion in knowledge over a six months' interval, notably in the ability to relate the immediate perceived environment to an illustrated map representation.

Children of the whole junior school range were studied by F. M. Prior (1959) for ability to represent a model village in map form, an exercise used by Piaget and Inhelder in *The child's conception of space.* Systematic errors were made, associated with age, in left and right, foreground and background, and in the dispersal of features over the map. The youngest children tended to group all features according to their logical relatedness. All trees were clumped together regardless of their true spatial arrangement. At 8 years there was still difficulty in coordinating the two dimensions which affected the representation of differences. By about 10½ on average the children had reached an understanding of the principles involved.

Questions about the children's ability to see and imagine perspective have ramifications in many aspects of the curriculum. Piaget and Inhelder used a perspective problem to illustrate the egocentricity of young children's thought. They set up a scale model of three mountains and placed a doll at different angles in relation to the mountains. The child had to imagine how the mountains would appear from the different perspectives, and select from a number of photographs. The young children, from 4 to 11, were usually unable to free themselves from their own sightlines, a result found also by Lovell in children from 5 to 6 years.

Flavell (1968) has extended this whole notion of training skills in perspective to apply to larger aspects of communication and of being able to appreciate the role and perspective of another person. Several of his exercises, which are particularly suitable for later childhood and early adolescence, involve spatial orientation, as with the three mountains problem, but also the further requirement of being able to verbalise to another in relation to one's own perspective. For example, a task was set up with telephonic communication between two people. Each had a fairly complicated map of a route in front of him. One of them was shown the route to be taken and had to communicate his knowledge to the other, by reference to the map which they both had, and then by putting the instructions into words, since direct contact with the map was not available. This is a situation in which 'You are bound to find it' is not allowed as an answer.

The programme of studies Flavell used in his researches is founded on the assumption that spatial perspective is on some sort of a continuum with the kind of perspective involved in seeing issues from another person's point of view. It would be interesting to know to what extent, and in what respects, the learning of geography militates against ethnocentricity. Another line of study that possibly reveals xenophobia, or xenophilia, on a smaller scale, is the study of people's concepts of 'neighbourhood'. Interesting differences are found among people in regard to what area of a local map they will mark off as the boundary of 'their neighbourhood', and of course a lot of street-gang boundary warfare may come from over-clearcut concepts of what is 'mine' and what 'thine'.

Exercises in local town planning, such as where a new supermarket should be situated, have provided interesting leads for the study of people's daily habits and shopping routines. Why do women, on the whole, prefer to go down-town for their shopping, other things being equal; and what other things could make for equality? What determines which side of the road children will walk along when they leave a certain school; and how will this affect the siting of pedestrian crossings? These are problems in logical inference, as well as observation, and so take us on to the next section.

INFERENCE

As Peel (1965) says, 'The successful use of imagined hypotheses to explain phenomena always contains a deductive element in the comparison of hypotheses with data.' He, together with W. T. Rhys, have clearly seen the possibilities of geographical thinking being introduced in this way, and have also used their ingenious problems on farm husbandry to study the thought process of secondary age children (see p. 95). A different kind of inferential situation was published recently by Jahoda (*Impressions of nationalities*, 1966) which has interesting possibilities of application to political geography. Jahoda wished to get away from the traditional approach to the study of national stereotypes. He provided his respondents (they were adult students in this case) with a small amount of information, which purported to come from belief-attitude surveys, about a particular national group. These items of information consisted of percentages of the population who adopted certain positions in relation to religion, to politics, to civil liberties and to higher education. The choice had to be made from eleven countries, each of which was rated for its likelihood of 'fitting the bill'. The inference involves a degree of historico-political knowledge, of course, as well as the ability to make inferences from statistics, but in the achievement of the task, great scope is given for the challenging of one's 'brand images' of other nations.

ATTITUDE

Mention has been made already of the use of local geography to investigate notions of 'the neighbourhood', 'round the block', 'up the street'. 'What is my neighbour?' is a question not only for religious education.

Psychologists have also been interested in children's concepts of nationhood, and again Piaget is a pioneer in the study done by Piaget and Weil (1951) to illustrate the way young Swiss and French children perceived 'being Swiss' and 'being French'. Again, the egocentricity of the young child is illustrated: the Swiss child always sees the Frenchman as a foreigner even when he is in France, whereas the Swiss is never a foreigner wherever he is situated. They, and many other investigators, have uncovered the strong preferences of young children for their own country.

A study by Jahoda (1962) of Glasgow children's ideas and attitudes shows how hazy are the ideas of young children (they were 6–11) about Glasgow, Scotland and Britain. Jahoda distinguishes four stages in children's conceptual growth in relation to these ideas. At stage 1 the child has no conception of Glasgow as a unitary whole: thus, the young child living in Glasgow, might well reply 'Glasgow – oh that's where my Mummie goes shopping.' At the next stage there was no conception of Glasgow as a part of Scotland and at the third stage there was no conception of England and Scotland as being parts of Britain. He also asked the children to represent the four concepts spatially, by aligning or superimposing flat boards which roughly represented the four comparative areas. Sometimes the child would repeat, parrot fashion, that Glasgow is part of Scotland but could not represent this spatially. One finding that must give geography teachers pause is that, throughout all his studies, middle-class children were found to be superior to working-class children in their appraisal of these geographical ideas.

Tajfel, with associates from several European countries, is currently producing several studies of children's attitudes to other countries. One study done with Oxford school children (Middleton, Tajfel and Johnson 1970), demonstrates that among primary school children there is a stable and consistent preference order and that it roughly corresponds with the order of scores on a number of items of information. Another study, done with the same children, examined their ability to understand that people of another country would act on principles guiding their own conduct. This tendency to attribute reciprocation was found to be related also to preference order.

CULTURE

The point has been made that a child's ability to attain concepts, and even percepts, may depend upon its general stage of development and upon its particular experiences with visual material. In our culture, children are able from quite a young age to identify objects from two-dimensional representations of them. Binet found that children, at the age of 3, could identify the same picture in succession, but found difficulty in interpreting a series before the age of 7. There is a limited ability to see a scene as a whole: children are readily distracted by one detail that is of immediate interest, and may fail to see the point if visual presentation alone is relied upon. Malter, showing a process chart of the passage of wheat through a flour-mill, found only a quarter of 10–14 year olds able to interpret the diagram well enough to mark the points of entry and exit: even when labels were introduced they were often ignored. M. D. Vernon (1946) likewise found that even students at colleges of education sometimes had difficulty in apprehending graphs, histograms and pictograms. This is in a culture which has, by and large, a high degree of sophistication concerning the two-dimensional representation of three-dimensional objects.

A profitable vein for cross-cultural investigation has come from the attempts of ethnographers and psychologists to investigate the performance of non-European peoples in relation to the well-known optical illusions – illusions, that is, as seen in our culture. Among the foremost investigators in this field were W. H. Rivers and W. McDougall who took the Müller-Lyer illusion with them on the Torres Straits Expedition. Since then, Segal and his associates have used these illusions to test hypotheses concerning the effect of the terrain and the customary shape of houses on the perception of the indigenous people. Jahoda (1966) did similar studies among the Lobi people, the Dagomba and the Ashanti in Ghana. The hypotheses were that open parkland in rolling country would effect greater susceptibility to the horizontal–vertical illusion, which would be likely to be seen in perspective, and that the 'carpentered environments', of rectangular houses would increase susceptibility to the Müller-Lyer illusion. Among the Bantu people, too, with their round huts, Allport found evidence of a lessened effect of the rotating trapezoid illusion.

Our understanding of other ethnic groups probably needs to be pursued further than a study of their customs and economies, into the whole area of the way they perceive, learn, understand and remember. The recent work by P. E. Vernon (1969) causes us to think again about what constitutes 'intelligence' in some other countries and about the way that economic arrangements and child-training practices both depend upon and contribute to the particular thought codes and personality dispositions of the people.

References

J. S. Bruner, (1960) *The process of education*, Vintage Books.
(1967) *Towards a theory of instruction*, Belknap.
J. H. Flavell, (1968) *The development of role-taking and communication skills in children*, Wiley.
F. Galton, (1883) *Inquiries into human faculty*, Macmillan.
G. Jahoda, (1962) 'Development of Scottish children's ideas and attitudes about other countries', *Journal of Social Psychology*, vol. 58.
(1963) 'Development of children's ideas about country and nationality', *British Journal of Educational Psychology*, vol. 33.
(1966) 'Impressions of nationalities – an alternative to the "stereotype" approach', *British Journal of Social and Clinical Psychology*, vol. 5.
(1966) 'Geometric illusions and environment: a study in Ghana', *British Journal of Social and Clinical Psychology*, vol. 57.
J. D. McAulay, (1966) 'Second grade children's growth in comprehension of geographic understandings', *Journal of Geography*, vol. LXV, no. 1.
M. R. Middleton, H. Tajfel and N. B. Johnson, (1970) 'Cognitive and affective aspects of children's national attitudes', *British Journal of Social and Clinical Psychology*, vol. 9.
E. A. Peel, (1965) 'Intellectual growth during adolescence', *Educational Review*, vol. 17.
J. Piaget, (1929) *The child's conception of the world*, Routledge.
J. Piaget and B. Inhelder, (1956) *The child's conception of space*, Routledge.
J. Piaget and A. M. Weil, (1951) 'The development in children of the idea of the homeland and of relations with other countries', *Institute of Social Science Bulletin*, no. 3.
F. M. Prior, (1959) 'The place of maps in the Junior School', unpublished Dip. Ed., dissertation, University of Birmingham.
M. D. Vernon, (1946) 'Learning from graphical material', *British Journal of Psychology*, vol. 36.
P. E. Vernon, (1969) *Intelligence and cultural environment*, Methuen.

7 Perceptual problems

HERBERT SANDFORD

Our knowledge of the physical and physiological aspects of perception is considerable, but much less is known of the psychological aspects and still less is known about perception when applied to specific problems in learning geography. We must avoid the temptation to apply to our subject the findings of more general investigations into perception. Much of the research into the legibility of type and into reading skills, for instance, appears to be inapplicable to the lettering on maps. It is also convenient here to ignore those perceptual problems that, though relevant to the teacher of geography, are also relevant to teachers of other subjects. Sensory discrimination, for example, varies greatly between children and can be related to certain differences in their attainment in many subjects.

Nevertheless, all the senses appear to play some part in specifically geographical learning tasks. It would seem reasonable to state that the more senses the child can bring to bear upon a geographical phenomenon, whether it be alpine pasture or urban decay, the more readily will it find its proper place in the child's understanding of the subject as a whole. The evidence in favour of audio-visual and other aids, however, is not as clear or as consistent as one would wish (Coppen 1968), and their intensive use is often an expression of faith. Nevertheless, it is not for trivial reasons, nor merely to add interest, that we want the child to heft the class specimen of galena, to handle the asbestos, smell the crude oil, taste the rock salt.

But pupils and students cannot directly perceive all the objects in the geography they are learning; there is a limit to the amount of fieldwork that can be undertaken just as there is a limit to the size of the display case. Reality must generally be studied at second hand and the means to that end are such aspects of geography as 'picture study' and 'map reading'. However, the closer we can bring the learner to the direct experience of reality the more nearly we achieve our aim. A very considerable number of technical innovations have come to our aid and the child's sensory experience can be enriched within the confines of the classroom to his better understanding of the world outside. Movement, sound and colour, as well as a suggestion of depth or solidity, now enrich geographical pictures, and, though we may never experience Aldous Huxley's 'feelies', there is every prospect that developments in holography may bring us close to the experience of total reality.

Maps, too, are becoming visually more meaningful, though problems of scale will always set a limit to what can be shown on them. The use of 'natural' or 'earth' colours and either hill shading or moulded relief is transforming our maps and globes, and there are now a number of animated maps that add the dynamic element that is missing from conventional ones (Cornwell and Robinson 1966).

THE PERCEPTION OF PHOTOGRAPHS

Research into perception in geography teaching has been concentrated on the problems posed by pictures and maps. In the field of geographical picture study the work of Long is substantial, and involved a large sample of children. The investigation concerned the undirected or free search of geographical pictures by pupils aged 10 (Long 1953) and aged 11–15 (Long 1961). The older children were also set questions to test their powers of observation, recognition and interpretation during directed search. A final report is awaited.

The clarity of the objects in the photographs and the amount of contrast and detail in them appeared to determine their likelihood of being perceived. Ambiguous features were recognised more by shape than by size. Selection was apparently at random but with a tendency to concentrate upon the centre of the pictures. Mental set, prior learning and the imagination all seemed to be involved; physical features were largely ignored, familiar objects were more readily noticed and some children could project themselves into the scene. The older children were more selective in what they described but did not appear to perceive more. Even these older children attempted few interpretations and all were markedly idiographic, 30% referring to the *houses* in one picture, for instance, but not mentioning the *village* into which they were grouped. They had a poorly developed sense of scale. This affected perception as well as interpretation so that hills became mountains in the minds of the children and all cultivated land was called flat.

THE UNDERSTANDING OF MAPS

Research into children's mapwork has been particularly active during the past decade. The more substantial of this work has concerned atlas maps, earlier work having concentrated upon large-scale topographic maps or upon fictional atlas-type maps.

Of considerable importance is the work of Bartz (1965). Bartz reached few general conclusions but she has given us the first detailed account, supported by evidence, of the difficulties experienced by children in forming useful and appropriate percepts when using atlas maps. Her sample was small and unrepresentative but there can be little doubt that had she used a larger and more representative sample, she would have identified the same kinds of difficulty though their incidence might have been different.

Individual children were given short informal oral tests on maps in *The World Book Atlas*. A high proportion of the children experienced difficulty in using the scale, latitude and longitude, compass direction, insets and symbols, especially relief symbols and lettering. Bartz found not only that these difficulties indicated incorrect concepts of the nature of maps and of the world, but that they also followed from the formation of erroneous percepts when confronted by the atlas map. Symbols were perceived but were not fully understood and therefore not used appropriately in map reading and interpretation: 'If the child could possibly think of an interpretation for the symbol based on some previous learning or association, then he will use this *before* searching for legend information' (Bartz 1965, p. 32). In the case of altitude tints, she quotes the equation of green with grass and of brown with desert. The children were unable to distinguish between different styles and sizes of type. A general tendency was to interpret the map too literally (p. 54).

Bartz had concluded that the most important symbols on the map were those that formed the lettering. In a useful subsequent survey she showed that the important work that has been accomplished in the field of type legibility is largely inapplicable to maps (Bartz 1970). We need research that is specifically concerned with them. Shaw and Dreyfus have made eight selections of type faces which were printed on the same base map of France (*Monotype Recorder* 1964) and this is the kind of material that is needed for such research. Fortunately, Bartz has now reported on an experimental cartographic legibility investigation (Bartz 1970, pp. 103–112). More limited attention has been given to the perception of other map symbols and some of this is referred to in a most useful paper by Wood (1968).

PERCEPTION OF ATLAS MAPS

My own investigation concerns the atlas mapwork of English secondary school children. (This was aided by a grant from the University of

London Central Research Fund.) The initial investigation was confined to 340 pupils in a London grammar school and was a study in depth of their free search of an atlas map (Sandford 1967). The children were given a general or politico-relief map of Asia and were asked to write down what the map told them about that continent. The interesting and sometimes surprising results led to the construction of an objective test which was given to a stratified cluster sample of 1,600 secondary school children studying geography in London and the Home Counties (Sandford 1970). The test consisted of a battery of three interpretative test exercises each made up of eight multiple-choice questions about a map in Philips' Elementary Atlas: a political map of the world, a relief map of Africa and a pair of thematic maps of Australasia, one of annual rainfall and the other of 'natural vegetation'.

The test was referred to as one of 'map realism', that is, it was intended to test the ability of the children to form accurate concepts of the world when using atlas maps. The pupils were instructed that the map might not provide the correct answers: the maps would guide but not direct them. A typical question was Item 17, 'How many towns are there in New Zealand?' with alternative answers of '2', '3' and 'more than 3'. Three towns were in fact shown on the map. Testees responding '2' (7%) were considered not to have perceived one of the three towns that were shown on the map, those responding '3' (42%) were thought to have read the map literally, but those responding 'more than 3' (51%) were held to have understood that atlas maps can show only a selection of place names and that in reality there were more towns than the three shown on the map. Correct responses were therefore made by children who could perceive the map adequately and could interpret realistically the information upon it.

The whole investigation is not yet complete and the free search and the objective test are to be followed by more detailed studies of specific problems. Some useful interim conclusions have, however, been reached.

In the easiest test that twelve experienced geography teachers could devise, the mean score was as low as 10·02 (SD = 2·99) out of 24. Yet it seems that most teachers assume that little or no help need be given to children in atlas mapwork and use atlases in class less frequently than sales would suggest (Sandford 1970, p. 15). An analysis of published books of atlas map exercises suggests that many teachers have no clear idea as to what they expect their pupils to be able to do with an atlas; whether to locate places, to study distributions or use it as an introduction to the geography of a new area or region (Sandford 1970, p. 122). This is in strong contrast to the clear direction given to the use of large scale topographic map sheets.

The results of the investigation so far appear to show that there is a hierarchy of mental processes involved in atlas mapwork. The first stage is simply the *perception* of the symbols, yet the proportion of errors among the testees was surprisingly high; 7% in the New Zealand example quoted above, and 17% failed to perceive both parts of Pakistan.

A map presents the child with a very complex perceptual field and one which consists largely of embedded figures: dot, line and patch symbols – and lettering – are superposed. There occurs a severe perceptual overload and the immediate memory, so essential to visual search, is strained; percepts become distorted and memory traces fade.

To handle such a complex image a correct choice of strategy is needed. An appropriate mental set is necessary in order to select from the mapped information that which is relevant to the problem – 'I am looking for towns in New Zealand,' for instance. An appropriate scanning strategy is also required for efficient visual search. This will vary with the problem: in the free search investigation there was a tendency to read the map like a book, from north-west to south-east, and it would be difficult to regard this as a generally appropriate strategy (Sandford 1967, pp. 92–4). Boldness, familiarity and interest, frequency, and pattern, all influenced the children's choice of symbols to record.

The second stage is that of *apperception*. In order that adequate percepts be formed, the symbols must be understood for what they are and not for what they might appear to be. That is to say, the appropriate concepts or referents must be associated with the symbols so that their message can be conveyed to the map user. Some children thought the low parts of Siberia to be under meadow and Kamchatka to rise like a flight of steps because they had attached incorrect associations to the altitude tints.

The atlas map is only a model of the real world (Board 1967). It is subject to a 'scale filter'; for example, the finest drawn river on a school atlas map may be as much as seven miles wide by the scale, so there must be a rigorous selection of phenomena to map and an equally rigorous simplification of all irregular lines. Thus even in very simple mapwork the symbols must be understood to have not one clear value but a range of values of varying likelihood.

Many children did not have this level of understanding: 53% thought that because there were no railway stations mapped between Bombay and Madras, there were no stations; 62% thought that because the map did not show any minor headlands and inlets around Lake Victoria, there were none. The mean score of the 1,600 testees for questions involving the selection of data was 1·49 out of 3 and for the simplification of line it was 0·89 out of 3; these principles were not well understood by the children.

The third stage is the performance of simple mental operations leading to the recognition of patterns and to making statements about position, direction, shape, area, altitude, length and so forth. An ability to handle number came before an ability to handle density and there was a progression from positive, through comparative, to superlative statements. These can be referred to as *verbal techniques.* Although apparently very simple, these operations proved too difficult for some children. 11% of the testees perceived the Sydney to Brisbane flight path as longer than from Sydney to Adelaide and 20% equated the size of Lake Victoria with that of the much larger Madagascar.

In stage four attempts are made to assess length or to compare sizes, heights and so forth in quantitative terms. These can be called *numerical techniques* and include the usual uses of scale, compass and coordinates that, together with the preceding stages, constitute map reading as distinct from map interpretation (Löbeck 1957). Such tasks are based on upadequate percepts but the numerous errors may have been 'mathematical' rather than perceptual. 31% of the testees could not give the straight-line distance from the Cape of Good Hope to Victoria Falles within a margin of error of 8%.

Stage five is *verbal interpretation*; making simple statements about what can be inferred from the map. A proficiency in map reading was a necessary prerequisite for meaningful interpretations. The older children tended to justify their interpretations. For instance: 'There are no rivers in Arabia (evidence), so it can't rain much (reasoning) and must be a desert (conclusion)' (Sandford 1967, p. 157). The increasing attention paid to interpretation (and also to pattern recognition) by older children did not support the contention of Long and others that the younger children are the more able to comprehend the picture or map as a whole.

We can also anticipate a sixth stage in children's atlas mapwork, that of *numerical interpretation.* In the free search investigation the child who said that there is a poor system of railways in China had no way to express this numerically, but with the introduction of quantitative techniques into the schools it would now be possible for him to calculate an index of connectivity.

Two controls appear to operate in both reading and interpretation. A perceptual error at stage one necessarily leads to mistakes at later stages, while an inadequate grasp of the reality behind symbols leads to errors at any stage from the simplest perceptual task (children saying, for instance, that there are 'no rivers in Australia') to imaginative interpretations ('many of the Asian seas are coloured red, black, white and yellow'). It seems important for children to acquire a set of 'yardsticks' against which to make meaningful comparisons between global features. In the objective test, 26% of the pupils thought that ships have to take it in turns to pass through the Strait of Gibraltar and 19% thought that large ships are not allowed.

These two controls over mapwork (those of perception and conceptual understanding) do not seem to be independent. Just as conceptual understanding of reality seems to enable some children to form more useful percepts, so the simplified view of the world depicted on the map seems to have been accepted too literally by most children. These children appear to have a mental map of a world that is as small as it is uncomplicated. For many of them coastlines are smooth, railway lines straight, towns few and terrain level. Features are compact and unchanging over time, and distant ones are relatively small, especially when compared with similar features in the homeland (Sandford 1967, p. 250).

In the free search investigation the younger children tended to confine their mapwork to simple observation of the map and to simple operations comparing sizes, for example, but the older children used numerical techniques more freely and made many verbal interpretations. In the objective test of map realism all pupils were required to attempt questions involving stages one to five but there was little difference between the ability of the younger and that of the older pupils, the mean scores for school years 1 to 4 being respectively 9·11, 9·89, 10·43 and 10·97 (sample mean 10·02, SD = 2·99).

Atlas mapwork undoubtedly seems to be too difficult for many children; less than 1% achieved 75% success in the objective test and the mean rate of perceptual error was 31%. Analysis of variance showed that, at the 1% level, the boys were significantly better than the girls, and both the older children and those taking a GCE course were also significantly higher scorers. Scores were slightly higher for questions on human geography than for those on physical geography.

SOME IMPLICATIONS FOR PRACTICE

What is being done to raise the standard of school atlas mapwork? Brown doubted the value of map interpretation until children are fourteen years old (Brown 1960) and Satterly doubted the value of any mapwork in the junior school (Satterly 1964). Yet the tendency is towards using maps with ever younger children and teachers are urged to make more regular use of them with children at all ages.

Bartz has expressed the prevailing view that our school atlases should be simplified and make more allowance for the pupils' difficulties. Progress in this direction is rapid and one would expect symbols to be more clearly perceived and better understood. There are three main trends to be detected in the design of school atlases. In the first place there are the numerous small adjustments to legend, relief representation, scale, gazetteer, insets and so forth that have been recommended by Bartz and others. Philips' Primary Atlas illustrates many of these: they are directed at specific sources of difficulty.

In the second place there is the more rigorous selection of data, especially of place names, as done by Baddeley for the Oxford Junior Atlas. This is intended to reduce the volume of 'real noise' – the complex reality that, if mapped, would blur the message and make the map unclear - but this limits the kind of interpretation possible from the map.

The third trend is to modify the map in a manner that might appear to complicate it. Just as the relief map has become the general or politico-relief map, so some publishing houses are adding to the general map certain vegetal, cultural and even demographic data. Such maps can be held to give a more complete picture of reality and so enable the child to form more meaningful percepts.

The difficulty is to choose a balance between paucity and abundance of information in order to achieve the optimum level of 'faithfulness' (Board 1967, pp. 706–08). According to the use to which a map is put (location, distribution studies, or for general background information) any particular symbol is seldom redundant (helping in, but not essential for, conveying the message) but may be either irrelevant (playing no part in conveying the message) or relevant. Not all relevant symbols, however, survive the scale and data filters of the map makers.

The solutions to the problem of low mapwork attainment – deferring mapwork and simplifying the maps – would seem to be inadequate unless the child can gradually be brought to the meaningful use of adult atlases by the time he or she leaves school. In addition there are difficulties not to be overcome in these ways, problems of scale and generalisation in particular. There is, however, a third approach which has received comparatively little attention. Rather than avoid the difficulties, it may be possible to help the child learn to overcome them.

Seventy-eight first-year grammar school children were given a short course intended to improve their atlas mapwork (Sandford 1967, pp. 192–235). The course sought to 'bridge the gap' between the large-scale topographic map (advocated frequently but less often practised) by taking children through a series of exercises on maps of ever decreasing scale and commencing with large-scale local plans. Their mapwork was tested both before and after the course and there was a distinct improvement in their perception, techniques and interpretations. Such exercises increased the pupils' familiarity with atlases and in the objective test it was found that the 74% of children who possessed their own atlas, and the 66% who used atlases apart from their schoolwork, were significantly higher scorers.

The course also sought to 'bridge the gap' between reality (conceptual understanding) and the atlas map by using pictures in conjunction with the maps. This did not, however, lead to an equal improvement in map realism. Although in the objective test 86% of the children preferred atlases to contain pictures, their higher scores were not significant. Knowing the reality behind an atlas map appears to be something that must be learned no less than objective facts, but the two differ in a number of ways. That Tokyo is the capital of Japan is a single detail; it is either right or wrong, it cannot be applied to any other thing and is independent of the map. On the other hand, the idea that the existence on the map of a number of town symbols implies the actual existence of a greater number of lesser towns, villages, hamlets and homesteads is of general applicability; it has its exceptions, it can be applied to Sumatra as much as to Russia, and its use is dependent upon an understanding of the map as a means of communication.

There would seem to be a difference in the ways in which these two kinds of learning are acquired. Perhaps the separate facts are learned rapidly and in isolation; they are precise and presumably the child is aware that he has learned something. On the other hand, learning about the possibilities and limitations of maps seems to be a slow process based upon the child's total experience of maps and of the features they are meant to represent. The child acquires this facility gradually, sometimes without even being aware that he has learned anything. Attention could well be given to devising improved courses to speed this process.

References

B. S. Bartz, (1965) *Map design for children*, Field Enterprises Educational Corporation, Chicago.
(1970) 'An analysis of the typographic legibility literature', *Cartographic Journal*, Vol. 7.
(1970) 'Experimental use of the search task in an analysis of type legibility in cartography', *Cartographic Journal*, vol. 7.
C. Board, (1967) 'Maps as models', *Models in geography*, R. J. Chorley and P. Haggett (eds.), Methuen.
T. W. Brown, (1960) 'Mapwork and the use of maps in schools', *Geography*, vol. 45.
H. Coppen, (1968) 'The search for evidence: what do we know about the ways in which audio-visual aids help learners to learn?' *Visual Education*, August–September 1968.
B. Cornwell and A. H. Robinson, (1966) 'Possibilities for computer animated films in cartography', *Cartographic Journal*, Vol. 3.
A. K. Löbeck, (1957) *Things maps don't tell us*, Macmillan.
I. L. M. Long, (1953) 'Children's reactions to geographical pictures', *Geography*, vol. 38.
(1961) 'Research in picture study', *Geography*, vol. 46.
Monotype Recorder, (1964) Broadsheet issued with no. 43, Monotype Corporation.
H. A. Sandford, (1967) 'An experimental investigation into children's perception of a school atlas map', University of London M.Phil. thesis.
(1970) 'A study of the concepts involved in the reading and interpretation of atlases by secondary school children', University of London Ph.D. thesis unpublished.
D. J. Satterly, (1964) 'Skills and concepts involved in map drawing and map interpretation', *New Era*, vol. 45.
M. Wood, (1968) 'Visual perception and map design', *Cartographic Journal*, Vol. 5.

8 The development of logical thinking

WILLIAM RHYS

Ever since the early 1920s Piaget and his associates have been seeking to analyse the intellectual techniques and logical processes employed by children at various stages in their growth towards full mental prowess. The extensive programme of research carried out at Geneva under Piaget's direction has generated a succession of complementary studies in Britain and elsewhere, and while his findings have to some degree been refined and modified in the process, the essential validity of his analysis has been amply confirmed (Wallace 1965, Lunzer 1968). Relatively few enquiries have been concerned with children's conceptual growth in geography, where attention has been focused almost entirely on certain limited aspects of geographical understanding as displayed by children of primary-school age (e.g. Prior 1959, Marsh 1966, Lunnon 1969). Apart from the seminal contribution made by Inhelder and Piaget (1958), what is known about the development of logical thought during adolescence has been derived from enquiries in such fields of study as history (Hallam 1967) and religion (Goldman 1964).

Of the many studies that have been published of children's development in general, those concerned with the development of spatial concepts probably have the greatest relevance for geography (Piaget et al. 1956, 1960). Geographical investigation has long been concerned with the description, analysis and interpretation of phenomena in terms of their spatial distribution and interrelationship, and indeed it has been argued that 'the whole practice and philosophy of geography depends upon the development of a conceptual framework for handling the distribution of objects and events in space' (Harvey 1969).

THE DEVELOPMENT OF SPATIAL CONCEPTS

As adults, we are so familiar with seeing the world in Euclidean terms*

* During the last decade geographers have become aware of the inadequacies and limitations of the Euclidean concept of space and have begun to

that we may fail to recognise that, for the child, there are problems to be solved. Far from being the starting-point of spatial awareness, the capacity to visualise and comprehend space in accordance with Euclidean concepts is the product of a long sequence of development. Piaget takes the view that children pass through a clearly defined progression, in which spatial relationships are built up through the organisation of actions performed on objects in space, at first by motor activity and later by internalised actions which culminate in operational systems.

During the first 18 to 24 months of life the coordination of sensory experience and motor activity produces an awareness of a limited and highly localised 'practical space'. From the appearance of language in the middle of the second year until the child reaches the age of 11 or 12 years, there extends the period of 'concrete thought'. The development of language permits the internalisation of actions into thoughts, and allows the child to evolve mental images of relationships which previously he had carried out at the sensory-motor level. The first spatial concepts that a child can understand and represent to himself are topological, that is, operations which involve such notions as proximity, separation, order, enclosure and continuity. Discriminations on the basis of these properties are usually quite well established by 7 years of age. They then form the basis for the development of more comprehensive systems and are steadily integrated within the projective and Euclidean concepts of space, which being more complex in organisation come later in the child's development. Projective concepts come when the child begins to appreciate how objects appear when viewed from different positions, and can locate them relative to each other without the aid of measurement (Piaget 1955). Euclidean space involves the representation of the world of objects within a comprehensive system of coordinate axes of reference.

The gradual emergence of an objective spatial framework at the representational level has been demonstrated by an experiment in

---

employ a variety of higher-order geometries in order to discuss the complexities of socio-economic space as opposed to the relative location of phenomena in physical space. Subsequently, there has been a considerable resurgence of support for the concept of geography as a 'geometrical science', especially amongst those concerned with advanced research (Chorley and Haggett 1970, Haggett 1965). The adoption of such sophisticated systems as the geometry of 'Riemanian Spaces' for widespread school use is, however, far less likely, in view of their complexity and strangeness.

which a group of children between 4 and 10 years of age were asked to construct a plan of part of Geneva which they knew quite well, from such familiar walks as their routes from home to school (Piaget et al. 1960). The youngest children could only orientate themselves spatially in terms of direct practical action, for example, by acting as guides on foot. Transition to true representation which requires understanding temporally divorced from action, took place only gradually. The first attempts were in terms of personal recollections of journeys actually made, distorted by subjective interest. The intuitive judgments expressed were unstable, inconsistent and contradictory.

From 7 or 8 years of age onwards the children gradually became able to represent changes of position objectively and to achieve a partial coordination of landmarks, but the system of reference built up round each landmark was not aligned so as to agree with the others nor coordinated into a unified whole. Eventually, by about 9 or 10 years of age the children were able to plan the total layout as a whole from the outset. Egocentric relationships had given way to relationships between objects, the subject being able to relate his own movements to the sum total of positional changes which are possible within a framework of fixed references.

Even so, the objective reference system which the 10-year-old may employ is essentially the product of direct personal exploration, and as such is severely limited in its scope. In their study of geography, children are frequently called upon to examine territories which stand outside the bounds of immediate personal experience, where contact with reality is made through transmitted information, expressed in a variety of representational forms, such as photographs, maps and diagrams. It could well be that a 10-year-old child, when confronted with a situation of this kind, would find difficulty in managing those very operations which he could handle with ease if presented concretely.

THE EXPERIMENTAL INVESTIGATION

In order to ascertain the quality of judgment that could be obtained from pupils at successive levels of understanding when confronted with such a challenge, the author presented several problem-situations of a geographical nature to a representative group of children (Rhys 1966). These problem-situations were devised to probe the adolescent's emergent capacity to make a realistic and reasoned appraisal of human action within areal units set well beyond the limits of direct personal experience (Table 1). Each unit was quite distinctive in terms of loca-

	Problem unit	*Theme*	*Data*	*Questions set*
1	Antonio Arango, Magdalena Valley, Columbia	Soil erosion	text	3
2	Narok, East African Rift Valley	Masai migration	map	1
3	Grain-growing, Portage Plains, Manitoba	Extensive monoculture	3 photos map	3
4	Nara, Island of Honshu, Japan	Rice-growing village	text, map, and photo	2
5	Park, Island of Lewis, Outer Hebrides	Crofter-farming	map and statistical diagrams	3

Table 1 The problem situations

tion and in the particular fusion of human and physical forces which operated within the local field-of-action. The employment of carefully edited case-study material ensured the use of a wide range of data in verbal, pictorial, statistical and cartographic form. The questions set were designed to focus attention on some critical or illuminating feature within a given situation, as a test of the children's reasoning capacity rather than their factual knowledge. The answers to each question were grouped together as an independent response sequence and analysed in accordance with the method previously applied to children's reasoning from passages of prose (Lodwick 1958, Peel 1961).

There were 120 children involved in this inquiry and they ranged in age from 9·8 years to 16·3 years. Thus they covered the statutory period of secondary education, with an extension at each end of the age scale, to ensure the inclusion of a group well established at the concrete-operational level, plus a group which ought to be stabilised at the level of formal-operational thought. It was hoped that this would provide an opportunity to tease out, in as much detail as was practicable, the sequence of development likely to occur between the two extremes.

Though contrived for a common purpose, the problems presented differed from each other in certain vital aspects, such as their global location, the technical resources of the local community, the richness and complexity of the local environment, the way in which the data

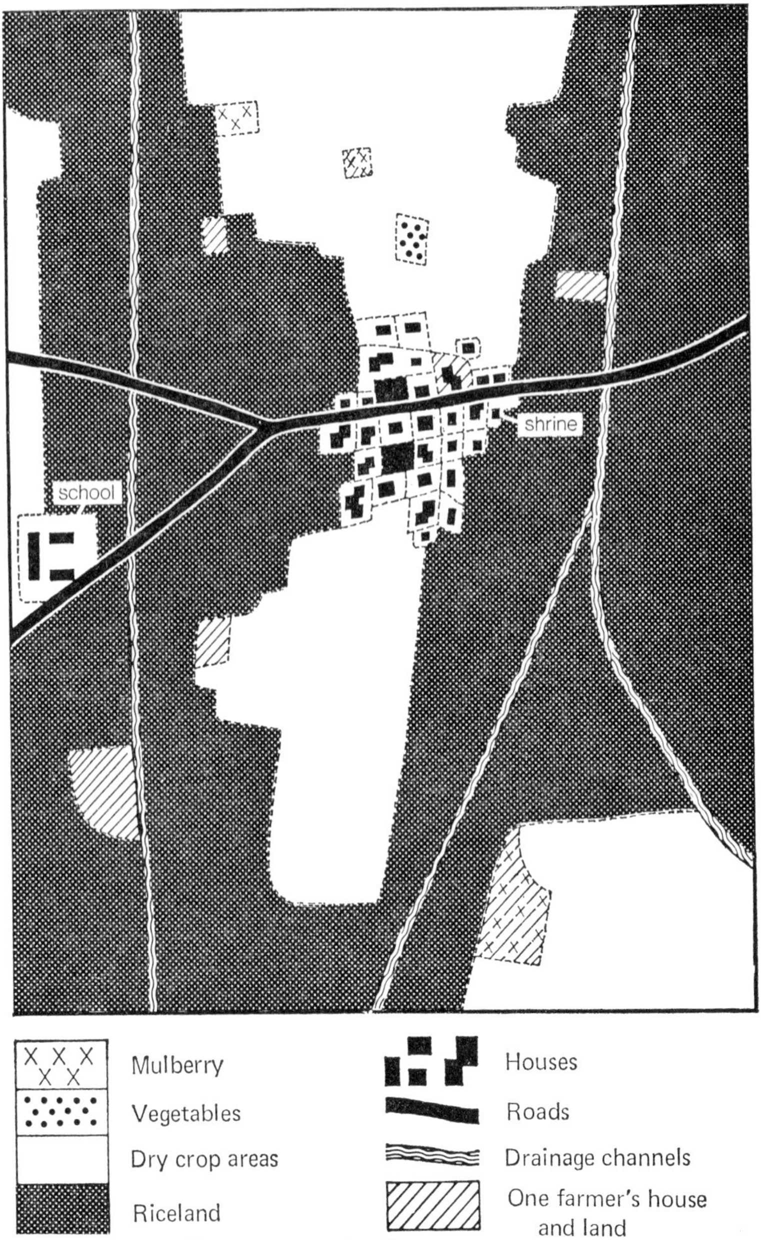

Figure 1 A small Japanese rural village

Source: G. T. Trewartha, *Japan, its physical, cultural and regional geography*, Methuen, 1948.

D

Category	*Age*	*Mental age*	*Principal features*
I	11·0 and below	12·0 and below	Not reality orientated
II	12·0 to 12·6	13·0 to 13·6	Reality orientated; single piece of evidence used
III	circa 13·6	14·0 to 14·6	Several pieces of evidence combined; able to relate cause and effect
IV	14·6 and above	15·6 and above	Comprehensive judgment based upon hypothetico-deductive reasoning

Table 2 Major response levels

were presented, and the level of difficulty posed by the questions. The children's responses inevitably reflected this variety, yet though the 12 response sequences varied in detail, they proved to be closely akin in general form, with certain of their more noteworthy and distinctive features tending to recur in accordance with a common pattern (Table 2). The number of responses placed at each level varied with each question, and individual children tended to fluctuate between one level and another when checked across all 12 response sequences, with the exception of those who were stabilised at either the first or the fourth level.

The principal features that characterise each of the successive stages of development can be illustrated in detail by reference to the response sequence that follows. For problem 4, a map, a photograph, and a short text were combined to convey a reasonably realistic picture of intensive subsistence tillage, with rice dominant, in an area of dense population. Both the questions set on this particular problem-situation were designed to focus attention upon those aspects of the traditional rural scene which contrast most markedly with British farming practices, and which are currently succumbing to change in Japan itself. The second question asked was related specifically to the map (Figure 1).

Question: 'The British farmer normally lives away from the village with his land grouped around his home in a single piece. Why do you think the Japanese farmer lives in the village with his land scattered in a number of separate places?'

Response sequence

I 1 'To be nearer the shops and their friends.'

2 'They might think it better to have it scattered. They might not like a big field and would prefer little ones.'

3 'He couldn't have land round there because the village is there so he has the land scattered.'

II 4 'Because some pieces are by the river and he needs the water for his rice.'

III 5 'It's scattered because he has to take what land he can get. He has two pieces near the drainage channels and others in dry areas where he's got vegetables and mulberry, because he can't grow anything else. He can have different crops at the right height.'

IV 6 'All the best land is needed for their farming and they can't afford any for the houses. If you relate the size of the house to the size of the plots of land, it would take up a lot of room. They want to use the best soil available for the crops and try to put the house on the poorer soil, so as to lose as little as possible. Because most of this bad soil is all in one place, rather than lose a high percentage of good soil they have the houses placed in one community.'

DISCUSSION AND CONCLUSIONS

The limitations imposed by concrete-operational thought are gradually removed during the years from 12 to 15, when the adolescent develops an ability to make use of propositional operations within a conceptual system which can be equated with a self-contained 'structured whole' (Inhelder and Piaget 1958). The conceptual system is self-contained in the sense that the adolescent's power of operational thought is no longer confined to practical problems and concrete situations, since he can now make use of hypothetico-deductive reasoning to deal with problems and possibilities which he has not encountered before.

The progress made by the adolescent in his development of Euclidean concepts, may be considered (*a*) in terms of the child's capacity to structure the field-of-action under review, and (*b*) in terms of the need to locate it within an extended Euclidean construct.

(*a*) Whilst the 10-year-old child may be able to take an area that he has experienced at first hand and represent it in some form of his own construction, when he is asked to analyse the material contained in a map of some place remote from his own experience, he is faced with a cognitive challenge of a different order. The youngest children quoted in the response sequence set out above were quite unable to accept the implications of the question in any realistic sense, and the answers given displayed a high degree of spatial confusion. As response 3 shows, many tended to react at the perceptual level, striving to conjure up some advantage to account for the obvious visual contrast between the compact nature of the village and the scattered pattern of farm plots. By about 12 years of age, the children could make a limited though realistic analysis of the map, related to single pieces of evidence tied to sub-sections of the spatial field, considered in isolation (e.g. response 4). Later, observations and analysis became progressively more skilled, perceptive and detailed, as in response 5, where the pupil quoted could combine several pieces of evidence to yield a fairly thorough analysis of the map in question. Finally, at the most mature level of judgment, the field-of-action could be organised as a whole from the outset. As response 6 demonstrates, there was a widespread tendency to scan the total situation in a reasoned way and to produce a judgment that could be supported by specific pieces of evidence.

(*b*) The meridians and parallels that geographers use provide a framework of coordinate axes of reference covering the whole globe. They form a comprehensive spatial 'container' that is wholly independent of the material it contains and dissociated from personal action.

The construction of an accurate mental picture of the world as a whole demands that each individual 'private world' should be reconciled with the external 'public world' in which places can be orientated within an abstract system of reference. An investigation by Blair (1964) into the difficulties experienced by children in map-comprehension, indicates that many children in the lower and middle years at secondary schools became uncertain and confused when presented with spatial distributions lying outside their personally constructed framework of reference. Only in the final, upper levels, were the children completely at ease with spatial distributions which were dependent upon a socially transmitted 'external frame of reference'.

These findings were supported in general by my own investigation, especially where the children had to relate the area concerned to its national or continental setting before they could comprehend the problem-situation in its entirety and provide an adequate explanation. This is expressed most clearly in problem 3, which was presented purely in photographic form, supplemented only by a single reference map to aid location. The area chosen for study formed a representative portion of the grain-growing region of Manitoba. The second question asked was specifically directed towards an oblique aerial photograph, which conveyed a vivid impression of a small prairie township in relation to the surrounding farming area. The children were then asked 'Why has this small town grown up here where the main road and railway cross each other?'

Those aged 10½ years and below were quite unable to grasp the implications of the question, and were apparently unaware of the extended frame-of-action to which these specialist grain farmers had geared their activities. They treated the photographed area as a discrete segment of space, unrelated to the larger area of which it formed a part; e.g.:

It makes it easier for people to go there because it is in the middle.

Such limitations were not overcome until the children could set the observed area within a received frame of reference, or make use of external evidence to locate the local area within its continental setting; e.g.:

The wheat is stored in those elevators and then loaded onto the train. It's taken away by train to the Great Lakes and then shipped by lake steamer and then ocean ship, to Britain.

Responses of this quality were not in evidence until after about 12 years of age.

This analysis seems to indicate that the children could not locate the areal unit under review with any degree of precision, nor orientate themselves spatially within that context-of-action, until they were 13 or older. These abilities are closely related to each other and they depend on the child applying, at the level of formal-operational thought, those Euclidean concepts which he has formed earlier at the concrete-operational level. A repeated sequence of development is thus required at the level of abstract thought. The spatial confusion displayed by the younger children suggests that they could neither conjure up a complete and accurate mental picture of the phenomena being studied, nor link them together in spatial relationships with any degree of certainty.

A map, as a system of communication, employs a complex artificial language to describe selected aspects of man's environment. The transmitted data, expressed in codified form, represent a simplified structure of reality. If a student can translate its symbolism into tangible imagery, the map may then act as an analytical tool, helping him to discern causal relationships amongst the spatial distribution it describes. Interpretation and explanation are thus open to the geographer in his use of maps. But the interpretation of symbolised material can only take place on the conceptual level, making use of those 'cognitive structures which link the individual's present perception and learning to his previous experience' (Vinacke 1952). A pupil who lacked the necessary knowledge and experience would be unable to translate or decode the cartographer's message. Responding intuitively to some visually dominant feature would be of little avail in itself, without some awareness of the underlying structure of reality.

The youngest children quoted in the Japanese village response sequence were obviously unaware of the true significance of the data being examined, and resorted in consequence to illogical guesswork. The concentration of buildings into a tight cluster at a particular spot, and the scattered distribution of farm plots, can only be interpreted by reference to some qualifying factor, such as surface configuration, soil fertility, land use or social organisation. Before an adequate explanation can be constructed one needs to draw upon concepts and generalisations which stand outside the test material. This is not achieved until about 13½ years of age, when a limited amount of deductive analysis becomes possible. Although the accounts given remain descriptive in form, cause and effect relationships could be plausibly stated, involving extended reasoning and dependent upon a wider background of knowledge.

This cumulative improvement in the quality of explanation offered is further strengthened by a progressive advance in the children's capacity to take account of the appropriate cultural viewpoint, and to appraise the area under review as though through the eyes of the people who live there. A realistic and reasoned appraisal of human activity within a spatial context requires an awareness of 'the interaction of man and land as exemplified in particular places' (Fisher 1970), where egocentrically determined value transference would inhibit true understanding. The problem of the perceived environment is under active investigation by geographers at present (Harvey 1969, Kirk 1963). Egocentrism, or the tendency for individuals to judge the world from a single viewpoint – their own – whilst apparently unaware of differing viewpoints or perspectives, is one of the fundamental, recurrent themes of Piaget's work. There is considered to be a continual advance and retreat of egocentric behaviour as the child progresses through the successive stages of his development, resurgence occurring whenever the child is confronted with some new cognitive challenge. It is not surprising, therefore, to discover a further outburst of egocentric thought with entry at adolescence into the realm of the possible and the hypothetical.

It was characteristic of all twelve response sequences that many of the younger children expressed judgments of an egocentric character. Where the situation under review could be equated with something familiar, the course of action referred to would be structured or organised purely in terms of past experience. On the other hand, where it could not be equated with something within the child's experience, there was a pronounced tendency to pass judgment in terms of some individual whim or personal preference attributed to the group concerned. Such attitudes are exemplified by the first two responses quoted in the Japanese village sequence, where human wishes took precedence, with very little to suggest that local circumstances might impose some limitation or restraint upon individual enterprise. In contrast, the responses placed in category IV revealed a capacity for objective judgment, where these older children could take into account the technical resources and expectations of the local population, as well as the restraints imposed by the environment. It is here, therefore, that the adolescent can orientate himself culturally, as well as spatially, within the foreign environment he is called upon to examine, and thus achieve a comprehensive explanation. This achievement depends on the emergence of a capacity to reason formally with hypotheses and propositions, expressed in precise verbal terms.

According to Piaget, the child will make what he can of what he sees or encounters, by virtue of the structures of thought possessed at his particular level of development. In order to comprehend and then to explain a problem-situation of a geographical nature, one requires the capacity to handle effectively a great number of variables operating in conjunction with each other. Before adolescence this would be well beyond the reasoning capacity of the child. The experimental investigations of Piaget and Inhelder (1958) into the powers of reasoning employed by children at different age levels, when confronted with scientific problems, have shown that the ability to deal with problems involving several elements or variables does not arise until past the age of 12. A complete and satisfying explanation could not be achieved until all the factors involved could be combined and analysed at the level of formal-operational thought.

It has been argued that a gradual transition may be discerned during adolescence, with the largely descriptive form of thought, which is used at first, giving way to a comprehensive, detailed and fully adequate power of explanation (Peel 1965, 1968). The results of the author's investigation would strongly support this contention. The growth and development of the adolescent's capacity to reason propositionally with material of a geographical nature is seen to be a slow and gradual process with each stage in the overall sequence of development shading off gradually, and at times almost imperceptibly, into the next. Though it is difficult to define age limits with precision, four major response levels may be detected (Table 2). Their principal characteristics may be illustrated once again by reference to the Japanese village response sequence listed above.

At first the situation is not appreciated, and the answers given involve tautology, irrelevance and denial of premises. The reality-orientated responses which follow employ judgments passed purely in terms of content, though expressed in propositional form. There is a gradual progression from unqualified inferences dependent upon isolated pieces of content, to a more adequate descriptive analysis, where the older pupils could interrelate important sub-groups within the total range of causative factors seen to be in operation. Finally, at the most mature level of judgment, a more sophisticated and elaborate analysis could be organised in terms of some positive assertion or hypothesis, to which a wide range of evidence could be related to sustain a relatively thorough explanation.

The child's intellectual advance is made possible through a process of dynamic adaptive interaction between the child and his environment. When confronted by a fresh cognitive challenge, the child has to resolve what is, in effect, a discrepancy between his current level of intellectual functioning and the demands exerted by the problem so encountered. When asked to come to terms with 'worlds' far removed from his own, the adolescent has to achieve 'equilibrium by active resolution and compensation' (Peel 1965), in order to resolve the external disturbance and effect a complete explanation.

The extent to which intellectual progress can be accelerated has yet to be clearly established (Hooper 1969). Certainly, in geography, carefully structured experience in field-work can refine key concepts, illustrate fundamental processes, and establish a secure basis for further advance (Everson 1969). Similarly, the use of operational games can sensibly reduce the number of variables involved through the creation of a simplified model of reality, and thereby help the child to cope 'with a good deal of advanced material long before that material can be consciously absorbed at the level of formal concepts' (Walford 1969). It remains true, however, that even the most enlightened teaching will be of little avail unless the child is in possession of those structures of thought which allow him to absorb the material provided and profit from the experience.

References

D. Blair, (1964) 'A practical study of the ability of some secondary pupils to handle the representation of spatial relationships', unpublished Dip. Ed. dissertation, University of Liverpool.
University of Liverpool.

R. J. Chorley and P. Haggett, (1970) *Frontiers in geographical teaching*, Methuen.

J. Everson, (1969) 'Some aspects of teaching geography through fieldwork', *Geography*, vol. 54.

C. A. Fisher, (1970) 'Whither regional geography?' *Geography*, vol. 55.

R. Goldman, (1964) *Religious thinking from childhood to adolescence*, Routledge.

P. Haggett, (1965) *Locational analysis in human geography*, Edward Arnold.

R. N. Hallam, (1967) 'Logical thinking in history', *Educational Review*, vol. 19.

D. Harvey, (1969) *Explanation in geography*, Edward Arnold.

F. H. Hooper, (1969) 'Piagetian research and education', *Logical thinking in children*, I. E. Sigel and F. H. Hooper (eds.), Holt International.

B. Inhelder and J. Piaget, (1958) *The growth of logical thinking from childhood to adolescence*, Routledge.

W. Kirk, (1963) 'Problems of geography', *Geography*, vol. 48.

A. R. Lodwick, (1958) 'An investigation of the question whether the inferences that children draw in learning history correspond with the stages of mental development that Piaget postulates', unpublished Dip.Ed. dissertation, University of Birmingham.

A. J. Lunnon, (1969) 'The understanding of certain geographical concepts by Primary School children', unpublished M.Ed. thesis, University of Birmingham.

E. A. Lunzer, (1968) 'Children's thinking', *Educational Research in Britain*, H. J. Butcher (ed.), University of London Press.
(1968) 'Formal reasoning', *Development in Learning*, vol. 2: *Development in human learning*, E. A. Lunzer and J. F. Morris (eds.), Staples Press.

J. F. Marsh, (1966) 'An investigation into differences between children in the formation of concepts of town and country', unpublished M.Ed. thesis, University of Aberdeen.

E. A. Peel, (1961) 'The growth of pupils' judgements in thinking comprehension,' unpublished account of research at Princeton, New Jersey.

(1965) 'Intellectual growth during adolescence', *Educational Review*, vol. 17, June 1965.

(1968) 'Conceptual learning and explainer thinking', *Development in Learning*, vol. 2: *Development in Human Learning*, E. A. Lunzer and J. F. Morris (eds.), Staples Press.

J. Piaget, (1955) *The child's construction of reality*, Routledge.

J. Piaget and B. Inhelder, (1956) *The child's conception of space*, Routledge.

J. Piaget, B. Inhelder and A. Szeminska, (1960) *The child's conception of geometry*, Routledge.

F. M. Prior, (1959) 'The place of maps in the Junior School', unpublished Dip.Ed. dissertation, University of Birmingham.

W. T. Rhys, (1966) 'The development of logical thought in the adolescent with reference to the teaching of geography in the Secondary School', unpublished M.Ed. thesis, University of Birmingham.

W. E. Vinacke, (1952) *The psychology of thinking*, McGraw-Hill.

R. Walford, (1969) *Games in geography*, Longmans.

J. G. Wallace, (1965) *Concept growth and the education of the child*, NFER, Slough.

9 Children's vocabulary

DENNIS MILBURN

The formation of geographical concepts is closely associated with the development of an appropriate vocabulary. Geographical terms are presented to children through their own experience, through visual stimuli, through the written word, and by speech. Each of these factors is interrelated in the evolution of concepts, though one factor may be more dominant than others at various stages of development.

The following analysis is based on the results of an investigation carried out over a period of five years. It attempts to review the major difficulties experienced by children in their understanding of current geographical vocabulary. The size of a school vocabulary in geography is also estimated, and in the light of the results of the investigation basic recommendations are made to help the development of such a vocabulary.

In geography we have to consider how far verbal images and text-book information lead to an understanding of facts and activities which may take place far away from the classroom. If children are given frames of reference which are too rigid they may find it difficult to discard them later, and they may also find it difficult to use them in their appreciation of relationships. This factor could be seen in the large number of children who stated in the tests that oases were *only* found in the Sahara. Other research has shown that adults with a high standard of attainment in geography have been able to construct a hypothetical model of, for example, erosional processes, but have been unable to apply it to the actual landscape. In the cognitive domain the simple communication of the correct version of an idea is not always enough. Nevertheless, our conceptual development depends to a large extent on verbal symbols. Within the bounds of a 'subject' we also depend to an even greater extent on the technical vocabulary of that subject as a skeleton for our thinking.

DEVISING A MASTER LIST OF GEOGRAPHICAL TERMS

For the overall size of a geographical vocabulary we could refer to geographical dictionaries in current use. For example, in the Penguin edition of *A Dictionary of Geography* there are 1,336 geographical terms, while in *A Dictionary of Geography* by F. J. Monkhouse there are 3,400 terms. However, some terms are obviously used more frequently than others. From the investigation referred to, the following figures emerge as to the number of terms used for work in geographical studies in primary and secondary schools:

	By 4th year in primary school	*By 5th year in secondary school*
Number of terms obtained through frequency of use in the classroom	147	315
Number of terms obtained through a sample analysis of text books	167	368

The geographical terms used in classroom teaching were collected, with the assistance of teachers, in three primary and three secondary schools over a period of five years. During collection such terms as names of countries, tribes, races, peoples, animals, plants, products, rivers, seas, and oceans were omitted. By a series of control tests with children of all ages, including sixth-formers and students, a 'master list' of terms was compiled, i.e. those terms which were in most active everyday use in schools, up to and including the Ordinary level examination. These 315 terms were used as a basis for testing the individual interpretation and definition of geographical terms of 1,000 children, 500 in primary schools and 500 in secondary schools.

This 'master list' of geographical terms now follows. It contains the 315 terms that occurred with most frequency; the 147 terms of highest frequency in primary schools are in italic.

Geographical terms of highest frequency in use in the sample schools

afforestation
agriculture
airport
alluvium
alp
altitude
anticline
antarctic circle
anthracite
anticyclone
antipodes
aquifer

archipelago
arctic circle
arête
arid
artesian
arm
atlas
atoll
avalanche

bank
bar

barometer
barchan
barrage
basalt
basin
bay
beach
bench
bight
block
bluff
boll weevil

bore
boulder clay
bourne
braided
breaker

cairn
campos
canal
canyon
cape
cataract
cave
chain
chalk
channel
chaparral
chinook
clay
clint
coal
coast
col
combe
confluence
coniferous
continent
contour
conurbation
convection
coral
core
corrie
crag
crag and tail
crater
creek
crevasse
croft
crust
cuesta
cyclone

dam
deciduous
delta
denudation
deposition
depression
desert
distributary
doldrums
downland
drowned valley
drumlin
dry farming
dry valley
dune
dust
dyke

earthquake
embankment
entrepot
equator
equinox
erosion
escarpment
estancia
estuary
export

fault
fault line
fen
fiord
firth
flint
flood
flood plain
fog
fold
ford
fossil
front
frost

gap
garrigue
geography
geology
geyser
glacier
gorge
granite
grike
groyne
gulch
gulf
gully

hail
hanging valley
harmattan
haze
headland
heath
hill
hinterland
hogback
hook
horse latitude
horst
humus
hurricane
hydro-electric power

ice
ice age
iceberg
ice cap
ice floe
ice sheet
impermeable
import
inlet
irrigation
island
isobar
isotherm
isthmus

joint
jungle

kaolin

karst
kopje

lagoon
lake
latitude
lava
levee
limestone
llanos
loch
loess
longitude
longshore drift
lough

magma
magnetic pole
mangrove swamp
map
maquis
marble
market
market gardening
marsh
mediterranean
metamorphic
meteor
meteorology
midnight
mirage
mist
mistral
monsoon
moor
moraine
mountain
mouth
mud

ness
nodal point
nomad
north pole

oasis
ocean
outcrop
ox bow

pack ice
pampas
pass
pavement
peak
peat
peneplain
peninsula
permeable
plain
plateau
plunge pool
polje
port
pot hole
prairie
promontory
pygmy

quartz
quicksand

radial drainage
rain
rainbow
rain guage
rain shadow
raised beach
range
rapids
ravine
raw materials
reef
relief
ria
ridge
rift valley
river
river capture
river terrace
road
rock

sand
sandstone
savanna
screes
scrub
seaport
seasons
sedimentary
selvas
serac
shale
shield
shingle
ship canal
shoal
silt
sleet
smog
snow
solstice
sound
south pole
spit
spring line
stack
stalactite
stalagmite
steppe
straits
strata
strath
stratosphere
subsoil
sun
swallow holes
swamp
syncline

tableland
tarn
thermometer
tide
topsoil

tor	u-shaped valley	*watershed*
town	*upland*	water table
trade winds	vale	wave cut platform
transhumance	*valley*	weathering
tributary	*village*	*well*
tropic	*volcano*	whirlpool
truck farming		*wind*
tundra	wadi	wind gap
typhoon	*waterfall*	wind rose

The individual interpretation of words depends on the range of a personal vocabulary. The Plowden Report states 'it has been estimated that a child needs about 3,000 words to begin reading' (vol. 1, sec. 55). A general assumption after referring to such authorities as Smith (1941), Thorndike and Lorge (1968), Vernon (1950), and Terman and Merrill (1937) is that at the mental age of 5 a child can use 2,000 words and the average adult can use about 10,000 words. The ratio of 'technical' (i.e. purely geographical) terms to everyday terms used in geography is approximately 2:1.

Vocabulary research is usually conducted on a basis of word frequency. Thus in Thorndike's *Teachers' word book of 20,000 words* a well-known geographical term such as 'river' is listed among the 'first 500 commonest words' in the English language, whereas the word 'Cambrian' occurs only once in 4,000,000.

In the 'master list' there are 96 geographical terms which are words of high frequency in everyday usage. As well as relating these to the Thorndike lists they can be compared with other word lists, such as Faucett-Maki (1939) and the Interim Report on Vocabulary Selection. Within these 96 words there are a number of homonyms (basin, cape, plain, etc.) and a number of homophons or near homophons (beach-beech, desert-dessert, etc.). Nevertheless, 35 of the words in the master list are words of very high frequency in all word counts. These are as follows:

beach	export	market	sand
canal	flood	marsh	sea
cave	fog	midnight	sleet
channel	frost	mist	snow
clay	hill	moor	sun
cliff	import	mountain	valley
coast	island	ocean	volcano
dam	lake	rain	waterfall
dust	map	river	

It is not usually thought necessary in teaching to pay more than cursory attention to the definition of words which are in common usage. Nevertheless, the test material showed that children could define an island as 'a little kind of box in the middle of the road' and a valley as 'a little village'. Similarly, most adults would use the term 'river' without realising that children may have concepts which are half formed and entirely at variance with an adult's concept. Thus a river could be defined as 'a long pool' or 'a dug ditch'. The most elementary geographical terms need checking with younger children, particularly, as will be seen later, if they are homonymic.

Having decided on the 315 terms of highest classroom frequency, it became possible to select those appropriate to the type of work carried out in schools in each school year, from the first year in the junior school to the fifth year in the secondary school. It is interesting to note that this total of 315 terms is approximately one-tenth of the total number of terms in F. J. Monkhouse's dictionary, and that this equates with Thorndike's 'first 1,000 most common words' as being one-tenth of the average adult vocabulary.

GEOGRAPHICAL TERMS DERIVED FROM TEXT BOOKS

Before the tests were given the whole range of terms used in classroom teaching were set against a sample of terms used in school text books. It is necessary to make some digression into the range of terms used in geographical text books. Sixty-five texts were studied in detail. Forty-six of these were especially written for primary school children, and the remaining nineteen comprised three 'sets' of secondary school books.

Following the same criteria used in compiling the 'master list', the following overall results were obtained:

	Number of terms used	*Percentage of terms defined within texts*	*Percentage of terms illustrated*
Primary texts	187	59	32
Secondary texts	368	42	50

In the primary texts the number of 'physical' terms is very high. Using the criteria: landforms, climate and weather, soils and vegetation, 123 out of a total of 187 are 'physical' terms. In the secondary school texts 266 out of a total of 368 terms are 'physical' terms.

There is not space here to make detailed comments on the analysis of the text books and their presentation of geographical terms, but some specific examples can be given. There is, in some of the primary school series, a marked lack of uniformity in definitions, at times bordering on the incorrect. For example the term 'delta' was defined as a river 'with nine channels', in another as a 'mangrove swamp', and in another book a picture appeared of a delta which looked exactly like a lily pond. Similarly, a levee was described as a feature where 'farmers have been building these banks for thousands of years'. Again, 'the Loire enters the great *plain* which geographers call the Paris *Basin*'. Finally, fourteen of the primary texts had no scale line on any of their maps. It would seem to be advisable that terms should be defined with even greater care in primary texts, and the fact that so many primary school pupils are encouraged to search for details in more than one book adds further emphasis to this point.

Contradictions in definition occur in some cases in secondary school texts, but not to such a great extent. In some cases a comparison of, for example, diagrams of rift valleys could be confusing, since they range from the characteristic 'block' illustration to one which resembles the classic cross-section of a denuded anticline. In secondary texts there were some indications that problems could arise by making over-generous assumptions as to what the reader might know. This was seen when specific terms were used in an adjectival manner, e.g. 'karstic plateaux, Dalmatian coastline, Garrigue hillsides'. This could of course be overcome by the use of a footnote, a glossary, or a dictionary.

Some series also showed a marked preference for locating features at one point only on the surface of the earth. In this way 36 out of the 49 references to an oasis related to the Sahara and 27 out of 30 references to fiords were related to Norway. However, it is impossible to prove which precise piece of information a pupil has learned from a text book. His learning is an amalgam of classroom teaching, the provision of material, and wider experience gained outside the classroom.

It is probably not surprising that the number of terms used in text books (368) is fairly close to the number collected in classrooms (315). Classroom terms tend to reflect text-book information. Teachers themselves also tend to use a well-defined hierarchy of terms which reach them mainly through the printed word and which they themselves pass on to pupils as a semi-perpetual geographical vocabulary.

TESTING THE UNDERSTANDING OF SELECTED GEOGRAPHICAL TERMS

As has been mentioned, tests were given to 500 children in three primary schools and 500 in three secondary schools. Two of the schools were in Central London, two in the suburbs, and two in the Midlands. An attempt was made to cover the widest possible range of socio-economic backgrounds.

The tests, as will be seen in the following table, ranged from testing the understanding of between 47 and 215 geographical terms. In addition the secondary school test was given to groups of sixth-form students and first year students in higher education who had obtained Advanced Level geography.

The test subjects were asked to define the terms under the questions 'Tell me something about this word' and 'What does this mean to you'. In the first two years of the primary school, verbal answers were accepted and written down by the testers. Drawings and diagrams were accepted at all levels. In marking the tests, full credit was given to any explanation which suggested a grasp of the essential meaning. Thus the term 'correct' in the table below is a very relative term.

The overall results from the tests now follow:

	Number of terms in test	*Average attempt* %	*'Correct' definitions* %
Primary school (junior)			
1st Year	47	53·1	8·8
2nd Year	81	43·2	12·2
3rd Year	165	39·3	14·6
4th Year	215	42·3	29·7
Secondary school			
1st Year	215	78·1	34·5
2nd Year	215	80·0	52·0
3rd Year	215	86·9	55·3
4th Year	215	89·3	57·2
5th Year	215	95·3	61·2

The average overall rate of attempt in the primary school was that 44·47% of the terms were defined. In the secondary school the overall average was almost double this figure, 85·9%.

As the tests progressed it became possible to isolate those terms which presented difficulties in definition at various age levels. They were not always obscure terms. For example, the term 'alp' had a very high attempt rate, but was also always defined as a range of mountains. The following table shows those terms in the tests which presented difficulties at four levels of school development:

First year of primary school (junior): No. of attempts by 100 children		*Last year of primary school*	*First year of secondary school*	*Fifth year of secondary school*
Avalanche	11	*alp*	alluvium	*alp*
Channel	18	antarctic	*alp*	artesian
Geyser	10	bar	anticyclone	*barrage*
Haze	5	*basin*	*barrage*	bluff
Heath	12	canal	*basin*	*col*
Marsh	21	cape	cataract	*distributary*
Moor	21	chain	*col*	*equinox*
Mouth	33	cliff	*confluence*	*flood plain*
Plain	15	*confluence*	corrie	gulch
Pygmy	10	continent	deposition	hogback
Swamp	6	equator	*distributary*	*isthmus*
Tributary	6	*erosion*	*equinox*	*mist*
River	65	estuary	*erosion*	*solstice*
		fog	*flood plain*	*swallow hole*
		gorge	gulf	*transhumance*
		irrigation	hinterland	*water table*
		lake	isobar	*wind rose*
		marsh	isotherm	
		mountain	*isthmus*	
		mouth	meander	
		north pole	*mist*	
		ocean	outcrop	
		plain	rainshadow	
		river	*solstice*	
		snow	stack	
		swamp	*swallow hole*	
		tributary	tarn	
		valley	tor	
		wind	*transhumance*	
			tributary	
			water table	
			wind rose	

Terms in italics occur in more than one column.

It is only possible within the short space of this chapter to look at a few brief examples from the many thousands of answers which were made in the tests. Of particular interest is the effect of homonyms on primary school children. As Ervin and Foster (1947) point out 'where meanings differ the child sticks to the most common meaning'. Thus "cape" is primarily an article of wear, and "ford" is a car. "Fault" was defined as in "it is your fault", "peak" as "on your cap", and "relief" as "a thing that did not happen". On the other hand some children gave meanings which were rarer than the geographical meaning: thus "latitude" as "you have it your own way".'

The homophonic terms were often difficult to separate from terms which were merely misread. Thus 'gorge' was often defined as 'George', and 'moor' as 'more'. Terms misread ranged from 'artesian', defined as 'good at painting', through 'irrigation' – 'going to another country' to 'aquifer', defined as 'where you keep arrows'. There were many other examples of the misreading of terms used in geography.

However, many primary school children made good attempts at verbalising the difficult concept of 'river'. 'A long pathway full of water' came as early as age 7, whereas the idea of flow came at 8, 'an everlasting flow'. The direction of flow was sometimes a problem: 'a line of water leading in from the sea'.

Valleys on the other hand caused great problems. Definitions ranged from 'down and up' (age 7), through 'the bottom of a mountain' (age 8), 'a dip between two hills' (age 9) to 'a river-chiselled ditch' (age 10). However, there were also definitions such as 'a little town' (age 7), 'a low village' (age 9) and 'lots of houses' (age 10).

Other examples which show that children have a concept which is adequate for them are: beach, 'the edge of the land near the sea', coast, 'the edge round the land', channel, 'where people go who can swim furthest'; cliff, 'a hill with a flat front', mountain, 'a high sort of hill'. Hills and mountains gave rise to many and varied definitions, the most normal feature being to use the concept of 'hill' as a basis for describing a mountain. Children were also able to give graphic definitions of features of which they had no experience, for example: volcano 'a tall mountain that spits fire'; though sometimes the description was animistic, 'where men blow rocks up'.

As was mentioned earlier in the chapter, there is a danger in primary school teaching that simple terms, such as beach, hill, and river, may be used in geographical study without further explanation. Similarly it is also often assumed that some mystical learning barrier is passed at the age of 11, and that fully developed concepts are readily available for abstract and analytical thought. As was seen in the previous table, however, many very basic terms are still imperfectly understood in the early years of the secondary school. Terms such as 'tributary' still being defined as 'a place where water is kept'. Even at fifth-form level a river basin was still equated with a river valley. There was also confusion with the actual bed of a river, but the most general misconception was to equate a river basin either with the lowland area liable to flooding, or the flood plain itself. At sixth-form level a basin was still being defined by some as 'the region between the banks or bluffs of a river'.

Other difficulties arise when geographical terms are themselves imprecise, as in the case of 'gorge' and 'canyon'. The fact that they are often synonymous makes their use more difficult. When pressed to define the difference, if any, the structure of thinking was that if a gorge had been formed by a river, then a canyon, because it had a different name, must have been formed by some other process.

Though there was a marked increase in verbal fluency as the tests progressed through the secondary school years, it did not follow that such an increase was correlated with the development of concepts. In some cases fluency only illustrated the lack of such concepts. Thus an excellent physical description of the Rhine rift valley was marred by attributing the valley to glacial action and the 'stepped' sides to soil creep. There were also cases where verbal explanations used terms which themselves reflected larger concepts, as in the case of terms such as 'equinox' and 'solstice'. Probably no other two terms tested, produced such rambling and amorphous answers, revealing the need for the detailed conceptual understanding which lies behind the verbal definition.

In general it could be deduced from the tests that, by the end of each main period of general education (i.e. at 11 and 16) pupils in the sample know approximately 62% of the geographical terms which are used in schools. However, they vary considerably in their ability to use them as aids to their own development.

Nevertheless, since a large number of terms in the 'master list' are physical terms, a large amount of practical work could be done either with equipment (sand trays, weather instruments, etc.) or during field work.

After the tests had isolated the terms which proved difficult at various stages of development, teaching experiments were set up to investigate situations in which those terms and their associated concepts could be learned. The overall result was that the understanding of most terms improved if subjected to concentrated study. In the primary school there was a marked increase in the use and precision of vocabulary after active experience. In the secondary school, where the two main areas of difficulty appeared to be the difficulty of understanding data relating to climate, and in particular the relationship of the earth and the sun, understanding again showed a marked improvement after practical investigation. There was, however, more resistance in the secondary school to reinvestigating material which had already been covered. This is referred to by Jersild (1947) as a 'natural disinclination to return to base'. In a sense a pupil feels aggrieved at having to reconsider those facts he claims to 'know'. However, as Bloom suggests (1965) 'more complex aims in cognition require far more sophisticated learning experiences' and this factor is of additional importance in promoting the awareness of relationships.

In the primary school, therefore, it would appear to be particularly important to ensure that geographical terms which are common to everyday speech are carefully presented in their geographical context, particularly if they are homonymic (bank, cape, ford, pass, mouth, well, etc.).

By the age of transfer to the secondary school it is often assumed that simple concepts have been fully assimilated, and that the pupil is ready to move to a study of overseas areas with relevant concepts of space, time, and relationships well established and ready to build on. From the tests it appeared that a considerable gap still remained between the awareness of a term and the ability to use it in a constructive way.

THE PROBLEM OF REGIONAL OR IDEOGRAPHIC TERMS

Those ideographic terms which relate to specific regions did not appear, from the tests, to be as important in geographic understanding as is often implied in schools (sudd, paramos, kopje, etc.). If a specific area is not dealt with in regional studies, then it is unlikely that the term will arise. In the introduction of geographical terms into schools, therefore, we need to draw a distinction between terms which have a ubiquitous meaning regardless of location, and those ideographic terms which are used for a particular feature in a particular location. Thus it is more important that children have an adequate conceptual understanding of such terms as 'flood plain' and 'transhumance' (both terms which are still presenting difficulty to fifth-form pupils), than mere verbal facility in describing ideographic terms such as campos, fjeld, puna or shott. Indeed the more detailed regional studies become, the less useful these terms become. The 'estancia', which has a definite regional connotation related to Argentina or Uruguay, becomes a 'fundo' in Chile, even though the agricultural economy is similar. Similarly, a term such as 'pampas' has different meanings in different parts of Latin America. The Argentinian pampas is the geographical 'type' area, but in Eastern Bolivia flat, fertile plateau areas at around 11,000 ft are also called 'pampas' as are the flat areas in the Atacama desert in northern Chile. The only common feature here is 'flat' or 'plain-like' since neither the Bolivian or Chilean pampas has a climatic relationship with the temperate grassland pampas of Argentina.

Similarly, it could be deduced from the tests that, if terms are used too specifically in teaching, one could reach a point where terms remain in isolation. For example, all oases are thought to be in the Sahara, and rift valleys are defined as a place rather than as an example of a particular type of physical feature.

CONCLUSION

The range of a child's geographical vocabulary and his true understanding of it may be markedly different. Development will not only depend on his educability; it will also be related to the amount of geographical material covered and the way it is presented in the learning situation. As was mentioned earlier, the understanding of most terms can improve if subjected to concentrated study, but a true understanding of basic terms, such as 'tributary', is an essential prerequisite to geographical studies.

The concepts, principles and elementary hypotheses which may have been formulated in the primary school are developed in the secondary school. However, review and relearning may still be essential since there is always a natural tendency to regress to simpler operations, particularly when new problem-solving situations are encountered.

Correct verbal expression is to be encouraged, for, along with active experience, it helps to consolidate learning (Luria 1961). Though some definitions are learned by rote and some concepts are difficult to verbalise, these should not be reasons for not attempting to develop children's geographical vocabulary. The acquisition of concepts and active vocabulary are complementary aspects of the process of intellectual development.

References

B. S. Bloom, (1965) *Taxonomy of educational objectives*, Longmans.

L. J. Cronbach, (1943) 'Measurement of knowledge of precise word meaning', *Journal of Educational Research*, vol. 36.

S. M. Ervin and J. F. Foster, (1947) 'The development of meaning in children's descriptive terms', *Journal of Abnormal Social Psychology*, vol. 61.

T. J. Eskridge, 'Growth in the understanding of geographic terms', *Research Studies No. 4*, Duke University Press.

L. Faucett, (1939) *A study of word values statistically determined*, University of Tokyo.

O. Garnett, (1960) *Fundamentals in school geography*, Harrap.

A. T. Jersild, (1947) *The psychology of the adolescent*, Prentice-Hall.

J. J. Kirkpatrick and E. E. Cureton, (1949) 'Vocabulary item frequency and word difficulty', *Journal of Applied Psychology*, vol. 33.

A. R. Luria, (1961) *The role of speech in the regulation of normal and abnormal behaviour*, Pergamon.

D. H. Russell, (1954) *Dimensions of children's meaning vocabulary*, University of California Press.

M. K. Smith, (1941) *Measurement of the size of general English vocabulary*, Genet Psychology Monograph, no. 24.

M. Terman and M. A. Merrill, (1937) *Measuring intelligence*, Houghton Mifflin.

E. L. Thorndike and F. Lorge, (1968) *The teacher's word book of 20,000 words*, Teachers College Press.

P. E. Vernon, (1950) 'Estimation of the difficulties of vocabulary', *British Journal of Educational Psychology*, vol. 20.

10 Children's attitudes to other nationalities

JOHN CARNIE

For most pupils school geography is essentially an extension and explanation of what they know about a world they have in small part experienced directly and in large part only heard of, and nowadays seen indirectly. Their growing understanding of the world, its countries and peoples, possibly even its landforms and climatic regions, is likely to be influenced by prior perceptions of and feelings about salient features of certain lands, natural phenomena, nations and races which have attracted their attention, perhaps from their earliest years. Relatively few pupils will go on to make geography a study in which insight and objectivity predominate.

Recent investigations into attitudes towards people of different nation and race have shown that much of what children learn and remember in their junior and secondary years is affected by previous experiences and prevailing attitudes well beyond the influence of traditional teaching methods. Geography teachers tend to disclaim responsibility for the encouragement of international goodwill among their pupils,* yet research evidence strongly suggests that children's ideas of other lands and peoples are at least as much determined by attitudes towards them as by knowledge of them.

Children of junior school age show a great diversity in their range of factual recall about different peoples and countries; they also vary greatly in the extent to which they are inclined to be accepting or rejecting about known out-group differences. But they are on average moving to a pre-adolescent peak of friendliness towards other natio-

* When 500 geography teachers, university lecturers and sixth-form pupils were asked to put in rank order thirty statements about the value of learning geography in school, on average the statement that 'geography deepens the pupils' appreciation of other peoples' way of life' was ranked first while the statement that 'the study of geography helps to foster international goodwill' was placed nineteenth.

nalities and races, when the majority will be most inclined to notice similarities with and tolerate differences among foreign peoples, and only perhaps 10% to 20% will be generally suspicious or hostile in outlook. The factors affecting their individual attitudes are bound to be complicated: personality and intellectual ability, home characteristics and community background, the mass media, school and classroom experiences, may all be having their influence. Yet it is possible to note certain developmental factors which have led up to this stage of maximum toleration around the age of 10 and to point to some probable subsequent trends.

THE ATTITUDES OF INFANTS AND LOWER JUNIOR CHILDREN

As an infant the child will have collected clues from its environment about certain frequently mentioned foreigners. In particular the names German, American, Russian, African (or Negro) and Chinese, may have become associated with a collection of diverse facts through hearing about 'The War', the space race, and peoples who are very different. So a crude concept of, for instance, the Chinese may have been formulated by the age of 6 or 7. Mention of the Chinese may then elicit fragments of adult stereotypes about people with yellow skin, slit eyes and pigtails, living in junks and eating rice. Such a pleasant but out-dated figment may have already been somewhat tainted by a whiff of Oriental menace from a television film revival or from an elder brother's comic, but is unlikely to develop into or be supplanted by a stereotyped view of the menacing Chinese Communist until fuller exposure to the mass media and adult prejudices in later adolescence. Concepts of various salient out-groups not directly encountered will similarly emerge from the early fragmented knowledge of the 7-year-old, growing to some kind of coherent mental picture adequate to meet his needs as an adult: more or less detailed, more or less accurate, more or less stereotyped.

Concepts about other nations and races develop like all other concepts which individuals hold, through classification, assimilation and adaptation; but they have one peculiarity, that they are themselves concerned with the characteristics of people. It seems that the first stage in the formation of such concepts is the identification by the child of his own ethnic or national group. This is likely to occur early, where the child is growing up in a mixed community, when racial awareness is frequently observed at the age of 2 or 3 (and own-group valuation, high or low, follows soon after), and often not until 6 or

7 in a homogeneous society when it is a matter of recognising one's national membership through such diffuse items as a country's name, its chief symbols (head of state, flag, capital) and perhaps its main claims to fame. It is not surprising that West European children of this age are reported to hold exaggerated views of the characteristics of their own nation, to the extent that these ideas might be acknowledged as the first recognisable signs of stereotyped thought, developing in relation to the in-group as part of the process of learning to distinguish it from out-groups. But this mode of thinking of one's own nation is not normally extended to other national groups by the junior child; his knowledge of other peoples is too fragmentary and their existence too remote for him to be able to make the kind of generalisations that characterise stereotypes. In so far as he repeats scraps of adult stereotypes, for instance of the Chinese, the young child is merely using what he believes to be correct information in an effort to make a more complete identification of a group whose name he has become familiar with. Only later, in adolescence, does the stereotyped way of thinking become commonly extended to foreign peoples.

In a heterogeneous society, however, the process may be accelerated. In the United States, for example, it has been observed that elementary stereotyped concepts of a racial group contacted closely or heard about frequently may develop from as early as 5 or 6 years. Recent Commonwealth immigration into the United Kingdom has to some extent brought this same element of multi-communality into play in the growth of English children's racial concepts. Its influence will vary with the nature of the encounter, for the contact may be direct and frequent, as when immigrants are living in the child's own neighbourhood, or less direct, when they are living in another part of the town; or it may be that the immigrant presence in a distant part of the country provides only a more vivid form of that kind of indirect experience which the child normally draws on, perhaps brought more closely home to him because for one reason or another the immigrants become newsworthy and a matter for adult comment and mass media reportage.

In areas of the United Kingdom where adverse comment about coloured immigrants predominates, white children might be expected to develop stereotyped ideas of them at quite an early age. But where community relations are more harmonious and adult opinions not censorious, direct and often pleasant experiences of the normal human variety of coloured people and of the characteristics they have in common with white people may give the junior child a chance to go on thinking of them as individual beings, at least well into adolescence. When teachers take the opportunities thus offered of helping their multi-racial classes or their all-white classes in our newly multi-racial society, to examine the geography of the homelands of some of these coloured immigrant children, the understanding and interest which can arise from well-handled situations may give further support to tolerant views of peoples who are different.

Once the major in-group has been clearly identified and labelled, the 6- or 7-year-old child's categorisation of the characteristics of other national and racial groups can get under way. Usually this is done on the basis of a belief that the world outside is populated more by peoples who are different than by those who are similar. This would appear to be a normal stage in the intellectual development of children, it being simpler for them to recognise differences between objects than to make the kinds of generalisations which allow comprehension of similarities. But this tendency is normally reinforced by adults, for parents often comment in simple terms on differences in the appearance and daily lives of such peoples as the Chinese and African, to some extent in response to their children's enquiries, and teachers find much interest among their pupils in infant and lower junior school classes when stories are told and elementary studies made of life in some distant lands. However, in almost inevitably establishing a way of thinking about out-groups which emphasises differences rather than similarities they may be fostering the view that others are disconcertingly strange: an outlook which diminishes slowly during the junior years as many children come to realise that people of other lands can be thought of in a variety of ways just as can people they meet.

In the last two decades television has become a major new factor in this development, bringing to the viewer's attention a diversity of detail about life abroad. But the young child tends to abstract only those items of information which are meaningful to him: the 6- or 7-year-old finds support for his ideas of the strangely different ways in which people outside his own country live and behave, and confirmation of his play-derived notions that countries are often in conflict with each other. War, especially the Second World War with Germany, is conveyed so vividly on the television screen that children of this age often have the impression that the conflict with Germany continues: 'They shoot our people don't they?' (boy aged 8). Only in later junior years do most children begin to grasp the more complicated concept of countries coexisting more or less peacefully. Competition between the USA and Russia in space exploration in recent years has brought these two countries' peoples also very much to the attention of young children; for the 6- or 7-year-old the impression gained of Russians tends to be a favourable one, but views of Americans are complicated by varying degrees of awareness of violence in the USA and of involvement in the war in Vietnam.

It is not surprising then to find these two aspects of cognitive growth, the identification of one's own national group and the differentiation of others, being accompanied and influenced by elementary evaluations. When the child first realises that he is a member of a certain group, his nation or race, he will naturally tend to prize this membership and value the characteristics of the group, however crudely recognised. Since this socio-centrism occurs at the age of 6 or 7 when the child is still likely to be thinking in concrete and absolute terms, of good and bad, right and wrong, friend and enemy, the salient features of his own group may come to be regarded as very desirable, and those of other groups, especially their differences, may be considered less worthy. For the younger child classifying of peoples will be in its simplest form: liked and not liked, in terms of favourable and unfavourable attributes. From the earliest age the child will have heard the name of its own nation used in an approving manner. If his country is England, the word English has probably come to be equated with 'nice', while to be 'not English' may be 'not nice'. As he becomes older, however, there will be associated with the term 'English' not only a favourable emotional attitude and a few more or less stereotyped ideas, but also a variety of information about physical and social characteristics which in time he may realise are shared partially or wholly with other national groups. The older junior child is developing new cues for nationality and the two acts of making an intellectual and an emotional judgment may be separated. Yet it is possible that for some children the simple, unfavourable evaluations attached to the names and characteristics of major out-groups, in the first awareness of them, may persist. This is likely to have some bearing on the kind of information both noticed and remembered about the groups in later years.

Unfortunately for the growth of race relations, the negative evaluation in our society placed on being black or dirty may become associated with coloured people at just that stage of junior development when, as has already been noted, value judgments are at their most elementary. Then, especially if apprehensions are confirmed by expressions of adult hostilities on the part of parents or other persons with prestige in the community, suspicious attitudes may be established which it will not be easy to eradicate. Differences of appearance and perhaps also of ways of living, which might come to be appreciated by many older junior children, may as a consequence be seized on by some as excuses for rejection, rationalising the child's unconscious fears of people who looked at some time to be threateningly different.

THE ATTITUDES OF UPPER JUNIOR CHILDREN

Investigations of the development of junior children's ideas of nation and race from the age of 7 to the age of 10 or 11 indicate a steady increase in knowledge of other lands and their peoples, and a marked rise in favourable attitudes. Several cross-sectional studies (in particular the major UNESCO investigation reported by Lambert and Klineberg, 1967) have suggested that friendliness towards foreigners reaches a maximum around 10. Groups of children examined at 6 or 7 have tended to show the uncertain knowledge and wary attitudes already described. Other groups at 14 have been found to have more differentiated attitudes, but also to be generally less friendly towards foreigners and to be showing signs of thinking along adult stereotyped lines. A recent longitudinal study* of the growth of junior school children's ideas of nation and race, however, indicates that the reported peak in favourable attitudes at 10 may be in effect a notional one and that in fact the upward trend in junior children's friendliness towards foreigners continues almost unabated right to the point where they leave for their secondary schooling. The downward curve in international and interracial goodwill appears to begin when various factors come into play together in adolescence.

The increase among junior children in the amount and variety of knowledge they can relate about other lands and their peoples has been described by Gustav Jahoda (1962) for a sample of Scottish children. These children moved from a stage most frequently found among 6- to 7-year-olds in which few foreign lands could be named and only snatches of concrete detail could be given about them, to a stage often reached by children aged 10 to 11 in which there was growing accuracy of geographical concepts, with political and economic ideas appearing, and an increasing emphasis on the inhabitants of other lands and their

* By the author, unpublished.

personal characteristics and behaviour. Jahoda and Tajfel (1965) have shown that 9- to 11-year-old English and Scottish children, as compared with 6- to 8-year-olds had come to possess more cues for nationality and were increasingly capable of differentiating their own people on the basis of actual physical characteristics rather than being influenced by emotional attitudes towards them. Yet this growing knowledge does not necessarily lead to more favourable attitudes. For instance, while younger children in Jahoda's sample seemed often to be attracted to such exotic features of a country as they happened to know of, some of the older children seemed repelled by the strangeness of certain foreign peoples they had found out about.

Nevertheless, in general, older junior children seem more tolerant than formerly of differences between their own national and racial group and other major groups. They are also more able to recognise similarities between their own people and other peoples, partly because their growing interest in human behaviour helps them notice more than the elementary facts about lands and ways of life that first attracted their attention. It was observed in the UNESCO study that the 10-year-old period seemed to be a critical one because at that age children seemed most ready to consider other people as similar and were particularly inclined to be friendly towards them. There was also at this age a maximum readiness to like peoples who were generally seen as dissimilar. Among 14-year-olds a decline in openness and friendliness was noted.

These later junior years are usually thought to be a period of relatively good adjustment for the child, comfortably set in his own limited and secure social milieu, looking out with interest at the world beyond. His subsequent growing awareness of himself and of his possibly precarious position in the extended social context he enters as an adolescent may provide the setting for a tendency to become suspicious again of out-group differences, which he will now know more about, and be more inclined to pick up and adopt critical views of foreigners.

For many children moving from the age of 10 or 11 into adolescence, there is a likelihood that a broadly tolerant and accepting attitude towards other nations and races will persist; for some there will be the possibility of growth towards the reciprocating way of thinking which underlies positive interracial and international understanding. For others, interest in different nations and races and associated feelings of friendliness towards them will be replaced by relative indifference and unfriendliness when, in later adolescence, conformity to adult stereotypes of the international scene begins to replace the more individualised and personalised views of the 11-year-old. Finally, some children at as early an age as 10 or 11 will have minds set suspiciously, furnished with assumptions about the inferiority and hostile intent of various nations and races, already closed both to the possibilities of sympathetic understanding and to change.

The direction which developments of interracial and international attitudes take in early adolescence may be determined by the child's specific experiences and circumstances at that time but they are at least as likely to be influenced by what he has come to know of, and how he has come to think about various races and nations in preceeding years. It is commonly accepted that the mode of thinking of some children and adults tends to be broadly intolerant (for instance, of ambiguity, of weakness, of differences)and of others broadly tolerant. Where nation and race are concerned, already by the age of 10 there appear to be two distinctly different ways of describing and presumably thinking about foreign peoples. The UNESCO study showed a clear difference between those children who were generally friendly towards other nationalities and those who were generally unfriendly. Such children who were well-disposed to foreign peoples usually made a limited range of favourable evaluations about them, but had a diversified knowledge of them and their lands, while those less well-disposed made more diverse evaluative statements (frequently critical) but could relate less about them. This suggests that even in the junior years a process of selective perception has been at work on the growing amount and range of information about other peoples and lands reaching the child. What is noticed and remembered to some extent depends on whether it supports either accepting or rejecting views of the out-groups, and this in turn may depend on whether the infant and younger junior child's tendency to be wary about foreign peoples and their differences has lingered on or been replaced by friendlier attitudes.

The rapid increase in the amount and variety of information which children from 8 to 11 can recall about various national and racial groups occurs, despite the fact that in upper junior classes they are frequently given little opportunity of learning about such peoples through school geography lessons. This is in sharp contrast to their infant and lower junior days when, as has been noted, the lives of peoples who are different is a common theme. Now if they learn in school about life in other lands, it is likely to be through individual and class projects or through their own reading of class and school library books. Their interest in foreign peoples probably remains, but their experience of geography, in so far as it is teacher-directed, tends to be in other areas.

Children of 10 or 11 cite teachers and parents less as sources of information in this field than do 6- and 7-year-olds. Television now becomes a major acknowledged source. Its effects can be seen in the kind of detail related, for instance of social institutions and modern developments, and in the children's increased awareness of international affairs. Though the schools have apparently given little attention to such matters, there are signs that peaceful relations between countries are now being understood and international obligations appreciated. Jahoda and Tajfel's study of a sample of English and Scottish school children showed that the number who classified relations between five countries as friendly doubled between the ages of 6 to 7 and 9 to 11; the younger children's emphasis on war had apparently been modified through exposure to information about relationships between countries in a peaceful context. A growing willingness to give aid more to foreign lands and less to the homeland has been found in 'Who shall we help?' tests among American (Rogers and Long 1966) and English children of junior school age. But at the same time, while it is increasingly likely that Germany and Japan are being seen as enemies of the past and not the present, ('They're on our side now' – boy aged 10) there is a growing awareness of East–West differences and a tendency to be more suspicious of Russians than formerly. The extensive Leiden study (1965) of West European children aged 6 to 12 has shown a remarkable change towards the conventional picture of the international situation of the moment.

Teachers of upper junior school classes and geography teachers of lower secondary classes might well ask themselves whether these changes should be left to occur without some organised contribution on their part, especially since a correlation does seem to exist between the extent of a child's favourable attitudes and the amount of knowledge he holds of a land and its peoples, and since, despite the quite sophisticated information they have in some areas, most children of 10 and 11 seem to be fairly ignorant of the basic geographical facts which underlie the ways of living and behaving of such key nations as the Americans, Chinese and Russians.

The extension of knowledge and understanding of other lands and peoples which does occur among older junior children seems in part to be due to the nature of their conceptual development at that age. Jahoda, concluding a report (1963) on the growth of ideas about country and nationality held by 6- to 11-year-old Scottish children, wrote of the great intellectual distance they had traversed in the space of a few years: 'At the outset, their responses reveal an almost complete ignorance about the wider geographical or social world surrounding them; some five years later the outlook of most of them is no longer fundamentally different from that of mature adults. During the intervening years they have acquired a set of conceptual tools enabling them to organise their environment meaningfully and to make the main distinctions conventional in our society.'

The 'conceptual tools' referred to will, however, be varyingly available to children of similar age but different developmental level. (In Jahoda's sample, for instance, there were marked differences between the levels of geographical understanding reached by children from schools in middle-class and working-class areas.) From a Piagetian point of view the later junior years will be for some children the closing stage of the period of 'concrete operations'. These more advanced children, and perhaps others having particularly relevant experiences, will already be using abstract thought processes to order their perceptions of the world and its peoples in a logical and objective way. For others, such knowledge will still be largely held in a prelogical form, based on concrete data accepted uncritically as the truth and perhaps abounding in contradictions and wrong assumptions.

However, there is some evidence (for example in McNaughton 1966) that carefully planned approaches to social studies material among children of upper junior school age might increase the number of abstract observations they make about foreign peoples (for instance concerning their behaviour) and thus accelerate the development of logical and objective thinking about them. This is in line with other programmes, such as Bruner's 'Man: a Course of Study', being tried out currently in the United States. Since it seems likely that children of 10 to 11 who are capable of formulating abstract concepts are more inclined to make favourable judgments about foreign peoples, there again appears to be a case for some intervention on the part of teachers.

THE ATTITUDES OF SECONDARY SCHOOL CHILDREN

Unless the maximum use is made around the age of 10 to 12 of opportunities to extend children's knowledge of certain key nations and races, and to encourage understanding of them, the trend of change for many individuals subsequently in adolescence is likely to be towards a withdrawal of sympathy from, if not a growth of actual antipathy for, salient foreign groups.

The possibilities for alternative developments lie partly in the fact that older junior and younger secondary school children appear to go through a stage when their attitudes towards the peoples of various nations and races are particularly diversified. One study has shown, for example, that when children of 8 to 11 are asked to choose friends from and apply descriptions to various ethnic drawings, coloured people seem to be increasingly acceptable in these individual terms; but when tests are given to find the children's attitudes towards the same people as potential neighbours and as members of certain nations, there is an increasing tendency to reject them in such group situations; adult opinions and international affairs, both apparently in the main conveyed through television, seem already to be having an effect on inter-group attitudes.

The UNESCO study has shown that 14-year-olds are still typically thinking of members of other nations and races as much in individual as in group terms. They still refer to what they see as the good and the bad characteristics of people who might be more simply described by adults in stereotyped ways as either good or bad. Negroes, for example, who had been frequently regarded as different, bad and dirty by 6-year-olds were described in more varied terms and increasingly liked by the samples at 10 and at 14. The older children seemed more interested in the behaviour of peoples and less in their appearance. While younger children appeared to think of foreigners as different if they had clearly visible physical differences, and on these grounds tended to reject them, 14-year-olds thought of differences in terms of personality, characteristics and habits; if they categorised foreign people as different, they were probably making a negative evaluation of their personalities and customs and not just their appearance, and if they rejected them it would be for these reasons.

The opportunity for the teacher at the lower secondary school level would appear to consist in part in helping pupils learn accurate details about some key countries and in part in maintaining the pupils' interest in the individual characteristics of the peoples of the world's major races and nations, perhaps largely through sample study and way of life geography. Such approaches, especially if supported by the kinds of vivid indirect experiences which can be provided by a variety of visual aids, extends knowledge of and increases understanding of the patterns of behaviour of people in other lands, reinforcing the general view of children at this age that other groups share the same human characteristics as their own group. With older pupils, careful programmes in the social sciences and in current affairs are also needed to provide the kinds of explanations and insights which match their growing intellectual powers. Even if children enter the secondary stage of their education with views of other nations and races which are generally positive and favourable, much needs to be done to encourage those attitudes of reciprocity which are so essential a basis for international and interracial goodwill but which cannot be fostered until a capacity for abstract thought has developed.

In fact what happens in adolescence, as demonstrated in the wide range of UNESCO samples, is that the junior child's tendency increasingly to recognise similarities among other peoples levels off after the age of 10 and then begins to decline. Similarly expressions of liking for foreigners start to fall off. By 14 Lambert and Klineberg were reporting that the stereotyping process had begun to mark many young adolescents' thinking of foreign people.

This apparently strong tendency among older adolescents towards agreeing with the consensus and conforming to group standards through adopting stereotyped views appears to have several causes. Perhaps for some there is a realisation that suspicions of foreign groups only part-admitted previously are shared by others and can be voiced. There may be a need for some to express themselves in socially approved ways which are best done in general terms likely to be easily understood by their peers; they may also be influenced by the simple forms used in the mass media, which increasingly provide information on foreign lands and peoples for the adolescent. Still others may feel that they must adopt adult ways of thinking and expressing themselves about various matters, including world affairs, whose complexities may be beyond them.

Blanket descriptions may be adopted and repeated without there being any underlying hostility, but the habits of thought engendered make it possible that, unless challenged, unfavourable attitudes and even prejudices may be established.

There thus appear to be two key problems affecting the growth of international and interracial attitudes among children: that the affective characteristics of the young child may interfere with his cognitive development and make it difficult for him to approach an objective understanding of his own group in relation to others; and that, though most junior children pass on to a stage where they are at least prepared to recognise the similarities and accept the differences of foreign peoples, pressures subsequently in adolescence are towards conformity to a more distrustful view of other nations and races. In both areas school geography could be making important contributions in fostering a realistic understanding of the world, without which children's ideas of certain key lands may remain deficient and of their peoples become distorted.

CONCLUSION

Teachers planning geography lessons with older primary and younger secondary school children might usefully recall that their pupils are passing through a crucial period in the development of their ideas of and attitudes towards foreign peoples. In their classes will be some whose understanding of salient foreign groups has developed slowly and who are still mainly preoccupied with national and racial differences. Their limited views leave them open to the growth of prejudiced ways of thinking in adolescence. Work in geography which encourages such pupils to see similarities in ways of living in foreign families and communities and helps them understand the reasons for differences, and which draws their attention to modern developments in other lands, especially if these approaches are supported by vivid detail and visual aids, should make it possible for many of the pupils to move on to a stage of recognition of similarities and tolerance of differences before the more critical views of the adult world begin to impress their minds. Such work may at the same time be of help to pupils whose views of foreign peoples by 11 or 12 appear to be the most advanced and tolerant; for it seems that such children, more receptive than others to information and ideas about the world outside their homeland, may develop an early awareness, through the mass media in particular, of international and interracial tensions and of stereotyped adult views of certain foreign peoples which may result in some of them also developing prejudices.

In fact it seems likely that a programme of work in geography during the middle years of schooling which includes full and sympathetic treatment of the life and lands of the key racial, national and religious groups of the world is essential for all children, for some will still be in need of the chance to acquire the kind of information which may open their minds to the common humanity of men, while others already tolerant will need support for their favourable ideas as they become exposed to adverse adult views of foreigners. In later secondary years, while the insight of history and some of the social sciences will become increasingly helpful, school geography will continue to have a part to play in providing the kind of illuminating information which at the least drives wedges of doubt into critical assumptions about other peoples and at the best encourages acknowledgement of the equal right of all peoples to a proper place on the earth's surface.

References

G. Jahoda, (1962) 'The development of Scottish children's ideas and attitudes about other countries', *Journal of Social Psychology*, vol. 58.

(1963), 'The development of children's ideas about country and nationality', *British Journal of Educational Psychology*, vol. 33,

G. Jahoda and H. Tajfel, (1965) 'The emergence of national concepts and attitudes in children', paper to the British Association.

J. Jaspars, J. van de Geer, H. Tajfel and N. Johnson, (1965) *On the development of international attitudes*, Psychological Institute, University of Leiden.

W. E. Lambert and O. Klineberg, (1967) *Children's views of foreign peoples*, Appleton-Century Croft.

A. H. McNaughton, (1966) 'Piaget's theory and primary school social studies', *Educational Review*, vol. 19.

V. R. Rogers and E. Long, (1966) 'An exploratory study of the development of social sensitivity in elementary school children', *Journal of Educational Research*, vol. 59.

11 Motivation

GERALD HONES

The situation can be all too familiar to a teacher. Instead of the lively response that was hoped for, even expected, from the class, there is instead a depressingly resistant attitude – or, what is sometimes even more discouraging, a neutral, apathetic air which suggests that the pupils have decided that the ideas they were intended to be enthusiastically involved with are not even worth opposing!

What has gone wrong?

The teacher has conscientiously met all the generally accepted theoretical requirements for the situation (objectives clearly defined, materials collected, method devised, and so on) and considered them all in terms of the actual pupils concerned. No one could apparently have done more to ensure the success of the operation and yet the living evidence, in the form of a truculent boy or a bored group of girls, demonstrates failure, at least to a degree. No wonder we feel a kind of despair on such occasions and somewhat cynically wish that we could put the educational theorist into that self-same situation, with the pundit forced to experience the realities of the classroom.

We know that we have, in some way, failed to motivate our pupils.

Of course, our misreading of the situation may have been caused, or exaggerated, by factors over which we could have little or no control, with the extra complications testing the flexibility of our approach, our ability to meet the unexpected. On some occasions we should be prepared to meet the problems because they are predictable: the extra effort required for the final periods of the week is no myth, and we should be foolish to ignore the effect that the style of the lesson preceding ours on the timetable can have on a situation, but there is always the possibility of an influence for which no particular planning is possible. One can then only make the necessary adjustments in an extemporary way, setting out to recover the rapport lost during the distraction of a disciplinary descent by the headmaster, or to recapture the motivated interest lost temporarily to the helicopter landing on the playing field.

FACTORS AFFECTING MOTIVATION

Nevertheless, our degree of success in motivating our pupils must be recognised as largely of our own making. Before considering, however, the particular motivation issues concerned in the teaching of geography, let us examine them briefly in broader educational terms.

In accepting that every individual pupil, as well as the teacher, has developed self-concepts which markedly affect his behaviour, the complexity of any classroom situation with all its interactions must be recognised as the outcome. Basically the attitude of individuals and of a class depends on the quality of the relationship between the teacher and the taught. In searching for improved motivation on the part of the learners (who would themselves be reacting differently if they were working with different classmates or in a different sized group) the teacher is always handicapped by the fact that it has not proved easy to translate the results of psychological research into some working hypotheses which could be directly applied in the classroom. It is not always easy to analyse precisely what the processes are which lead to a situation in which children are motivated, if one is involved in the situation. It is easier for someone outside the situation to see clearly what is happening, but unfortunately few teachers are observed while teaching; and when they are, the observer may often obtrude into the social relationship involved.

When one attempts a simplified portrayal of the situation involving one pupil, the complexity of the interrelationships soon creates problems. Undoubtedly the physical and social environment is of paramount importance in learning situations, and such factors as room size, composition of form unit, type of school organisation, or flexibility of timetable, inevitably exert a major influence on what is being done, and how successfully.

Equally important is the support of a range of resource materials, available to both teacher and pupil. The effects of financial restrictions on supply are exaggerated whenever there is any change of emphasis in the classroom, whether in terms of the subject or teaching method.

Within the physical and social environment, affected (but not controlled) by such tangible factors as the type of desk or table available for mapwork, or the less easily defined attitude of staff colleagues towards the modifications of the timetable necessary to permit some practical work, the teacher and pupils are involved in a highly complex, continually changing pattern of interaction. The quality of pupil motivation derives from the degree of success achieved by the teacher in 'reading' the precise situation in process. Enthusiasm, knowledge, sympathy, and the other oft-stated qualities are only really successful when the style of approach is flexible, constantly being tuned to the required wavelength.

The key figure is, of course, the pupil. Although all teachers know full well that every class has its own 'chemistry' or character, a group quality that can vary because of such external influences as a threat of football being cancelled, or internal changes in balance when a dominant personality is absent, it is, nevertheless, the individual pupil that the teacher wishes to 'reach'.

Once the signal from the teacher's transmitter has stimulated a reply from the pupil's transceiver, the aim must be to increase the resonant effect. This entails the teacher's micro-pulses being constantly (even automatically) adjusted to match the needs of the transceiver, in terms of either wavelength or volume. Although naturally both pieces of equipment have operating limits, outside which they would not be able to interact, maximum response within those limits of tolerance will only be achieved by a mutual process of tuning.

It is easy to believe that poor pupil motivation is often attributable to the fact that the teacher has visualised the potential motivation only in terms of the teacher's own 'cluster of understandings, skills, appreciations, attitudes, and feelings', which are 'in effect the sum of their reactions to previous stimuli' (Gorman 1969) and failed to appreciate that motivation can only really succeed when the pupil is reacting positively to the situation because it makes good sense when based on the *pupil's own* 'cluster of understandings etc.'.

Defining the curriculum as 'a structure erected on a base of reciprocal personal relationships', Derek Morrell (1969) summed up his feelings by saying that 'if there is positive reciprocity of feeling and aspiration as between the teachers and the taught, satisfying to both, there is a describable curricular reality: the teachers are contributing to the learning which is taking place, they are helping to create new realities. But if there is no such reciprocity, if there is a total absence of mutual emotional satisfaction, the curriculum remains simply an idea in the minds of the teachers: it lacks reality, even though the teachers and the children go through the motions of scholastic activity.' If we are to accept that as teachers 'we are concerned with human beings whose feelings and aspirations are far more real and immediately important to them than the cognitive development which is the educators' main stock-in-trade', then, even if not wholly convinced, we must build this into our thinking about what to teach, as well as when, and how.

MOTIVATION AND CLASS TEACHING IN GEOGRAPHY

It may well be that, as geography teachers, we have often assumed falsely that our pupils have a basic, natural interest in our subject – particularly when we have viewed this in terms of competition with the demands of other subjects! – and, as a result, not appreciated the need to attempt to see the teaching situation from their viewpoint. It may be trite to state that 'learners ultimately learn what *they* actively desire to learn; they do not learn what they do not accept' (Gorman 1969) but it is certainly worth continually reminding ourselves of this. It could be that as key figures in the classroom – perhaps too often dominantly central – we have continued to impress only our own set of values on events. By virtue of the very training which has led to our present position, for example, we may well be unconsciously exerting a type of academic imprint on the situation, in a form not really seen as relevant by the pupil.

This is not to say that freedom should reign, in curriculum or classroom, for it certainly matters a great deal *what* people learn, the *order* in which they learn, and *how* the learning proceeds. A structured learning process, however, can still be formulated while bearing in mind the basic idea that the geography taught should be 'socially valuable' as seen by the pupil (Scarfe 1971).

Clearly, if we are to follow what appears to be the logical extension of the type of planning which puts the individual pupil as the central figure, our teaching cannot always be based on the use of the whole class as the unit of organisation. Instead, there would be a need for more emphasis on individual pupils, or groups with some common core of interest, following different lines of action, which may or may not be parallel.

It could well be that this style of approach, probably very different from the way in which most of us were taught and even the ways in which we were trained to teach, will be needed even more often than hitherto if the number of 'mixed ability' classes in schools continues to grow. In any case, whatever one's feelings are about any positive moves towards the organisation of more classes in this way, it must be recognised that very few supposedly 'streamed' classes have not included an appreciable range of abilities within their compass. When one also looks at the diversity of interest, ability, and previous school background of many of the geography classes now operating in systems where subject 'options' can be chosen, it is generally very evident that the manner in which the class emerged has almost inevitably resulted in considerable heterogeneity. Yet, more often than not, this type of class is taught as a single unit.

Just as one accepts the need to use different approaches according to the age level, then equally the demands of different abilities must be recognised. To achieve real motivation of pupils across the whole spectrum, it is not sufficient to visualise a simple division between the able and less able pupils; rather, there must be genuine attempts to achieve some more sensitive gradation of approach. This matching with ability will also suggest that study should not always be organised along class lines.

The teacher needs to decide the actual balance of emphasis. Building into his decisions such variables as ability, interest, age, and future needs, the motivation of the pupils can be sought in a variety of ways. However, these decisions are made within the framework of the curriculum, which will itself have been formulated bearing in mind such general educational principles as that of structuring the learning so that it occurs on successively deeper levels, the new being associated with the old.

MOTIVATION AND NEW MOVEMENTS IN GEOGRAPHY

This already very complicated situation, in which educational theory often seems to clash violently with the practicalities of the classroom, now has added to it the effect of new movements in the teaching of geography. Whereas some will see these recent trends as merely yet another element to worsen an already confused state of affairs, to others they present the key to the whole problem, providing opportunities for improved pupil motivation. This belief is really based on the premise that the essential characteristics of the changes in the subject can be summarised as a move away from an emphasis on facts to 'an orientation concerned with concepts, methods, and values' (Ambrose 1970).

This is seen as a partial answer to the difficulties discussed earlier in terms of a teacher being able to stimulate different pupils by presenting them with exercises which require the learning of certain concepts for their solution.

The belief is that a teacher will be able more effectively to motivate his pupils to learn geography by the use of a flexible approach in which they are able to study within a framework, following lines of enquiry of their own choosing, rather than working along closely prescribed routes at the same time as the rest of the class. Once the basic problem to be studied is decided upon, perhaps even analysed first of all as a class exercise, the continuing activity using the related skills could well be completely individual in character. For example, after a basic class exercise involving the relationship of time and distance by studying alternative ways of travelling from London to Paris, such other variables as cost and personal preference could be 'built in' when pupils prepare a detailed analysis of a holiday journey of greater complexity of their own choosing. Whether they plan a trip to the Costa Brava, or a detailed itinerary intended to include opportunities for fishing in a variety of waters, the consideration of the problems and the process of decision-making should provide improved motivation.

The degree to which the exercise is structured is, of course, dependent on a decision by the teacher, based on previously defined objectives. If he wishes to emphasise the particular characteristics of travel by air, for example, he will require that this means of transport should be one of those considered in the holiday planning. The hope would be that the considerable element of choice still left to the pupils would lead to their being motivated.

This balance between guidance and freedom is often very sensitive and one must be prepared, on occasions, to modify plans in order to increase, or even maintain, motivation.

When I was working recently (with a junior class in a secondary modern school) on an exercise of this nature, two boys faced me with such a decision. Rather than work on their own 'holiday journey' like their classmates (who were by then using atlases, guide books, brochures, and timetables as they 'aimed' for Finland or Yugoslavia) this pair explained that they would like to 'invent' a game. Their suggested outline involved using different tourist destinations, routes, and means of transport, with limitations provided by time, money, and unforeseen hazards – the inevitable 'chance' cards. I agreed to their suggestion, believing that in developing their idea they could well achieve a great deal more than in following my original plan.

Of course, the hope was that their motivation (and that of their conforming classmates) would be increased by their involvement in the exercise, as well as by the impact of the reality of the data used throughout. These positive aids to motivation were, however, insufficient when following the same approach with a class of 'less able' pupils of the same age, probably because of insufficient guidance being offered in helping them to sort out the 'step-by-step' processes involved in the exercise. Unable to visualise the exercise as a motivating entity, these pupils probably required more immediate, short-term goals if they were to be encouraged by success – the periodic stimuli to maintain progress, the little pushes which keep the mental fly-wheel turning.

It is easy to see that, in trying to improve motivation through an approach such as this, one has sacrificed a planned overall uniformity of learning. Individual pupils will have learned a largely 'self-selected' series of facts related to their holiday plans. While some will now be able to locate Helsinki, others will be familiar with the Adriatic; one may have developed a good understanding of the airways of Europe, while another may be a new expert on car ferry routes. Only the teacher can decide what is to be included as the factual core of the exercise, common to all, and this would then be included in the structure. It is suggested, however, that although different facts were used by pupils in developing the central concept and practising the intended skills (planning journeys), they would be that much better assimilated through this method. Too often an emphasis on achieving a 'complete' coverage of a region, or topic, has resulted in a too hastily acquired layer of facts which, because they lack coherence, can easily be forgotten. In any case, the very definition of what precisely is meant by 'basic' or 'sufficient' knowledge is inevitably highly subjective and thus open to argument.

Just as it is the teacher who decides what to include in the course, so must the teacher be able to choose the approaches considered most suitable for any particular situation – and it is worth emphasising that more than one approach may be necessary at any one time. For example, a class of pupils with limited ability in the basic skills of reading and writing may cover such a wide range in intelligence that some form of individual work is essential. The actual pace at which each pupil is working should be geared to that pupil so that the encouragement of goals being achieved is regularly received. However, it may well be that some pupils, in the same class, will work better in groups with a type of cooperative motivation operating. No generalisation can be suggested: each situation merits individual consideration.

In addition, a pupil needs to be actively participating, rather than passively receiving, but the active work of drawing or calculating may well be only superficially successful. The powerful drive of real motivation is far more likely to be present when the pupil is not only active in the mechanical sense, but 'involved' in a deeper way. When the purpose of the learning situation is understood and accepted, there is a much greater likelihood of there being a genuine desire to learn, with the pupil accepting responsibility for his own learning.

EXAMINATIONS AND MOTIVATION

The effect on motivation of examinations (internal and external) can often be very marked. To many, examinations provide a very necessary stimulus, one which is regularly needed to maintain momentum, or develop reinforcement of learning through constant revision. Nevertheless, others believe that the carrot provided in the form of future success, and the required certification of a standard achieved, sometimes encourages progress of the wrong sort – possibly even in the wrong direction – with the accompanying threat of the stick making the poor donkey unnecessarily restless, never to be the same animal again!

How dominant a role in motivation of the pupil should examinations play? Can their influence always be in harmony with other motivational factors?

Many teachers at present feel that they must, if they are to help their pupils obtain the best possible examination grades, work in such a way that the other, basically more important, aspects of motivation are inevitably devalued; that it is the external examinations which lead to rigid, arid, meaningless learning. Yet it would seem essential that whatever motivation is afforded by the examination should be reconciled with the self motivation which comes from a basic interest in the subject.

If the syllabus offers the teacher both sufficient guidance and room for manoeuvre in choice of topic and method adopted, the responsibility for motivation rests firmly with the teacher. The syllabus should be defined as a framework of resources which could be drawn upon, rather than used as a determining influence. Similarly the abilities which the course is intended to encourage need careful definition and an examination framework designed which tests these very abilities, through a variety of testing methods.

If we are to make full use of all the aids to pupil motivation available to us, we must seek such cooperation from the examining boards. More emphasis is needed in the examination on testing the pupils' ability to handle source materials – and then assessing how well the relevant geographical concepts and skills are understood and applied to the particular situation. An increased dependence on 'teacher assessment' could well develop, with the added responsibility also allowing the teacher to feel free to encourage more independent study on the part of the pupil.

Herein lies the key to motivation for it is very much an individual emotion. It may well be that 'a shift from constant teaching to more independent learning may help to improve the relationship of master and boy on which so much of motivation depends' (Taylor 1971) but certainly not all the time. Knowing the overall situation in which the teaching is taking place and the pupils he hopes to see motivated, the teacher must be able to choose his topic, skill, or method as he thinks appropriate. Just as it is difficult to sit on the fence while keeping one's ear close to the ground, so there are problems when keeping a firm guiding hand on a loose rein, but good teachers have always done just this!

References

P. J. Ambrose, (1970) Charney Manor Conference, February 1970.

A. H. Gorman, (1969) *Teachers and learners*, Allyn & Bacon.

D. Morrell, (1969) Extract of talk to Anglo-American Alliance, *The Times Educational Supplement*, 19 December 1969.

N. V. Scarfe, (1971) 'Games, models, and reality in the teaching of geography in school', *Geography*, vol. 56, part 3.

L. C. Taylor, (1971) *Resources for learning*, Penguin.

12 On being adaptable

JOHN TALBOT WHITE

It is not unusual to meet a young teacher fresh from university or from a college of education, full of specialist knowledge of various branches of geography, confronted with a class of youngsters in a secondary school who have neither need of nor interest in what he thinks he has to offer. Many young teachers in training have expressed the wish to move into secondary education so that they 'can teach their subject', with an assumption that there will be an immediate transference of their acquired knowledge and skills to the youngsters they will teach. This can lead to the situation in which teachers attempt to 'water down' their learned notes to suit the ability of the children they encounter; the lower the ability, the more water they add, presumably to offer even the lower ability groups a highly diluted course of academic geography, rather like gruel for an infant with not many teeth and an indifferent digestion.

I witnessed a classic example of this when a young man wrestled with the finer points of river capture and a bewildered phalanx of ten-year-olds, on what seemed the sound basis of a very good example in the immediate area. Alas, his learning was in the way. It might have worked if he could have seen it with their eyes. But even if he had managed to use the appropriate vocabulary, I doubt if the children were ready for the concept. One of the main problems with the academic study of geography is that it can remove the essential elements of exploration and enjoyment. It can reveal the statistical bones of a country and leave the essence of the land untasted. But it is the living presence that has most significance for children; what it would be like to be there, to walk the streets and markets, eat the food, endure the climate. This 'presence' is more likely to be derived from first-hand experience (but this possibility is obviously limited) and by wide reading of good topographical writing, and awareness of current affairs. After all, most of us are involved in teaching not potential geographers, in the academic sense, but potential citizens and travellers.

I am not trying to decry academic learning or to doubt its use to the potential teacher. Indeed, my experience of children of primary and secondary range convinces me of the need to have a real enthusiasm for, and detailed knowledge of, one's subject. A group of boys who were almost completely illiterate in the conventional sense of the word once subjected me to a bombardment of the most searching questions about the nature of the universe which I was ill-equipped to answer. The longer one teaches, the more one is aware of one's own inadequacy in the extent of one's own knowledge.

I think a strong case can be made out for the need for specialist teachers in the primary school. This is already accepted in languages and music; it could be in geography. But there is a need to hide the files and notes discreetly away and start all over again when involved in the teaching process. There are two parts to the equation; one is our duty to the academic integrity of the subject, the other is to the needs and interests of the children we teach. To take an architectural analogy there is no point in constructing a house that no one can live in.

THE SYLLABUS

The basic material that a school geography department feels is necessary for the education of the pupils is enshrined in the syllabus. Most syllabuses at the secondary stage are related in some measure to future examination requirements, whether of O- and A-levels of the GCE or of the CSE or even, in some cases of the RSA. They are frequently planned on a continental basis, British Isles in the first year, then to the southern continents, North America and Asia, then to Europe, and a final fling at the British Isles the second time round. The problem here is that the syllabus in geography is based on no natural development, on no sequence of concepts from the simplest to the more complex. It seldom has the natural development of language study, of mathematics or of musical interpretation and skills. It does not even have the quasi-natural growth pattern of history, from earliest man to the present day. Its natural sequence from the earth itself to man's most complex achievements does not make the foundation for a syllabus as the former concepts are certainly no less complex than the latter. With younger children, the 'man' aspects of the geographical interplay are more interesting and more within their range of understanding than the 'land' aspects.

There is seldom any link between the ideas formulated in the primary schools and in the secondary stage. Many teachers at the secondary stage have little idea of what primary school children have achieved in terms of 'geography'. Attempts have been made to cope with this problem by means of the concentric syllabus, starting with the home area, or at least the homeland, and developing a theme, thence to foreign countries and ultimately to the world pattern. These topics are frequently of an economic nature, such as wheat, fish, meat, and other food crops in the first year, textiles such as cotton, wool and artificial fibres in the second. Some schools have constructed two syllabuses, or two stages of syllabus, one for the Lower School based on project work, the other returning to the more familiar pattern determined by potential examinations.

It is fair to say that most geography teachers are aware of the deficiencies of the syllabus at all levels and they are most aware of deficiencies when teaching less able children, especially for those who are unlikely to reach 'examinable status' and for whom that particular 'carrot' (or is it a 'stick'?) has little relevance. Having worked for some years with what I felt was a fairly useful syllabus based on the concentric idea, I was alarmed to find myself confronted with a conventional 'continental' syllabus. Now I am not so sure that the one had any particular advantage over the other. What mattered was not necessarily the material of the syllabus but the mode of interpretation when faced by the day-to-day confrontation with a variety of classes of every level of ability. Some sort of syllabus is necessary while we have external demands to meet. Some sort of syllabus is needed to give us a sense of pattern and direction in our overall work-plan. An attempt to produce a work-plan based on day-to-day revelations of children's interests is possible only for the brilliant teacher, working in an isolated situation, who can still carry the overall theme in his mind. In a large school with the probability of quite large-scale movements of children from class to class (especially in a 'streamed' situation) at the end of every year or even every term, there is a need for some consistency based on an agreed syllabus.

Most of the children are less aware of the gradual unfolding of a syllabus than are the teachers. A class of particularly academically-ungifted children once came roaring into my room when I was about to drive them determinedly through the southern continents and their self-appointed spokesman shouted 'Can we do China?' I couldn't explain that is was Nigeria next with all the delights of drawing the map of a cocoa farm, a film thrown in and even the real cocoa pod that I had treasured for just this moment to supplement the usual pack of plastic objects that helped us to see the progress of cocoa bean to chocolate. They could not see any real reason why we couldn't move from the Congo to China. They had probably forgotten the Congo anyway (we 'did' that last week) and China was on their mind. They explained that they had seen a Chinese juggler (he turned out to be Japanese, anyway) in some backwater of London the night before and this had prompted their interest. So I 'did' China. I think that a teacher is justified in breaking from a syllabus and 'using the moment' if the interest of his pupils can be gained fruitfully in this way. A natural disaster such as earthquakes in Peru or drought in the Australian out-back; a sensation such as the landing on the moon or the sub-navigation of the Arctic can all stimulate useful study of the places involved. Weather studies of the more dramatic type are best discussed when something happens to make them relevant. I remember finding the idea of insolation factors in the settlement pattern of the Alps suddenly became pertinent during a particularly hard winter when one side of the school playground started to open out into spring, while the other half still sulked in a dirty snow-laden winter. Overgrazing of the Kansas grasslands became reasonably comprehensible when we found that a photograph taken five thousand miles away looked just like the patterns in the cracked clay worn by too many erratic feet in the grass 'amenity area' around the school. Even one of the earth banks in the playground where the grass had long given up trying showed some classic erosion patterns.

Perhaps this all sounds a bit far fetched, but an attempt to bring reality (even by proxy) and relevance into our work always pays off in terms of the interest and reaction of the pupils. Such reality is usually locally based, and the study of the local environment can underpin much geographical study by developing basic concepts. This does not mean that 'local studies' should be tackled as an entity in themselves; better to make the best use of a landscape that is always there on the home doorstep and is available for constant reference when the need arises.

One or two examples have been given above and perhaps another would not be out of place here. I was merrily describing the four-course rotation of the Norfolk system of farming (or the way they are supposed to farm up there according to the book I was using); I say 'merrily' because the lesson lent itself to the construction of a black-board diagram that everyone would eventually copy, and enough margin was left for final embellishment by those lively characters who got on faster than the others, and would all finish nicely in the allotted time for that lesson. But the sun was shining on our suburban haven and the outside world looked much more inviting than the classroom, and Norfolk farming was almost as unreal as the export statistics for the major Australian ports. So we went out of the school and had a look at all the back gardens around the school area, complete with notebooks so as to salve my conscience. We listed all the 'crops' we found growing there and then classified them into 'flowers', 'fruits', 'vegetables', etc. In spite of the expected inclination to sleep in the sun, the children all worked very hard and then came the questions that made me feel I had carried out some worthwhile 'geographical' work. 'Why don't we grow oranges?' said one. Others made rejoinders about the climate. 'Then why don't we grow wheat? The climate is all right,' queried another. The lesson fizzed to a close with a heated discussion as to the possibility of keeping a cow or a goat on 'all that grass' as one child put it. They resolved to get a communal garden with all the grassy parts put together to keep a communal cow happy. Fortunately they had forgotten the idea before causing undue alarm in the district but we 'did' Norfolk farming shortly afterwards and the reasons for a rotation, the size of fields, the need for fertiliser, the use of livestock in the sequence all seemed a bit more interesting and understandable.

VISUAL AIDS

Usually, as with farming, we have to gain 'actuality' at second hand, by means of pictures, slides, film-strips, cassettes, and, best of all, movies. There can be little doubt that the good moving picture is the best of the visual aids but, alas, many of those available to schools are out of date and depict a way of life that is no longer true (there is at least one that still shows Eskimos hunting caribou and living in igloos). Another problem is that films must sometimes be ordered at least a term in advance and so the syllabus must be patterned to fit the expected film. In spite of all the visual interest of the film, I have always found even more genuine interest aroused by actual objects, such as a coconut (the whole thing, not just the flesh) or a cocoa pod, or a genuine cotton boll, a boomerang or an ostrich egg. Every school should have a 'museum' of such things: they are quite as relevant and valuable as the school library. It is almost worth 'doing' the eskimo if one starts off by wearing a really fine 'anorak' or 'parka'. Education can be so dull; the slightly theatrical touch, the occasional light relief is justified.

To return to the pictures. There are now so many good sources of pictorial images of a geographical nature that it is possible for the classroom to contain a fairly complete library of landscapes and the people that inhabit them. Such pictures, preferably big, preferably in colour, should be mounted on card or thick paper and protected with paper, varnish or other suitable transparent materials, classified and filed in such a way that children can use them independently. Many of the best still pictures are available in such a way that they cannot be used for classroom projection but they are admirably suited to individual study, which can be stimulated by work-cards associated with each picture.

Simple question sequences – even one question such as 'What is happening in the picture?' or 'Describe what you can see here' – are valuable in helping to make full use of visual material. Investigations have shown that children often interpret pictures quite differently from the trained geographer and it is as well for a teacher to know what the pupils see rather than what he thinks they are seeing. Their interest is awakened by people and animals rather than by buildings and landscapes and while we may want their interest to be focused on the latter, it is often better to start from the former, to move to the physical landscape from the people who live in it.

Another use of the picture is to leave the pupils to complete it: to give the picture of pit-head gear above a coal-mine or of a trawler at work in a rough sea and get them to draw below what they think is going on. I have often used a picture of an Eskimo crouched over a hole in the ice, holding a type of fishing rod, as the top half of a picture with the children being invited to complete the lower half. It is most intriguing to see the life beneath the Arctic ice that they imagined!

MAPS

Maps are the key method of geographical expression and the subject has an initial advantage with children in that most of them are attracted by maps and enjoy looking at them, working with them and drawing them. Unfortunately, many geography teachers think only in terms of the Ordnance Survey map and the atlas and ignore the enormous variety of maps that children encounter in their daily lives, in travel brochures, magazines, newspapers, television and in the streets. Even the plan of a traffic roundabout is a kind of map.

Many of the maps in use in classrooms are too large even for brighter pupils to grasp. I have found it almost an advantage when a map begins to break up at the folds so that I can cut it up into small sections, mount the sections on cards and use them as the basis for individual exercises. It is not difficult to organise a simple questionnaire that is applicable to a complete set of such 'maplets'. It arouses interest, for example, to grant a certain area (like a feudal overlord to his lesser brethren), to give the children the map of their 'estate' and ask them to fill up a questionnaire as a 'tax return' on their estate. Any device is useful, as with the pictures, to stimulate the children into detailed analysis of a section of a map.

Getting used to 'using' maps as a source of information and enjoyment often avoids the need for formal map-reading instruction. I was once criticised by a colleague for allowing children to colour in maps they had made in their own way. The roads turned out blue. He felt they should have been red. But the roads outside the classroom were all tarmac and quite definitely a subtle shade of blue. I saw his point but I was much more concerned that children saw the need for symbols on a map and produced what they felt were suitable symbols than they should learn *at that stage* what the 'official' symbols were.

PROJECTS

One of the devices in common use for all ability ranges is the project, frequently on a group basis. One group 'does houses', another 'clothing' (usually the girls), another 'transport', etc. Or a country is divided up into states or provinces or major exports, and each group undertakes a study of one of those sections. Unfortunately, such projects are often initiated with too little material to support them. Projects usually require much more resource material than the 'class lesson'. And they often seem to be more successful with the able children. The less able children need more specific tasks than the child-orientated project supplies (such lessons often start with 'choose your own topic' – which may be a topic for which little material is available). Specific tasks are needed and this necessitates a great deal of preliminary preparation by the teacher in getting work-cards made, pictures mounted and suitable books for each group and each child. I remember a girl threading an uncertain way to my desk from her 'group' and asking nervously whether she could 'write that page out' and the look of relief on her face when I said she could. I would not have dreamt of actually asking her to write the page out but she was obviously pleased with the prospect so I could see little harm done. Project work often leads to a subdued murmer of 'Yes, but what have we got to *do*?'

To summarise some of these points, there is a need when teaching youngsters of the lower ability groups for the relevant, the actual, the specific, the practical. The last word might conjure up visions of model-making, though I have always found this one of the most difficult of activities to organise so as to keep everybody happy, busy and usefully employed. It can drag on. The models gather dust on top of the cupboard between one Open Day and the next. Personally, I always make models to be broken up as quickly as possible. They are made of simple materials, preferably simulating the original materials of the object they are supposed to represent and always done to a strict time-limit; and they are 'pirated' as soon as possible for the next model. It is the making of the model that is the useful activity, though it should be captured in all its glory by means of photography before it is consigned to the junk-heap or the cupboard in the corner.

USING CHILDREN'S KNOWLEDGE

I am always amazed at what children know. I was gazing at a world map at the back of a friend's classroom recently when a very young girl toddled up, stood on a chair and wanted to show me where she had been for her holiday. Benidorm. And her finger was accurately pointing. Not to be outdone, another youngster came along to indicate Sydney in Australia and Cyprus as places she knew. Her voice had a hint of the boredom of the traveller who had seen too much.

It is often worthwhile, before initiating a study of a new area, country or topic to find out what the children know about it first. Though I do remember the annoyance of a teacher who had to do coal-mining, as it was on the syllabus, and nearly all the children came from coal-mining families. The teacher did not, and felt this gave the children an unfair advantage. I wonder if this reaction is as rare as one would wish. After all, the mobility of teachers often means that they find themselves in areas about which the children have much more knowledge than they do. This should be an advantage, giving the children the pleasant position of being the 'teachers' for a change, a change that they welcome. I learnt my humility the hard way. I was taking a field trip through a rural area that I knew well, discoursing learnedly on the types of livestock (incidentally, why can't we encourage children to know their cattle breeds as well as they know their cars?) when I felt an uneasy silence in my very young listeners. I wasn't to know that one of them had a prize from a Young Farmer's Club but he soon put me on the right track (most politely, I may add).

I walked closely by his side for the rest of the day and consulted him before opening my mouth again.

IMAGINATION

If I were to look for a final aspect of this perpetual problem of adapting geographical material to the needs of children of varying ability it would be that of imagination. There is a need to ring the changes, to use a variety of approaches, to vary the diet, for our own sakes as much as for the children who are our fairly captive audience.

The United States is a big country and rightly looms large in most syllabuses. The agricultural regions make a familiar (though one suspects, often inaccurate) map. The big cities make a useful source of encyclopaedic reference. It is also a place that lends itself to the new games techniques, building railways across the mid-West to the Pacific coast. It lends itself to mighty journeys drawn on huge wall maps or cross-sections built as a frieze right across the back of the classroom with all the variety of landscapes and human activities recorded. It lends itself to an historic interpretation from the Indians in their primitive paradise to the invading Spaniards and Russians and French and English, the hunters, then the cattlemen, then the homesteaders, then the industrialists and finally the rocket sites and spacemen, making an enormous strip-cartoon whether on all the available pin-boarding or in the individual exercise books.

But I learnt more about the United States (which I have never visited) from one programme on sound radio in which Alan Lomax interpreted the variety of American life in *song*. Blues, ballads, folksong, railroad songs, hillbillies; they were all there and brought the scene to life for me more than any written word or picture. Think of the countries that we remember for their songs. The tape-recorder and the record-player are now familiar tools in most schools and open up yet another avenue for the imaginative teacher in his quest for reality and variety in his teaching methods. After all, enjoyment is not the least important factor in this learning process.

References

E. W. H. Briault and D. W. Shave, (1965) *Geography in and out of school*, Harrap.

M. Long, (1964) *Handbook for geography teachers*, Methuen.

G. J. Cons and C. Fletcher, (1938) *Actuality in school: an experiment in social education*, Methuen.

M. Long and B. S. Robertson, (1966) *Teaching geography*, Heinemann Educational.

B. Brouillette (ed.) (1965), *Source book for geography teaching*, Longmans.

13 Games and simulations

REX WALFORD

The technique of simulation and gaming has achieved enough exposure in recent years for educationalists to look upon it as a serious business. The mushroom growth of simulation in military and business education has been the forerunner of its adoption in more general educational areas.

Geographers have been among the most interested and involved as the exploration of the technique has progressed from its infancy. The idea of the 'geographical game' is no longer the intellectual curiosity that it once was; neither has it remained the oasis of frenzied euphoria that some classroom practitioners once imagined it to be. It has already become a regular part of the curriculum for some teachers and an experimental activity for many others. Some thirty to forty geographical games and simulations, usable at school level are now (1971) available in published form, and up to a hundred others circulate in mimeograph or photostat. More importantly, current discussion about simulations focuses not so much on their justification and mechanics, as on their integration into the general syllabuses of schools.

Some of the earliest general reservations expressed about simulation reflected a belief that they were somehow a frivolous activity, compared with other methods of instruction; indeed, early developers were encouraged to eschew the word 'game' altogether. It would seem, however, that the noun is now acceptable and used in a technical and less evocative sense.

As long ago as 1938 Huizinga in *Homo Ludens* (republished 1970) had set out the general philosophy of seeing play as almost the essence of man's cultural activity; Roger Caillois (1961) and Eric Berne (1964) later followed this with more popular versions of the same theme, Berne's book achieving a breakthrough into the world of the colour supplements and the women's magazines.

Nigel Calder (1967) produced a variation on this theme which was of interest to geographers in his book *The Environment Game*, in which he wrote:

It is no pun or idle metaphor to see social institutions such as have existed since the dawn of agriculture as an elaborate game, the prizes of which are individual wealth and power. Constitutions and laws are the rules of the game and one ploy is to seek to change the rules to one's own advantage. Intelligence, money and force, and alliances of these, constitute the chief counters in the game, but the rules are biased in favour of those who are already winning and, as the winners are also in a much better position to cheat, most people at most times have been losers.

Calder contrasts his 'old game' noted above (and currently reproduced in an effective classroom simulation) with the possibility of no less than fifteen 'new games' which could be played by human beings – among them his 'environment game' – and points out:

> Let there be no mistake about it, a game there must be, human and material resources have to be deployed according to some set of rules. . . . So while by talking of 'games' we recognise the ephemeral character of social institutions that seem obsessively indispensable to those in the thick of the old game, we need not be cynical in our use of the word.

But even before this, geographers had become interested in the implications of game theory and subsequently in the possibilities of operational gaming which derive from it. Some game ideas for children were being tried out in the early 1960s, both in America (Gould 1963) and in Britain, where J. P. Cole's work (1967, 1969, 1970) was of stimulating significance.

TYPES OF SIMULATION

The basic idea of simulation as a teaching technique is to encourage students to 'put themselves in the place of others', to try to see a situation as someone else would have seen it, to attempt to resolve a problem by a realistic participation in it. In seeking to understand the world from a different point of view there is usually the end intention of trying to see what decisions would have been taken at certain times and for what reasons.

As far as geographers are concerned, the technique seems particularly appropriate for a time in which there is increasing concern about the spatial implications of the decision-making process. As at least the cruder precepts of the man-land relationship have become increasingly difficult to sustain, so greater attention is drawn to *how* and *why* decisions are taken which affect the spatial organisation of the environment.

And this can apply as readily to a governmental decision to farm new lands as to an individual's decision to take up a shop lease. In either case the decision-makers may perceive the environment somewhat differently from other onlookers; and their reasons for their decision are related basically to this 'perceived environment' rather than to any 'objective' environment which might be thought to exist.

The understanding of this new *terra incognita* in geography has become a major focus for study in recent years, and the 'behavioural' school of geography is making some intriguing contributions in this growth field of perception studies (Downs 1970). But the attempt to disentangle individual perceptions of the world through the refined tools of social science has necessarily limited application in the classroom. An alternative and more useful approach to the problem in schools may be through the use of simulation – a technique which tries to allow for human perceptions, intuitions and irrationalities by allowing them a place alongside the more analytical aspects of any study.

Simulation itself can take a variety of forms. Role-play, operational games, and mathematical simulations are all recognisably part of the same family, and the appropriateness of each one to particular tasks depends on the intentions of the simulation designer, as well as on the level of understanding which participants may have. A few examples, used in geography teaching, may help to clarify this terminology and provide a frame of reference for what is written later.

(*a*) *Role-play*. From the earliest days of their life children are accustomed to role-play situations. Play in the Wendy-house or with old costumes from the prop-basket enshrine the idea, and in the primary school there has been a long tradition of creative dramatic activity. Such play is often valued as expressive or therapeutic. Brian Way describes one such activity in his book *Development through drama* (1967).

. . . a simple situation is built up round the idea of coal-mining. Working at the singleton stage, each person experiences going to a low coal-face, and hacking away with a pick and then gathering the coal with shovels into trucks, and pushing the trucks through dark tunnels to the surface. . . . Then a coal-mine scene is built up using the whole class. Some work at the coal-face, some are in charge of transport, others look after lifts and so on. Then quite suddenly a new question is brought up, 'What is it really like in a coal-mine?' Many different thoughts will arise from the discussion—cramped conditions, dirt, heat, the darkness . . . so we return to improvisation, everybody now working down in the darkness by oil and candlelight . . . and so a simple group improvisation happens which includes (an) episode of (an) explosion. . . .

. . . we start discussion again. What, we ask, caused that explosion? And we discuss gas and where it comes from and how it accumulates in the mine – and we discuss what caused it to blow up, namely the naked lights. At once, we get the class to divide into small groups; they are all connected with mining – inventors, managers, engineers, and coal-face workers. Each group has the same problem, set them by the coal-mine owners . . . they must urgently find a way of lighting the mine that will not have the same dangers – and no one has yet heard of electricity or the dry-cell battery. This discussion is not academic – it involves real people with a real life-and-death problem; depending on the age-group they may find the answer. If they don't then we are standing by with the relevant information about Humphry Davy lanterns. But we do not leave it at that – we study them in detail and then have another scene . . . where the lantern indicates the presence of a pocket of gas. And so on. . . .

The aim of Way's lesson, as described, appears to be to evoke creative responses in the children, and it is intended for the 'drama' period in the timetable. But it would seem also to have valuable possibilities in regard to cognitive learning, and as such might well justify a place in the history or geography period also. The primary school teacher who takes his class to the 'simulation' coal-mine in the London Science Museum in relation to a project on Britain's power resources is surely engaged in the same kind of activity as that described above?

Role-play of this kind at more adult levels is less obviously 'dramatic' and active, but more sophisticated in style. It remains, however, essentially open-ended. One class in a London school, for example, simulated a meeting of a local town council concerning a proposed road-widening scheme. In order to appreciate the conflict of opinion and the reality of the problem, the group (of sixth-formers) were given by their teacher half-page biographies of some of the supposed combatants. These included the Town Clerk (anxious to give the town a modern image), the Town Engineer and Surveyor (keen on the scheme because it would greatly improve traffic flow), Chairman of the local Historical Society (anxious to preserve some threatened Tudor cottages), a Councillor who was a shopkeeper (undecided about whether the new road would increase custom or only encourage through traffic), a Residents' Association secretary (anxious about the cost on the rates) and so on. The class were armed with maps, statistics and other background information for the discussion. Seen in this context the apparently 'pure' geographical problem of where (or whether) to build the new road assumed some extra dimensions. The investigators of the problem – the students in the class – had nevertheless to try and reconcile interests and solve the problem by discussion, in this case by ingenious compromise that satisfied a healthy majority of those involved.

(*b*) *Operational games* The operational game situation differs from role-play in its additional set of rule structures. There is still the opportunity for the development of roles and strategies in a simulated way, but the rule framework of the game represents outside constraints with which the participants must reckon.

A simple fishing game, for example, might involve participants, or groups of participants in the simulation of (say) trawler crews about to set off on a typical fishing trip. A 'title card' given to each crew might give them distinctive details about the name of their trawler, its supposed capacity, its maximum endurance at sea, and the experience of their captain in certain waters. Since each trip lasts over a time period, the game would consist of 'rounds', each of which might represent a day's fishing.

The crews (or perhaps their captain) would have the opportunity to devise a strategy of search and a choice of route; they would do this with reference to a board or map which would represent the English near and middle water fishing grounds (or whatever other area the deviser of the simulation chose for an example). Perhaps a 'weather forecast' read out before the beginning of each round would regulate the amount of fish able to be caught in certain areas. There could also be chance cards regularly turned up to represent the unexpected bonuses or hazards which all crews meet from time to time. Most important of all, a 'chance' element could be written into each day's fishing. When trawlers had chosen to fish in a particular area on the map, the amount of their catch might be related to some kind of dice throw.

Such apparently random elements are built into the game not to make it less predictable or more exciting but to represent realistically the amount of chance factors which operate in real life. The good simulation neither over-values nor underestimates the amount of unpredictability in situations like these. The use of dice and chance factor cards aids rather than undermines the context of these decisions.

The game itself can vary in complexity depending on the needs and demands of the teacher. Certain aspects of the game described above (e.g. the individual constraints placed upon each trawler) could be jettisoned if a simpler simulation was desired; conversely, other aspects of the real-life situation could be written in (e.g. the problems of marketing the catch in addition to the search for fish). The level of the game's complexity should be matched to the abilities of the participants. Simple games represent relatively crude models of reality; sophisticated ones can introduce much more of the 'real situation'. Both kinds, however, seek to abstract the essentials for study.

(*c*) *Mathematical models* The mathematical model attempts the simulation of real-life situations, but usually without the personal element of role-play contained in the two types of simulation noted above. Its simulation aspects are controlled by the mathematics of probability factors, and by weightings given by the deviser of the model. Random-number tables may well be applied in relating such weightings to chance.

Some wellknown examples in this sphere relate to simulations of the development of towns; in these, weightings have been given to various grid-square areas (usually depending on their calculated 'attractiveness' for settlement) and then random-numbers have been used to hypothesise the way in which settlement might develop (Keeble, 1969, Hancock, 1970). (When this has been done in relation to historical data, the development of the model may have been intended to reveal what weightings produced the *existing* pattern). Morrill's (1965, 1969) now much-quoted simulation of the Negro ghetto areas in Seattle was worked out in this way; others have used it to try and predict further town-growth in particular areas.

Because there is no element of role-play in the mathematical simulation, the application of such models is suited to certain problems in physical geography. They represent a logical extension of the 'hardware models' (wave-tanks, sand-trays) with which physical geographers have sought to explain processes associated with the earth's surface. And since the mathematical model needs operation rather than participation, it seems also suitable for the study of problems associated with overall patterns of growth, diffusion, or contraction. It can help to reveal long-term trends and influences, but not small-scale situations where individual decisions need to be scrutinised.

THE IMPETUS FROM MODEL THEORY

Much of the impetus towards the use of simulation techniques in geography has derived from a current emphasis on the development of theoretical models. In Britain, the work of Chorley and Haggett (1968, 1970) set out the case for the increasing concentration of study towards such models and away from what were thought to be cul-de-sacs of idiographic study. In a world in which areal uniqueness was becoming demonstrably less obvious, and in which the region was increasingly difficult to define, the search for 'models' against which variations from the norm could be tested seemed more profitable. Such a search for patterns and regularities in the environment accorded appropriately with what was happenning in other social sciences, since more rigorous tools of analysis were encouraging a more coherent and wide-ranging methodology.

This work found its echo in schools where some teachers were finding existing approaches restrictive, and where two additional disadvantages to the status quo were beginning to be expressed. One of these was the feeling that the development of syllabuses built around an areal framework was unprogressive, since it led in many cases to an emphasis on 'covering the world in five years of geography lessons' rather than to any development of sequential ideas. The concept of the region assumed an important place in many such syllabuses but it was argued that such a concept was both over-sophisticated and inappropriate as a central base in many cases. At the 11-year-old level the idea of synthesising before many analytical tools were known seemed perverse; at the 18-year-old level the regional idea seemed only to half-explain many situations, since its emphasis was on a static rather than a dynamic picture of the environment, a 'snapshot' approach to a world in rapid change.

The problem of the 'data explosion' was also becoming urgent and impelled a re-examination of the danger of over-dependence on factual material. Though clearly a geographical education demands a framework of factual knowledge, the aim of teaching in schools is not the compilation of a mental gazetteer. The superfluity of current information has consequently aroused a renewed interest in the identification of key geographical concepts and ideas, beacons, set to speak, amongst the great sea of facts.

The example of the American High School Geography Project (at work in Boulder, Colorado, between 1961 and 1970) and the writings of Jerome Bruner (1960, 1966) have both been influential in stimulating thought and research about the restructuring of geography syllabuses around such fundamental ideas. Simulation approaches seemed appropriate to both these situations. The development of a practical application of a theoretical model clearly carried implications in relation to studying 'dynamic' situations; during simulations situations change, feedback takes place, the system adjusts accordingly and so on. And secondly, when related to other activities, the simulation makes it possible to study ideas in depth, since it represents the playing out of a concrete situation in which essential ideas have been deliberately emphasised for teaching purposes.

AN EXAMINATION OF SOME CRITICISMS

The development of simulation ideas has taken place over a period of years and it is now possible to examine the situation in the light of some experience. The experience, however, lacks as yet any major piece of research to shed light on long-term effects; and indeed some practitioners would argue that it will be difficult to design such research for a variety of reasons. In some cases, simulations themselves are the practical vehicles of change, acting as signposts towards new objectives and horizons in the curriculum, as yet glimpsed only imperfectly.

Experience has brought development and diversification of the technique, and has also helped to put claims and enthusiasms in perspective. Almost universally, the motivating properties of the technique have not been questioned; simulations *do* seem to work extensively in generating pupil involvement and interest during their actual duration. What have been questioned have been some of the academic foundations of what has been going on. It would seem appropriate at this point, therefore, to examine some of the reservations and criticisms expressed both generally about the technique and specifically in relation to its use in teaching geography.

(*a*) *Do simulations really teach?* Cherryholmes (1966) concluded that 'simulation does produce more student motivation and interest compared to other teaching techniques but there are not consistent or significant differences in learning, retention, critical thinking or attitude change.' C. R. Anderson (1970) confirmed Cherryholmes' research and other work reported by Boocock and Schild (1968), and concluded that between a group who had used a simulation game and another who had not there was 'no significant difference in learning factual information'. Taylor and Carter (1971) in a survey of simulation techniques in the urban planning field considered the validation of studies in some detail but relied mainly on 'a growing consensus of opinion'. They noted increasing use of simulations, but found it difficult to make conclusions about their effectiveness because of the relative infancy of the technique and the difficulty of applying particular studies (such as that done by Monroe on the Cornell Land Use Game) in a general context.

But as Kasperson (1968) noted:

> the measurement of learning itself is a thorny problem. In games it is difficult to establish evaluation criteria as to what the game is in fact teaching and to create tests discriminating among the various types of learning. Since games are not closed systems, players may introduce unanticipated and often unrecognisable values, behaviours and rules, thus thwarting evaluation efforts.

If research as yet returns a 'not proven' verdict on the technique, there would seem to be less reservation on the part of teachers who have used and continue to use it in their regular classes. But this enthusiasm may stem at least in part from the fact that desirable results are achieved by using simulation in conjunction with other techniques in the classroom; thus it is not easy to identify the distinctive contribution that the simulation itself may make.

This situation may be unsatisfying for researchers but entirely suitable for practical teaching purposes. Most advocates of simulation stress the need for preliminary 'briefing' and a following 'debriefing' once the simulation has been used. The simulation's motivating properties are seen as a way of opening up a situation for pupils so that further learning may take place as a result. One is well aware of the frequent report of the spin-off effects of simulation, with pupils becoming motivated to read further in the subject, to try the simulation again, and perhaps to design modifications and improvements in the light of their knowledge subsequently gained – the latter being an important extra use of the simulation itself.

In particular, many developers of simulation material stress that use of the simulation should be followed by discussion about the principles involved. The 'concrete operation' of, say, a farming game brings into play some of the aspects of the agricultural system; but the following discussion and work may *use* these operations and transform them into the level of 'formal abstractions'. The simulation prepares and informs for more committed consideration and evaluation of problems in orthodox classroom teaching modes. Thus, it may seem profitless to try and 'separate' the cognitive effects of simulation, without seeing it in a totally integrated class context. From the teaching perspective, it would be wise to remember that as much care needs to be taken in *using* the game, as in playing it.

(*b*) *Should not geographers always start from reality and not from a theoretical idea?* The nuance in a statement such as this sometimes implies that 'reality' is something *other* than what is being discussed in the simulation, and this is usually developed to mean the 'reality which can be observed in the field', the 'actual landscape' and so on. It is beyond question that the latter has a long history of importance in the discipline of geography, but it does not necessarily follow that geographers are concerned *only* with what is observable, or that they should use that as a *starting-point* for study. For instance, a visit to a farm can reveal the 'observable reality' of farmer, work-force, buildings and animals; but just as important are the less easily observed realities, the accountant's trust in the farmer's management decisions, the farmer's relationship with his men, the factors which encourage high-risk crops in the expectation of quick profits, etc. These are no less real for not being immediately observed. They form the stuff of which simulations are made.

It might be argued, however, that investigation of an actual case-study, through literature or direct contact, can deal with these relationships. The case for simulation study would not be made *against* case-study, but in relation to it. (Indeed, many simulation users compare their simulation with case-studies in their follow-up work.)

But the simulation might be used in preference to the 'actual case'; both because it is based on more than one case-study, and therefore combines elements of a wider background, and because it is structured to emphasise essential points and block out 'background noise' which can be a persistent confusion to inexperienced observers of the environment.

Thus the idiosyncrasies of a particular case-study can perhaps better be judged later rather than sooner, if seen in perspective against a simulation model – assuming that the latter has been reasonably and perceptively constructed. In addition, the use of simulation material in this way implies certain attitudes towards 'reality' by the user. The conscious or unconscious objectives involved in the use of simulations relate to the investigation of a model of a frequently recurring type of situation *in order that* common elements and relationships may be identified at other times in 'reality'. And this search for pattern, as has already been suggested, is a prominent theme in much contemporary investigation in both the physical and the social sciences. The case-study may also help to do this, but its function as a truly 'sample study' needs to be carefully examined before inferences are drawn from it. The perfect 'sample study' used as a simulation exercise would seem to be a most desirable goal for which to strive.

The teacher's own skills need to be used to firmly wed simulation of any kind to 'reality' as McLeish (1970) points out:

> In elaborating . . . models, we select particular elements to represent the most essential, the most salient or the most pregnant aspects of the concept (or relationship) for understanding the complete concept as it is in reality. By its very nature, the analogue model is at least one step away from reality . . . obviously this method has a number of disadvantages. The most significant of these is that a student, having understood the model, may remain convinced ever afterwards that he understands the reality as well. . . . But this disadvantage is not inherent in the use of the model; rather, it points to an incorrect and inappropriate use of the models presented to the student. It also testifies to the lack of clarity on the part of the instructor as to the desired outcome of the instructional process.

And the pursuit of 'reality' itself does not always imply the donning of the raincoat and heavy boots. L. J. Curry (1968) drew attention to this point recently:

> It is too often forgotten that geographic studies are not studies of the real world, but rather, perceptions passed through the double-filter of the author's mind and his available tools of argument and representation. We cannot know reality; we can only have an abstract picture of aspects of it. All our descriptions of relation or process are theories – or when formalized, better called models. Thus explicit model building . . . is no innovation, but rather a frank recognition of human frailty.

(*c*) *Simulations have undesirable elements* (e.g. they equate success with financial profitability, they are competitive, etc.). Criticisms of this kind are usually based on a restricted knowledge of the range and types of simulations which have been developed. Many simulations do *not* equate success with financial profitability (the 'values' used may well be a Satisfaction Index of points, or something of a similar nature); neither are all simulations competitive (some, indeed, stress the need for a cooperative approach to solve particular problems). Where financial profit is related to the aims of the simulation it is replicating as faithfully as possible the factors in the original situation (e.g. an industrialist seeking a least-cost location). Thus, the 'profit' motives which appear in some simulations do not invite judgment on the simulation itself, but on the particular set of circumstances which gives rise to it.

Indeed, there is often interplay between financial and other factors in an interesting way. In a frequently-used simulation concerning the process of route building, which uses the competitive situation of the USA in the 1860s as its context (Walford 1969), it has become more satisfactory *not* to define initially aims and values for participants. Some groups resultantly see competition with other groups as of greater or lesser importance in the situation; one group may be happy to define its own target as the building of a viable railroad, another may seek to reach San Francisco first, even at the expense of bankruptcy, a third may simply wish to achieve a West Coast terminus, a fourth (and perhaps initially poorer) company may be happy to have achieved a high revenue compared with their original capital. Discussion of these different aims and values enhances the value of the simulation and points out the differing viewpoints which can be held in a particular situation.

Similarly a simulation about urbanisation may hold in tension the differing concerns about profitability and environmental quality, even to the extent of seeing these in differing terms for each particular participant.

If different groups of pupils work at a simulation idea, they are not necessarily *competing* against each other; a simulation of town growth, for example, attempted by five or six different groups, may reveal interesting sets of alternative strategies for development; an illustration of the fact that there is not necessarily a 'right answer', and that an existing urban form may be only one of a number of consequences that have occurred in reponse to an original stimulus.

(*d*) *Simulations are dangerous* This is certainly an argument to be considered seriously, and it evolves from two differing viewpoints, one concerned about the possibility of wrong ideas, the other about the effects emotionally on children.

If simulations are effective motivators, runs the first argument, all the more reason that the models on which they are built should be 'correct' or at least highly tested sets of ideas. Since the idea of the theoretical model is difficult to evaluate (are its shortcomings due to mismanagement or erroneous assumptions in construction?) it may be possible to teach and persist with wrong ideas; models do not necessarily represent any kind of scientific basis for geography.

To this, one can only say 'Amen', and resolve to work with the best and most tested models that one has available. The onus is certainly on the user (and even more on the deviser) of models to satisfy himself that the hypotheses on which the simulation is built are reasonable ones; an indiscriminate adoption of simulations only *because* of their motivating properties would be a capitulation to expediency of the worst kind. But being aware of these dangers, recognising the limitations of models, and not elevating them to the status of idols is, one hopes, the alert response of teachers who trouble to use them.

The second criticism in this sphere relates to the general effect of simulation activity on children. It is thought that some children may become emotionally disturbed or vulnerable when involved in simulation activities (an incidental testimony to their motivating properties). In Project Simile's 'Star power' simulation, for instance, the following situation is intended. The game is a kind of analogue of world trade in which successful traders of 'chips' are allowed to change the rules to their own benefit at the end of each round. The game *depends* on the eventual frustration of poor traders in order to be successful; the organisers are enjoined to await a prospective revolt on the part of those who are losing and who dislike the rule-changing which goes on from the top, and then to step in and end the game – pointing out that this kind of revolt is similar to the frustration that underdeveloped countries feel in certain 'real-life' trading situations. Discussion about world trade and underdevelopment goes on from there.

The game clearly treads a tightrope towards class disorder; it is advertised as being for 'adventurous and courageous class teachers'. Nevertheless, it has achieved a considerable amount of exposure in American and British classrooms; it does make a powerful and well-remembered point, if adequately controlled. Those who use it would recognise its dangers, but consider that its advantages outweigh these on balance.

It is true, however, that the teacher using a simulation needs to be aware of the effect of the simulation on individuals; lagging behind, being dealt cruel blows by 'chance', making a rash decision can have its emotional effect on pupils; and for this reason it seems unwise to use structured simulation material with very young children. But it is possible for these vulnerable situations to be foreseen, and guarded against. Groups make better losers than individuals since responsibility becomes corporate; and since simulations rarely begin with groups being 'equal', it is usually possible to find rationalisations for poor performance if necessary. More fundamentally, it is important to stress the operating of simulations and games, rather than their winning; the practised user will often deflect attention towards aspects of events *in* the game immediately it has been concluded, rather than towards a climactic result.

Some of these dangers become self-evident when a teacher has had experience of a small number of simulation situations; a perceptive view of individuals within a class of students can usually give warning of mishap.

SOME PERSPECTIVES

It is important nevertheless not to overclaim for the technique. An understanding of the strengths and weaknesses of simulation should help not only to develop its promise as a pedagogic tool, but to place it in perspective. The most fervent advocates would not suggest that simulations are suitable for all purposes, nor that they should be used with unvaried constancy. But they help to do some things well, and if this seems in accord with current movements in the teaching of geography, they may have an important role in determining classroom approaches to fresh ideas.

Most important of all, it is vital, as has already been stressed, to see simulations thoroughly integrated into ongoing work, and not used as a spare 'entertainment factor' at some stage, possibly near the end of term. The fishing game described earlier, for example, would gain most from being at the heart of several weeks' work on the topic. In a primary or middle school, where 'Fishing' might well be a typical project topic, there would desirably be some preliminary lessons in which pupils mastered vocabulary, and basic elements of the topic; following the game, there would need to be a reconsideration of what was happening within it, and also further work developed from insights and stimuli derived during the game. Some kind of visit or visitor to the classroom would make additional impact. The value of the simulation would lie in its place at the heart of the topic, and in its role in involving many pupils in active and concrete consideration of its problems. Decisions and strategies might not be based on complete information, but they would be based on *some* previously understood material.

The range of simulation material now available to geographers is very large. Without borrowing too much from other disciplines, there is plenty of material available to cover many of the dynamic themes which geographers may need to consider – urbanising, locating, route-building and travelling, diffusing, colonising, transforming land surfaces, developing new lands, and so on. To see geography in terms of these themes is not to suggest that place has been abandoned as a central study in the discipline, but rather that the spatial characteristics of the environment need to be studied through process as well as through form.

And in addition, it may be added that the simulation approach to understanding the patterns and processes that shape the environment attempts to make no false dichotomies. By the nature of the technique, it does not stop short at considerations of 'geology, relief, soil, climate'; in Simons' (1966) dictum 'Any factor at all that seems to cause areal differentiation is the geographer's concern'.

Following this through may sometimes take simulation into fields that do not seem to be the traditional province of the geographer. But if this is so, it may cause a reconsideration of the geographer's proper field of study, rather than a rejection of the technique. If the geographer's task is conceived in terms of explaining the distributions and the interactions which make up the spatial organisation of the environment, such explanations cannot be adequate if they are selective. The geographer's particular expertise may be conceived in terms of the fundamental spatial concepts and ideas which he uses to explain such environmental organisation.

In general, simulations seem to motivate highly, and to encourage the study of such ideas in some depth. If they also encourage a total look at the process of decision-making as it affects the earth's surface, they may help to make clearer the true multi-disciplinary implications of the studies that geographers make.

References

P. J. Ambrose, (ed.) (1969) *Analytical human geography*, Longmans.

C. R. Anderson, (1970) 'An experiment on behavioural learning in a consumer credit game', *Simulation and gaming*, vol. 1, no. 1.

E. Berne, (1964) *Games people play*, Deutsch and Penguin.

S. S. Boocock and E. O. Schild (eds.), (1968) *Simulation games in learning*, Sage Publications.

J. S. Bruner, (1960) *The process of education*, Vintage Books.

(1967) *Towards a theory of instruction*, Belknap.

R. Caillois, (1961) *Man, play and games*, Free Press.

N. Calder, (1967) *The environment game*, Secker & Warburg, in paperback Panther.

C. H. Cherryholmes, (1966) 'Some current research on the effectiveness of educational simulations', *American Behavioural Scientist*, vol. X.

R. J. Chorley and P. Haggett (eds.), (1965, 2nd ed. 1970) *Frontiers in geographical teaching*, Methuen.

(1968) *Models in geography*, Methuen (sections available in paperback).

J. P. Cole and N. J. Beynon, (1969, 1970) *New ways in geography*, Introductory Book, Books I and II, Teachers' Book, Blackwell.

J. P. Cole and G. A. Smith, (1967) 'Geographical Games', *Bulletin of Quantitative Data for Geographers*, No. 7, University of Nottingham.

L. J. Curry, (1968) 'Climatic change as random series', *Spatial analysis*, B. J. L. Berry and D. L. Marble (eds.) Prentice-Hall.

R. Downs, (1970) 'Geographic space perception; past approaches and future prospects' in Board C et al. *Progress in geography*, vol. 2, Edward Arnold.

Geography in an urban age, (1969) Units 1–6, Teacher's Guides, Student Resource books, Student manuals, etc., Collier-Macmillan.

P. R. Gould, (1963) 'Man and his Environment; a game theoretic framework', *Annals of the Association of American Geographers*.

J. Hancock, (1970) 'An urban diffusion model', *Profile*, vol. 3, part. 1.

J. Huizinga, (1944) *Homo Ludens*, Temple Smith, in paperback Paladin.

R. E. Kasperson, (1968) 'Games as educational media', *Journal of Geography*, vol. 67, no. 7.

D. Keeble, (1969) 'School teaching and urban geography: some new approaches', *Geography*, vol. 54, part I.

J. McLeish, (1970) 'Systems, models, simulations and games in Education', *Instructional Simulation systems in higher education*, Cambridge Institute of Education.

R. L. Morrill, (1965) 'The negro ghetto: problems and alternatives', *Geographical Review*, vol. 55, reprinted in (1969) *Analytical human geography*, P. J. Ambrose (ed.), Longmans.

Project Simile, *Star Power*, 1150 Silverado, La Jolla, California.

M. Simons, (1966) 'What is a geographical factor?' *Geography*, vol. 51, no. 232.
J. L. Taylor and K. R. Carter, (1971) 'Gaming simulation', *Journal of the Town Planning Institute*, vol. 57, no. 1.
R. Walford, (1969) *Games in geography*, Longmans.
B. Way, (1967) *Development through drama*, Longmans.

14 School examinations

NORMAN GRAVES

The purpose of this chapter is to review and discuss examinations in geography, particularly in the United Kingdom and to a lesser extent in the USA. In doing this it will be necessary to trace briefly the development of examinations, to examine the various types of examinations and their levels of operation, and to assess their functions critically in the light of research findings. Certain suggestions will then be made about examining in geography.

BRIEF HISTORICAL SURVEY

School examinations, aside from internal school tests, virtually did not exist before the middle of the nineteenth century in English-speaking communities, whether in the UK or in the USA. During the second half of the nineteenth century written examinations were widely introduced in both countries, but their development was different in each country and will be treated separately.

In the UK, 1858 saw the setting up of the Oxford and the Cambridge local examinations and the London Matriculation examinations. In 1874 the Oxford and Cambridge Board was created to cater for the 'public schools' whose older pupils were seeking admission to these universities. These were followed by other examining boards, so that by the first years of the twentieth century there was a multiplicity of examinations which schools could use, some connected with universities and some not, like the College of Preceptors' examinations. The government therefore set up a consultative committee to look into school examinations in 1911. This committee reported that (1) there ought to be an examination for 16-year-old candidates and another for 18-year-old candidates; (2) the examination should be a test of liberal education; (3) the inspection of schools should be part of the examination.

After consultation it was agreed that the universities should administer the examinations and that the then Board of Education should provide a coordinating body, which when it was set up in 1917 was called the Secondary Schools Examinations Council. Thus, from the end of World War I to 1950, the two main examinations were the School Certificate Examination taken at 16 years and the Higher School Certificate taken at 18 years. Both were essentially based on written papers which in most subjects (apart from modern languages, mathematics, and the sciences – the latter including practical work) consisted of questions which required answers written in essay form. A change of some significance occurred during this period. Prior to the 1930s, it was usual for question papers to be set for particular schools. It was assumed that an examining board was merely assessing the result of one school's teaching based on its own syllabus. However, during the inter-war years there was an increasing tendency for question papers to be set for the whole entry to the examination. This led to criticisms that the general examination syllabuses were effectively controlling what teachers had to teach. When, in 1943, the Norwood Committee (which was an offshoot of the Secondary Schools Council) reported on the curriculum and examinations, it came down strongly on the side of limiting the effect of examinations on school work.

The practical effect was manifested in the decision to introduce in 1950 the General Certificate of Education (GCE). This, like the School Certificate and the Higher School Certificate, was to consist of two examinations, one for 16- and one for 18-year-old candidates; but, unlike its predecessors, each was to be a single subject examination, so allowing schools a maximum of flexibility in planning courses. It was also stated that only the most able need take the examinations which would allow them to obtain the necessary university entrance qualifications; others would be free of such embarrassments, and their education could develop along experimental lines. In fact the GCE examination at the O-level (16 year) began to be taken by a much broader span of candidates then the most able 20%, and a new examination, the Certificate of Secondary Education (CSE), was set up in 1965 to cater for those representing the 40% of the ability range below the top 20%. Thus the total number of examinees has grown enormously as well as the range of examined subjects. Until the advent of CSE, however, the techniques of examining hardly changed, in spite of the publication of *An examination of examinations* by Hartog and Rhodes in 1935 which was critical of existing examining methods, and in spite of the enormous amount of work done in the USA on objective testing.

In the USA criticisms of traditional written examinations had been voiced much earlier and led to some experiments with continuous assessment in the late nineteenth and early twentieth centuries. These experiments revealed that, though schools were given great freedom to educate their charges, the final qualification given to the students was of a variable standard. In the 1920s the New York State Department of Education began experimenting with objective type tests and by the 1930s these tests were well established in American schools. The College Entrance Examinations Board (CEEB) originally set up by some north-eastern schools and universities to regulate entry to universities, also began to experiment with objective tests in the 1930s, and this led to the creation of the 'Cooperative Test Service' whose main purpose was to 'supply colleges and schools in the US with measuring instruments to yield accurate and comparable measurements of defined achievements'. In 1948 this organisation was merged into the Education Testing Service (ETS) located at Princeton. The CEEB relies on the ETS for the tests which are administered as part of the board's Admissions Testing Program for applicants to certain colleges and universities. The tests given usually include (*a*) a Scholastic Aptitude test which yields a score of verbal reasoning and a score of mathematical reasoning (this is a three-hour multiple-choice test) and (*b*) a battery of achievement tests in English, social studies, mathematics, history and languages. Most candidates are required by the colleges to take three achievement tests, which are of one hour each, three being taken at one sitting. All tests, except that in English, are multiple-choice.

It may be seen that there are fundamental differences between the English and the American system of examinations, and that these differences originated in the inter-war period. They may be ascribed to the greater numbers in American secondary schools which became egalitarian in tendency long before Britain aspired to secondary education for all, and which made traditional essay type examinations difficult to mark. They may also be ascribed to the rapid development of psychology and the application of statistical techniques to the social sciences which made possible the development of aptitude and achievement tests. It should also be noted that whilst geography as a subject may be taken at O- and A-level in the GCE examination in England and Wales, no such subject features among the achievement tests of the CEEB's Admissions Testing Program, though some of the questions in the social studies test could be classed as geographical.

THE FUNCTIONS OF EXAMINATIONS

Many discussions on examinations are marred by an inadequate clarification at the outset as to what examinations are meant to do. We must therefore look briefly into the functions of examinations in the light of experience. The term 'examination' will be used to cover all types including objective tests.

In the first place an examination may be used simply to select a certain number of candidates for a post, or for a college, or for an apprenticeship. The examination is then a competitive examination and those who are among, for example, the first ten in the results list are chosen and the rest are not. The examinations for entry to the Civil Service have that function and no other. Various open scholarship examinations for entrance to some Oxbridge colleges have a similar function. To have 'failed' such an examination has no absolute significance in terms of one's competence in the subject of the examination. If there are five places to be filled and a candidate is sixth among a list of one hundred, then he 'fails', but presumably he is still competent. There are few examinations of this type in which geography as a subject is extensively involved, except perhaps in France where the *agrégation* and *certificate d'aptitude pédagogique pour l'enseignement secondaire* are of such a type.

In the second place there are a large group of examinations which are generally called qualifying examinations. Most of the GCE and CSE examinations are of this type. Their function is simply to set up some standard of achievement in various subjects and to determine whether a candidate has or has not reached it. In such examinations the pass/fail line is important, since the candidate is declared competent or incompetent according to whether he is above or below it. Since this is the most widespread type of examination in the UK we shall come back to it later. At this stage we need only note that, since the pass/fail line is often drawn at the point where scores are in the region of 50% of the total, it is drawn where there are often the greatest number of candidates. Thus the risk of putting someone on the wrong side of the line is correspondingly higher than if the pass/fail line were drawn at the 80% point. Most geography examinations are of the qualifying type. They are used as evidence that one has satisfactorily completed a course of study and they have widespread currency among employers in the UK.

In the third place some examinations are used in order to predict the candidates' performance in different subjects or skills. Most of these are termed aptitude tests since they are meant to discover whether a student has an aptitude for this or that. Thus the 'Scholastic Aptitude Test' of the CEEB is essentially meant to give some indication of the candidate's potential for academic study based on his performance on tests of verbal and mathematical reasoning. In Britain the so-called 11+ examination is of this type. It attempts to pick out those candidates who may benefit from an academic education. It may be pointed out here that, since the number of places in academic secondary schools is limited, then such an 'aptitude examination' also takes on the function of a competitive examination. Similarly, in Britain the existence of a limited number of university places leads to the A-level examination being used as a competitive as well as a qualifying examination.

Lastly, the many examinations used within schools are mainly attainment tests. Their essential function is to discover whether students have in fact learnt what they were expected to learn. Presumably if they have not, then some remedial action may be taken. Their secondary function of ranking pupils in some sort of order is in a sense incidental. Clearly many geography tests are in this category.

TECHNIQUES OF EXAMINING: THE ESSAY QUESTION

Whatever the functions of examinations, there is a common element which runs through all of them. They rely on candidates responding to questions, on the quantitative assessment of the qualitative differences between the responses, and on the drawing up of a list of candidates in rank order based on that assessment. But the form of the examination may vary widely, as well as the kind of knowledge that the examination tests. We shall ignore the oral type of examination, since it is not widely used in geography, although some CSE examination boards use it.

Let us begin by looking at the traditional essay-type question which is the main form used in British qualifying examinations. This type of question can be very easy to set but extremely difficult to mark, since to some extent it is open ended. Thus when a candidate is invited to 'Give a geographical account of the North Deccan' (Geography A-level Welsh Board, Summer 1966) it must be rather difficult for the examiner to decide what ought to have been included and what could be left out. It is, of course, tantamount to asking the candidate to write all he knows about the North Deccan, and in the end whatever preconceived scheme of marking the examiner may have had, he is forced to look at what candidates have in fact provided him with by way of answers, and try to work out a scheme appropriate to those answers. Inevitably such a scheme cannot avoid differences between markers, or between the same marker on different occasions. Thus the standard error of measurement of such an examination (namely the extent to which a mark merely represents a band of marks and not an absolute position on the scale) is necessarily high, and in many cases is not known. (Valentine, 1967).

Fortunately, questions of that type are not necessarily typical of geography examination papers, though there are still too many where candidates are expected to regurgitate factual knowledge. If the examiner is trying to test the candidates' powers of reasoning with the concepts used in geography, then the question must be set in such a way that the candidate is posed a problem involving the application of a principle or is asked to discuss certain issues. For example, one might ask candidates the following question: 'Define what is meant by "dynamic equilibrium" in relation to the study of landforms. Assess the usefulness of this concept in explaining any one landform in an area which you have studied.' In such a case, knowledge of an idea is being assessed as well as its applicability. There is no attempt to specify where the idea should be applied. It could be argued that such a question was less concerned with fact than with ideas and reasoning. Nevertheless, marking such a question would not be objective. The wording of an essay-type question is of great importance, since the bulk of the candidates could hardly be classed as highly sophisticated in the art of answering such questions. An ambiguous question may give scope for the sophisticated to explore its possible meanings, and in a sense expose its inadequacies, but most candidates are under the delusion that the examiner knows precisely what he wants and that the question is asking them to provide this. For example, there is now little excuse for using the term *geographical factor* in a question when this term has nowhere been defined and would appear to be incapable of definition (Simons 1966). Yet the term has been used frequently in examinations in the recent past at both the O- and A-levels of the GCE. Similarly, the term 'geography' has often been used as an all-purpose word whose significance varies with the context. For example the following three questions were set in the same examination paper in 1966 (London A-level):

(*a*) Assess the relative importance of motor-roads and waterways in the transport *geography* of north-western Europe, excluding the British Isles, Norway and Sweden.

(*b*) What factors, physical and human, help to explain the agricultural *geography* of either France or the Netherlands?

(*c*) Compare the *geography* of any two major seaports in north-western Europe.

It would seem that in the first question the word 'geography' is used to mean 'network', in the second to mean a whole set of concepts which could include 'the distribution of crops and stocks' or 'types of farm economy', and in the third to mean 'site, situation, trade and hinterland'. There is little justification for this sort of thing, which may leave the 18-year-old candidate wondering precisely what the examiner does want. It is also bad policy, since candidates may be encouraged to turn out the sort of vague answer which goes under the generic name of 'waffle'. It will also cause great difficulties in marking. Such questions are evidence that the examiner who set them may not be clear as to what sort of response he is expecting from candidates. This last point may be further illustrated by a question of the type:

Africa has only recently been fully explored. What geographical factors do you think account for this?

This is a searching question. Assuming the candidates ignore the adjective 'geographical' and simply attempt to enumerate the various factors which may have delayed the exploration of Africa prior to the twentieth century, it will involve them in assessing the influence of the Sahara as a barrier to communications in the era before air travel, the effect of the wind system on sailing ships, the problems caused by the regimes of African rivers to water transport, the nature of transport available at the different periods, the nature of the West African coast, the paucity of the road networks, the influence of vegetation on penetrability, the attitude of various indigenous inhabitants to foreign explorers, the differing attitudes of the explorers themselves, the influence of climate on disease and the state of medical science at the time, and so on. Not only does it demand a wide knowledge of physical, economic, social, technical and medical factors, but it involves their being able to assess these in the context of the nineteenth century and before. It would seem highly optimistic to assume that 16-year-old candidates could do this with any real measure of success. Why not, therefore, tailor the question to the sort of answer which candidates may be expected to give at that age?

This process of tailoring the question to the candidates may be illustrated by the question 'What are the factors which influence dairy farming in Denmark?' which is in the same form as the question on Africa. Now most candidates find it difficult to sort out the multiplicity of factors which influence dairy farming in Denmark and in fact tend to bring out snippets of remembered information and little argument. But suppose the question is reworded in the form 'Some of western Jutland is heathland, bog and forest. Most of the island of Zealand is cultivated and dairying is the predominant type of farming. What variations in relief and soils in Denmark help to explain these differences in land use? In which ways does the climate of Denmark help or hinder dairy farming?' Clearly one is then simply asking the candidate to concentrate on the relief and soil as influences on land use, and to assess the effect of climate on one form of farming. The instructions are clear, the question is limited in scope and some information is given in the question to help the memory.

More and more in the present day the tendency, in both GCE and CSE, is to provide candidates with information and ask them to reason from this information using a principle or technique they know. This not only helps the candidate, but it also helps the marker since it may limit the vast amount of irrelevant material that is often given in examination questions which are too open. But no essay question can ever be marked with a complete degree of objectivity and reliability, though many examining boards do their best (Bruce 1969). Whatever the difficulties of marking such questions, they are the only questions that test a candidate's ability to write in continuous prose a reasoned statement concerning the matter he is being examined on. The very fact that they are to some extent open-ended, enables the creative person to inject a note of originality in his answers. In practice, however, few candidates do this.

TECHNIQUES OF EXAMINING: THE STRUCTURED QUESTION

A modified version of the essay question is that in which the examiner attempts to get the candidate to arrange his answer in several parts. This is done by structuring the question in such a way that the candidate is more or less bound to structure his answer in a similar way. An example will make this clear:

Study the pictures A (the coast of West Wales at Fishguard) and B (Moorfoot Hills, Peeblesshire, Scotland)

(*a*) (i) Describe the physical features of the landscape in picture B
(ii) Contrast the use man makes of the land in both areas

(*b*) Account for the limited population of *either* the Highlands of Scotland *or* those of Wales.

(University of London GCE, Summer 1964)

Here the candidate is asked to write on three separate topics based partly on the evidence provided by photographs and partly on his previous knowledge.

At the 16-year-old level, this type of question is a great advance on the simple essay question. It helps the allocation of marks by breaking up the question; it limits the amount of irrelevant material that almost inevitably creeps into an essay question; it does not rely entirely on recall but tests the candidates' ability to apply previously acquired concepts (e.g. about physical features) from the observation of features on photographs. This type of question may be set using map extracts, statistics, or descriptions of areas as the documentary evidence. It can be used to test reasoning ability as well as powers of observation. It is not, of course, possible to mark such a question completely objectively.

TECHNIQUES OF EXAMINING: THE OBJECTIVE-TYPE QUESTION

As we have seen earlier, the disadvantages of both the traditional written examination based on essay-type questions and continuous assessment of students had led in the USA to early experimentation with objective-type questions. It should be clear that what is objective about such questions is their marking and nothing else. Candidates are asked to indicate the correct answer to a question for which only that one correct answer will be given a mark or maximum marks. Thus the marker has no latitude in allocating marks and cannot help but be objective in his assessment. In fact the marking may often be done electronically. Since the marking is objective, it follows that none of the problems which arise because of the different performances of different examiners on essay questions is present. Also since the questions may be answered quickly, they can test a much wider sample from a syllabus than can essay questions. The subjective element is introduced in the type of knowledge tested by the question.

In general such questions may be of the following types:

1 The multiple-choice-type, which are the most popular. For example:

Underline the correct phrase:

Most of Britain's oil imports come from

A Venezuela
B the United States
C the Middle East
D the North Sea
E Algeria

(SE Regional Examinations Board CSE Geography, Paper II Part A, 1970)

2 The true–false type. For example:

Underline the words true or false in relation to the statements below:

The rivers Marañon, Purus, Madeira and Negro all have their sources outside Brazil.

A True
B False

(SE Regional Examinations Board CSE Geography, Paper II Section C – Atlas Extract)

This type has the disadvantage that candidates have a 50% chance of getting the right answer even if they merely guess at it.

3 The matching type. For example:

Besides each of the towns below, which are in the south Lancashire–Merseyside industrial area, write down one of the industries or functions from the following list appropriate to that town.

Chemicals, textiles, inland port, soap manufacture, sugar refining

Liverpool ....
Manchester ....
Bolton ....
Port Sunlight ....
Widnes ....

4 The completion type. For example:

East Anglia is mainly comprised of the counties of Essex, Suffolk and .... on the .... side of England. It is an area largely covered by a superficial glacial deposit of ...., but underlain by gently dipping strata of chalk which outcrop to form low hills called the .... Heights and the .... Edge, forming the western boundary of the region. To the east the chalk disappears under younger rocks so that along the east-facing coastline there are no chalk cliffs facing the .... Sea in ....

or Suffolk. In the south the chalk is covered by the .... clay which underlies most of the county of Essex.

All these questions are very simple and have been chosen from the CSE level of examining. They are all concerned with questions of fact, which is an objection often made to objective-type questions. It is unfortunately true that it is much simpler to devise objective-type questions which test factual information, than to devise questions which test the capacity of candidates to reason. However, it is quite possible, though more time-consuming, to produce the latter type of questions, and on the whole such questions are more worthwhile since they test knowledge of concepts and principles and their application. Here are a few examples, in each of which the most probable answers would have to be underlined:

1 Town A is just 50 kilometres east of town B, but whereas A has 1500 mm of rainfall per year, B only has 650 mm per year. The probable reason for this difference in rainfall is

(*a*) Town A is surrounded by sea on three sides but B only on two
(*b*) Winds from the sea never reach B
(*c*) There are no water bodies near B from which the air could obtain its moisture
(*d*) There is a range of high hills between A and B
(*e*) The winds blow from east to west

2 Two wells were bored one kilometre apart down to a level of 60 metres below the surface of the land, which in that area was perfectly flat. In one well the surface of the water table was found at a depth of 50 metres below the surface, in the other well it had not yet been reached. The probable reason for this difference is:

(*a*) the rainfall was less in the area of the dry well
(*b*) the dry well was bored through sand whereas the other was bored through gravel
(*c*) the aquifer was dipping below the surface and at a lower level in the area of the dry well
(*d*) the rock was porous in the area of the dry well but pervious in the area of the other
(*e*) the aquifer is saturated in the dry well but supersatured in the other.

3 An industrial chemist has discovered a new process for making self-sealing tubeless motor-car tyres. He needs a little skilled labour, a great deal of capital for his plant, very few raw materials

apart from substantial quantities of the by-products of the petroleum refining industry. The capital is forthcoming from a consortium of chemical and petroleum firms. He expects to sell about 60% of his output to motor-car manufacturers at home and 40% to motor-car manufacturers abroad. The Department of Trade and Industry have given him permission to set up a new factory in any one of the following five areas. Which one will he probably choose if the respective costs of the sites are about the same?

(*a*) Milford Haven
(*b*) Dundee
(*c*) Southampton Water
(*d*) Tyneside
(*e*) Teesside

4 Hilltown in the state of Artifact was found to be the fifth largest town in the country. Its population was 200,000 whilst the population of the largest town in the country was one million. This is a case which seems to conform to

(*a*) the nodality principle
(*b*) the principle that the greater the size of the town the greater the number of its functions
(*c*) the theory that the population of the towns in a country form an arithmetical progression
(*d*) the law of urban growth
(*e*) the rank-size rule

It is, of course, possible to set such questions on maps or on pictorial or statistical evidence, so that the variety of questions can be very great. The questions may also be pitched at different levels of understanding corresponding broadly with the CSE, O-level and A-level of the GCE in English examinations. It is therefore possible to set a test for, say, 16-year-old candidates which would begin by very simple questions answerable by most candidates and gradually increase the intellectual level of the questions from simple reasoning to more complex problems until eventually only a few of the candidates would be capable of answering the last few questions. Any attempt at setting such a common paper must make use of objective-type questions, since essay-type questions would be difficult to set as well as mark for a wide range of ability. Further, the large number of candidates coming forward makes it more and more difficult to find enough qualified examiners of the essay-type examination papers.

The problem lies in the limited experience which exists in this country in the formulation of objective-type tests in geography. Although Ballard published examples of objective-type geography questions in 1923 (Ballard 1923) these were to a large extent ignored by examining bodies in Britain. A small-scale experiment was reported in 1954 (Daniels 1954) in which the performance of a group of fourth-year grammar school pupils on objective-type tests in geography was compared with their performance on essay-type questions for the O-level examination. This seemed to indicate no marked superiority for the objective-type test in predicting ability in geography. In 1964 the devising of objective tests in geography was reviewed and a small test constructed (Craig 1964). By then the problem of examining a vast number of CSE candidates in geography was becoming apparent and guides to the construction of objective-type tests were being published by the organisation that was to become the Schools Council. In 1966 a group of teachers and school inspectors reported the results of experiments conducted in testing geography in a new way in *Examinations Bulletin No. 14, Trial Examination in Geography* (Schools Council 1966). This expressed cautious approval for an examination using more objective-type questions, and yet at the same time expressed doubts about the value of such questions on the grounds that children may come to believe that there is always one correct answer to any problem. This latter criticism probably results from confusing teaching and testing. In any event many questions merely seek to obtain the most probable answer, so that the idea of there being only one correct answer should not arise. In 1967 an attempt was made to devise an alternative to the Joint Matriculation Board's O-level examination in geography and to test it out in a number of schools. (Mullins 1967). This experiment showed that it was possible to test similar material to that normally tested in the traditional essay questions by more objective questions in which the interpretation of data played a greater part than the recall of facts, and that such an examination had a high degree of reliability. A year later in 1968 the Godfrey Thompson Unit for Educational Research of Edinburgh University published a report on an experimental test in geography at the Ordinary Grade of the Scottish Certificate of Education (Pilliner 1968). This was an account of an experiment in which an objective-type question paper was designed to cover the same grounds as the traditional examination. A sample of 850 candidates throughout Scotland was subjected to both tests. The results indicated that:

1 The experimental examination discriminated among the candidates much more effectively than the traditional examination. That is, the candidates were more widely distributed along the scale of marks than they were in the traditional examination.
2 The standard error of measurement was small (7 score points out of 200 – i.e. a mark of 100 could really have been between 97 and 104) compared with the generally large standard error of measurement usually associated with traditional examinations.
3 The correlation between the numbers passing the traditional and the objective examination (and also those failing both examinations) was of the order of 0·747, thereby indicating that on the whole the two examinations were testing the same knowledge. Given the difficulty of reliable marking in the traditional examination, a closer correlation could not be expected. However, had there been a complete lack of correlation, then it might have been argued that this was grounds for suspecting that the objective test was not in fact measuring the same qualities as the traditional examination.
4 Boys on the whole did significantly better on both the traditional and experimental examination. This was a by-product of the experiment, suggesting that the geography taught seems to appeal to boys more than to girls, and that in particular boys do better when spatial ability is apparently involved.

The Scottish experiment seems to suggest that objective tests in geography could adequately test most of the content of O-grade geography and that in some respects such tests were better at measuring the candidates' performance. It would seem advisable, however, to submit candidates to both objective- and essay-type questions so that scope is given to measure (albeit with some margin of error) the candidate's ability to express himself on a geographical subject, as well as his knowledge of various parts of the syllabus and his ability to reason about geographical data. There is every reason to suggest, further, that objective tests could be devised to test geography at the A-level (18-year-old).

THE PRACTICALITY OF OBJECTIVE TESTS IN GEOGRAPHY

If the advantages of objective testing in geography are evident, this does not mean that all examining boards can suddenly begin to administer such tests. In the first place, it will be necessary for teachers and examiners to agree on the concepts, principles, skills and facts that they want to test. Traditional examination syllabuses are usually couched at such a level of generality that they do very little to help teachers decide what concepts are going to be examined – hence the inevitable recourse to examination questions. It may even be necessary to decide at what level the concept or principle is going to be examined; for example, whether knowledge of soils should involve knowledge of classification by texture and/or classification by pH value.

In the second place, a large number of items will need to be written, and tested on a sample of the potential examinees so that their facility and discriminating power can be analysed. Items which do not discriminate between able and less able candidates in geography are of little use (Schools Council 1964). At this stage all ambiguous questions will be rejected.

In the third place, the list once constructed will need to be validated so that the items are seen to sample fairly the knowledge which it has been decided to test. In the fourth place, the reliability of the test will need to be estimated. This is to ensure that the test is consistent in its measurement and that approximately the same result can be expected when the test is administered at different times (Anastasi 1958).

It will be clear that the considerable labour needed to achieve worthwhile objective tests in geography means that they cannot be achieved in an amateur manner. A central examinations research body ought to be created to service examinations. Such a body should employ not only subject specialists, but experts trained in psychological testing so that the examinations could be properly validated and tested for reliability. In other words there is a case for having a British Examinations Service on the lines of the American Education Testing Service. The Schools Examination Department of the University of London is already experimenting with such tests in geography for the O-level examination, and so are several CSE Boards.

COURSE WORK ASSESSMENT

An alternative method of assessing the work done by students is to examine the work they have actually produced during the time they have followed a course of study. The simplest case of this is the examination of theses for higher degrees. In such a case the student may have worked for one, two or more years on a topic or problem and at the end writes up his findings in the form of a dissertation or thesis. His work is therefore summarised in the dissertation and examined by competent persons. Here the complications are minimal, there is only one candidate involved and there are usually two or more examiners. However, when course work is assessed at a lower level the task of assessment is more complicated. First, there are usually a number of different pieces of work to assess. Secondly, they have been produced at different times during the course and they probably differ in standard as the candidate has improved his work over time. Thirdly, different candidates may have been given different assignments by their tutors so that the problem of comparison is increased. Fourthly, the total volume of work to be seen by an examiner may be excessive. In practice, teachers mark the course work and the marks are moderated as between different institutions. Moderation is the process whereby the marks given by one institution are harmonised with those given by another, in such a way that candidates are finally marked according to some universally applicable scale. The task of moderation is a difficult one involving the exercise of judgment on the part of the examiner-moderator and it would be rash to claim that this art has yet achieved a great degree of reliability, particularly in view of the factors mentioned earlier. It is difficult, for example, to compare an essay based on a minor investigation into the load-carrying capacity of a Pennine brook with one dealing with the development of a settlement in Dartmoor, if both are offered as examples of course work for A-level by different candidates in different schools. It would therefore seem reasonable not to base the whole of one's assessment of candidates on course work alone.

CONCLUSIONS

The development of examinations in geography has moved over the centuries from purely oral questioning through the written essay examination to the objective-type test. Every form of examination has its advantages and pitfalls. In geography a danger which exists in every form of examination is the tendency to test knowledge of facts rather than conceptual knowledge. We have seen that it is easier to ensure by their proper construction and validation that objective tests do test reasoning, knowledge of principles and their application, as well as some knowledge of fact if that is required. It would therefore seem to be sensible that the major part of a geography examination might take the form of an objective test. Since the ability of students to express themselves in clear continuous prose on a geographical topic is valued, it would also seem sensible to include, as part of the total assessment of a candidate, a mark derived from answers to essay questions and one derived from course work assessment. The logistics of the operation may, however, mean that the full treatment could only be given in examinations where the number of candidates was not excessive – perhaps at the A-level of the GCE rather than at O-level or CSE.

References

A. Anastasi (1958) *Psychological testing* (especially chapter 15), Collier-Macmillan.

P. B. Ballard, (1923) *The New Examiner.*

G. Bruce, (1969) *Secondary School Examinations: facts and commentary*, Pergamon.

J. K. Craig, (1964) 'A study of the construction of a series of objective tests of attainment in geography of secondary school pupils', unpublished MA thesis, University of London.

J. C. Daniels, (1954) 'Testing geography at the Ordinary level of the GCE', *British Journal of Educational Psychology, vol. XXIV.*

P. G. Mullins, (1967) 'An alternative form of examination in geography at GCE O-level', unpublished M.Ed. thesis, University of Manchester.

A. E. G. Pilliner, (chairman) (1968) 'An experimental test of geography at the ordinary level of the Scottish Certificate of Education', unpublished report of the Godfrey Thompson Unit for Educational Research, Edinburgh University.

B. S. Roberson, (1971) Geography Examinations at O- and A-level, *Geography, vol. 56.*

P. E. Roc, (1971), Examining CSE Geography, *Geography, vol. 56.*

Schools Council (1964) *The Certificate of Secondary Education: An introduction to objective type examinations*, Examinations Bulletin No. 4, HMSO.

(1966) *Trial examination in geography*, Examinations Bulletin No. 14, HMSO.

M. Simons, (1966) 'What is a geographical factor?' *Geography*, Vol. 51.

J. Valentine, (1967) 'GCE – a comedy and tragedy of errors', *New Education*, February 1967.

Aspects and techniques

15 Physical geography

GRAHAM STEVENS

Physical geography may be defined as an amalgam of geomorphology, meteorology and climatology. It continues to be one of the great strengths of school geography and at the same time it is an area of weakness. This paradox can be explained by a review of the current position. A summary of recent progress within the separate subjects will bring out significant implications for teaching.

THE PRESENT POSITION

There is a great variety in the teaching of physical geography in the lower secondary school. The different interests of boys and girls, the differing enthusiasms of teachers, as well as the differing abilities of pupils, are contributory factors to this variety. Two basic approaches are apparent. In one, there is a single year course in physical and mathematical (old definition!) geography, while in the other there is an attempt to cover the same topics over three years integrated within a concentric or regional syllabus. The physical content of fourth- and fifth-year geography is determined largely by the external examinations. Despite contrary pleas, a special section in the examination paper encourages the tendency to separate the teaching of physical and human aspects. This division is even more evident in the sixth form where the great majority of courses reflect a tripartite examination – mapwork, physical geography and regional geography.

The current situation contains four general characteristics. Firstly, a list of physical topics is remarkably repetitive for years one to three, four and five, and six and seven. For example, 'vulcanicity', 'types of rainfall' and 'deserts' will probably be taught at each level with differing degrees of complexity. Following from this, the second characteristic is the implicit notion that there is a discrete 'body of knowledge' in physical geography – that there are a certain number of facts and explanations to be assimilated by the pupils. Thirdly, the method of teaching is usually non-scientific. The keynotes are description and simplified explanation. Certainly the enjoyment, and perhaps the realistic appreciation, of physical geography has been increased by the growth of educational technology – video-tape, film-loop, movie film (Clark 1970), topographic map and slide. (It has been estimated that 40,000 slides were taken by 125 geographers on a recent three-week tour of Canada!) There remains, however, heavy dependence on exposition and standard text books. The fourth characteristic is the growth of fieldwork. A common pattern is whole or part days in the locality for the lower school rising to whole weeks in more distant places for the sixth form. These courses usually attempt to integrate the physical and human features of an area – the norm being qualitative description followed by simple causal relationships. Reports that the real landscape is disappointing to students since it is 'not like the text-book diagrams' are disturbing (Small 1966).

At present, the weakness of school physical geography is that, in many cases, it consists of little more than the acquisition of interesting 'facts' and simplified explanations about natural phenomena. It has often been stressed in the pages of *Geography* that many of these 'facts', or even the framework itself, are wrong (Dury 1963, Pugh 1964, Small 1966 and 1969).

One of the great strengths of physical geography is its continued popular appeal to young people exemplified by their keenness to participate in, and often pay for, experience 'through the bootsoles' and more recently by their positive involvement in activities concerned with Conservation.

CHANGES IN METEOROLOGY AND CLIMATOLOGY

The most important change is that meteorology is no longer seen as a separate area of study from climatology. In the sixth form, climatology has often been little more than a memorised, descriptive catalogue of average statistics within a dull numerical classification in which the causes of these average conditions were often ignored or inadequately explained. The shift in emphasis has been to a situation where explanation is of far greater importance than the cataloguing of mean data. The climate of a particular place need not be seen as a 'capes and bays' list of figures but as the result of dynamic meteorological concepts – 'meso-scale weather' in modern jargon. Thus meteorology is fundamental and not extraneous.

Satellites, large defence expenditures, and the growth of civil aviation have accelerated research in this field. At the simplest level, there is much new knowledge about the characteristics of convection

(Simons 1970), thunderstorms (Chorley and Haggett 1965, p. 46), hailstorms (Barry and Chorley 1968, p. 150), and depressions (Pedgley 1962, Barry and Chorley 1968 pp. 147–50). It is possible to devise descriptions of these systems which are scientifically valid but sufficiently simple for pupil comprehension. The important aspects at the lower school stage are careful observation of these phenomena in the locality. Colour film-strips will aid cloud recognition and the instruments of the school weather station will provide numerical measures which can be supplemented from published sources. Whatever the ability of the pupil, the diagrams that summarise the results will be simplified but can include accurate details of scale, e.g. width and height of the system.

All of these types of weather involve concepts from heat physics like condensation, evaporation and precipitation. For the pupil, as Chandler says, 'the necessary physics can often be provided as part of a wider training in science' (Cooke and Johnson 1969). For the teacher, the alternatives are to seek help from the physical science staff or to read and adapt some of the texts already mentioned. It is possible in the teaching of these phenomena to follow scientific method more closely – observation, production of hypotheses, testing of hypotheses by observation or experiment, and finally rejection or verification of these hypotheses. It is important that the educational situation appears 'open-ended' – that the student feels the possibility of more detailed observation, of more accurate experimentation, of newer hypotheses – that there is no 'final answer'.

The causes of these small-scale weather-systems are being increasingly well understood and are closely related to the fundamental concept in climatology today – 'the engine of the atmosphere'. Models of the general circulation of the atmosphere have a long history starting in 1735 with the 'Hadley Cell' which attempted to explain the trade winds as a result of equatorial heating (Chorley and Haggett 1967, pp. 100–03, Barry and Chorley 1968, pp. 128–34). An increasingly sophisticated pattern has been developed to the stage of Palmén whose model of the circulation is seen as the result of 'self-regulating attempts to equalize the major differences that arise from inequalities in the world distribution of heat' (Barry and Chorley 1968, p. 135). In brief, there is a surplus of heat between 40° N and 35° S and therefore energy must be transferred from the earth to the atmosphere and from low to high latitudes. The simplified model of the circulation emphasises four characteristics: convective instability near the equator, anti-cyclonic subsidence in sub-tropical desert areas, the variable wave pattern of the upper westerlies in mid latitudes, and subsidence near the poles.

An understanding of this general circulation is crucial at the sixth-form stage as a means of improving comprehension of the phenomena discussed above and dealt with in a largely descriptive way in the lower school. In particular, research into the upper westerlies of the northern hemisphere has changed ideas about the causes and movements of pressure systems. The Norwegian model of depression formation is replaced by the idea of 'divergence' of the upper winds just ahead of a crest or trough in the wave pattern. This leads in the lower atmosphere to 'convergence', and therefore air mass interaction near the surface is a result, not a cause, of depressions. It is now possible to stress the causes of a particular climate rather than its statistical averages by reference to this circulation model and a relatively few areas might be studied in this way. Another area of recent advance, and possible sixth-form study, is micro-climate. Direct measurement and project work in forest, mountain or urban areas could be undertaken and related to problems like air pollution (Chandler 1965, Scorer 1968).

CHANGES IN GEOMORPHOLOGY

'In spite of the general renaissance of science in the present century, physiography still remains largely qualitative. Streams and their drainage basins are described as youthful, mature, old, poorly or well drained, without specified information as to how, how much or why.' These words were written by R. E. Horton twenty-six years ago and mark perhaps the beginning of rapid change (Dury 1970, p. 117). It is encouraging that in the context of higher education these words appear historical and are becoming increasingly so in schools. Research in related disciplines, particularly hydrology, has been the main stimulus.

Two characteristics of this progress are the application of scientific method and increasing quantification. It is notable that much of the early headway in changing the concepts and methods of geography was within geomorphology but that the wider application of these methods has transformed human geography.

'Precision' is fundamental to scientific method and this starts with the accurate description of landforms. In place of vague estimation, quantitative measures of the shapes of landforms in the field are made (Leopold and Langbein 1966). This information can be supplemented by 'morphometry' which is the numerical analysis of information on maps, particularly useful in studying drainage basins and slopes (Morisawa 1968, pp. 152–66). The second aspect is process, where evidence of the forces acting on landforms in the field is obtained, e.g. the rate of weathering in limestone (Dury 1966, pp. 177–216). Much additional detail comes from experimental simulation, e.g. official hydrological stations.

Having obtained accurate information the next stage is 'prediction' – producing hypotheses about the formation of the landscape. These are then tested as far as possible in the field and the laboratory. This method produces new theories – an example of which is the 'dynamic equilibrium concept' which replaces the restricting framework of the Davisian cycle. In simple terms this concept states that, for example, slopes will develop within small areas at constant maximum angles where climate, lithology, soil, vegetation, and relief remain stable. A change in any one factor will produce a new equilibrium slope angle. The advantages and disadvantages of this framework are discussed fully by Small (1969).

The changes in geomorphological research are related to improvements in the techniques of storing and handling large quantities of numerical data by the development of computers. Simple statistical techniques plot the relationship between two variables, e.g. stream order and stream length (Dury 1966, p. 43). These lead on, since geomorphic phenomena are usually the result of several factors, to multi-variate analysis (Cole and King 1968, pp. 152–60). Another development is to introduce the concept of probability. Although the more sophisticated techniques require computation, there is obvious appeal in expressing complex relationships between many variables by means of the 'general systems' approach (Chorley and Haggett 1967, pp. 76–80).

The Sixth Form and University Committee report on geomorphology (*Geography*, November 1968) recognised this shift in emphasis from 'a superficial and uncritical learning of many over-simplified facts' to the need for studies in depth of a small number of carefully selected areas. It is clear that in the lower school there is great scope for 'precision' in the description of landforms seen at first or second hand. Facile, scaleless diagrams of, for example, unreal volcanoes, glaciated highlands, or hugely notched coast sections, are being discarded and replaced by a more scientific approach in which validity is maintained even at the simplest levels.

IMPLICATIONS FOR TEACHING

Not surprisingly, the teacher is faced with most of the problems and, in many ways, has the greatest difficulty in finding solutions. The first problem is 'the explosion of the data bank'. It has been estimated that if one read continuously for twenty-four hours every day it would be impossible to keep abreast of developments in only one of the subjects within physical geography. There are two important implications of this situation. Firstly, as ever-expanding information threatens to engulf him, the teacher is forced to emphasise methods rather than facts, ideas rather than memory, and this is to be welcomed. The second implication is that school physical geography reflects the quality of the standard text books on which the teacher depends for explanation and summary of current research. The books in common use are frequently out of date and non- or pre-scientific. Teachers can rectify this by their considerable collective purchasing power.

Another problem for non-science graduates is the difficulty of communicating numerically expressed ideas to arts-orientated pupils. The solution is many-sided, but one important aspect is 'in-service retraining'. On a recent statistics course for teachers in inner London, 90% of the participants were geographers. The exchange of ideas in such a situation is encouraging and this trend will be reinforced by the increasing number of schools with computer links.

The implications for the examination boards are of paramount importance and are possibly the easiest to introduce. This significance derives from the fact that, despite frequent denials, most school geography reflects the examination syllabus. The opportunity exists, therefore, for the boards to stress the scientific approach to the subject by emphasising the accurate observation of phenomena, by urging methods of study and analysis, and by encouraging individual hypothesising particularly in relation to a few areas studied in the field (*Geography*, Vol. 53 1968, Prudden 1966). Good-quality Mode III papers could be encouraged at every level since these can best reflect the particular needs of any school. The examination boards should be the vanguard of change rather than the guard's van.

The implications for the subject in schools are worth elaborating. New sixth form syllabuses, which unfortunately do not consider the non A-level candidate, have been published in *Geography* (November 1968 and January 1970) and these can be rapidly implemented. The problem of the lower school syllabus remains and is being studied by two Schools Council Projects at the moment, but the use of scientific method at this level has been stressed.

The greatest achievement of school geography recently has been the almost universal introduction of fieldwork (Cooke and Johnson 1969, pp. 70–78). It is clear that scientific method must be built into this achievement and 'field-teaching' – eyeballing and simple explanation – must gradually evolve into field-research as pupils move up the secondary school (Everson 1969). This should be possible due to the increasing numbers of permanent field-study centres (there are over 200 in the Snowdonia National Park alone!) where quantitative data can be built up progressively and long-term projects undertaken, e.g. soil-creep, meander movement, microclimate (Boardman 1969). This research aspect can be extended to schools where experiments with hardware models like stream-tables, ripple tanks (probably already in a Nuffield Physics laboratory!) and even with pit heaps can be undertaken (Chorley and Haggett 1967 pp. 727–74, Large 1969). With increasing experimentation on both the physical and human sides, the time has come to rename the geography room, the geography laboratory.

Lastly, it is necessary to make clear that the sort of work which is done under the heading of geomorphology and climatology belongs firmly to the physical sciences. It will be increasingly difficult for the teacher without a basis in natural science to teach these aspects of geography.

References

R. G. Barry and R. J. Chorley, (1968) *Atmosphere, weather and climate*, Methuen.

D. J. Boardman, (1969) 'The place of the school field centre in the teaching of geography', *Geography*, vol. 54.

T. J. Chandler, (1965) *The climate of London*, Hutchinson.

R. J. Chorley and P. Haggett (eds.), (1970) *Frontiers in geographical teaching*, Methuen.

(1967) *Models in Geography*, Methuen.

M. J. Clark, (1970) 'Physical geography on film', *Geography*, vol. 55.

J. P. Cole and C. A. M. King, (1968) *Quantitative geography*, John Wiley.

R. U. Cooke and J. H. Johnson (eds.), (1969) *Trends in geography*, Pergamon.
G. H. Dury, (1963) 'Rivers in geographical teaching', *Geography*, vol. 48.
(1966) *The face of the earth*, Pelican.
(1966) *Essays in geomorphology*, Heinemann.
(1970) (Ed.) *Rivers and river terraces*, Macmillan.
J. Everson, (1969) 'Some aspects of teaching geography through fieldwork', *Geography*, vol. 54.
N. F. Large, (1969) 'The pit heap as a venue for geographical fieldwork', *Geography*, vol. 54.
L. G. Leopold and W. B. Langbein, (1966) 'River meanders', *Scientific American*, vol. 214.
M. Morisawa, (1968) *Streams – their dynamics and morphology*, McGraw-Hill.
D. E. Pedgley, (1962) *A course of elementary meteorology*, HMSO.
H. C. Prudden, (1966) 'Suggestions for the teaching of peri-glacial processes in physical geography', *Geography*, vol. 51.
J. C. Pugh, (1964) 'Some avoidable errors in physiographic studies', *Geography*, vol. 49.
R. S. Scorer, (1968) *Air pollution*, Pergamon.
M. Simons, (1970) 'Atmospheric convection', *Geography*, vol. 55.
R. J. Small, (1966) 'Some criticisms of the teaching of geomorphology at A-level', *Geography*, vol. 51.
(1968) 'Geomorphology in the sixth-form course', *Geography*, vol. 53.
(1969) 'The new geomorphology and the sixth-former', *Geography*, vol. 54.
(1970) 'Climatology in the sixth-form course', *Geography*, vol. 55.

Urban geography

MICHAEL STORM

Geography in schools has been characterised by a remarkable neglect of urban topics. Supporting evidence for this assertion could be assembled from a variety of sources; text books on Britain rarely devote more than a third of their pages to the towns (Lowry 1960), and fieldwork handbooks, whether dealing with methodology (Archer and Dalton 1968) or supplying itineraries (Dilke 1965), generally show a preponderance of rural techniques and locations. Over the last decade or so there has been a considerable growth of interest in urban studies, stimulated largely by the emergence of teachers whose college or university training placed more emphasis on urban geography. School texts have appeared which are exclusively concerned with urban topics (Storm 1965, James and Walford 1969, Turner 1970), and fieldwork programmes now customarily incorporate investigations of urban landscapes (Bull 1969, Bradley 1970). Nevertheless, any discussion of the teaching of urban geography in schools must start from a consideration of its presistent relative neglect.

THE NEGLECT OF URBAN GEOGRAPHY IN SCHOOLS

Explanations might range from the severely pragmatic (adolescent pupils on rural field study exercises are, at the very lowest assessment, experiencing an alien environment, with healthy open-air activity; in a town, there are hazards from coffee-bars as well as traffic) to the ideological – teachers, after all, are not immune from the pervasive anti-urban sentiments which have imbued most writing about towns with a blend of aesthetic rejection and moral distaste (White 1964). But the principal explanation is to be found in one of the traditional objectives of school geography, which is to establish 'some of the simpler relationships between facts of geographic environment and human activities' (Archer and Thomas 1936). This is certainly the view of the subject retained by most laymen, who see geography as an attempt to explain the nature and distribution of human activities by reference to certain immutable 'geographical factors' such as climate, relief, rock and soil types. From the teacher's viewpoint, standard 'geographical explanations' are more conveniently demonstrated or discovered in a rural context; a transect across the Berkshire Downs will illustrate vividly the controls which structure exercises upon scenery and land use. Even here, the pristine clarity of man-land relationships will be marred by county planning policies, national location decisions, the quirks of local land ownership, and the structure of agricultural subsidies; but within the urban fabric, the 'controls model' is clearly more difficult to apply.

Nevertheless, the treatment of towns in school geography may be seen in terms of the traditional types of geographical explanation. Thus, an analysis of the components of urban study would reveal a notable preoccupation with the *physical siting* of towns. Pupils who know nothing of the ranking of Shrewsbury, and the possible effects of nearby Telford New Town on Shrewsbury's regional centrality, will be found to possess a surprisingly detailed knowledge of its defensive position within a loop of the Severn. The haziest knowledge of employment and population trends in Greater London will often be combined with an ability to sketch with commendable accuracy the layout of Roman London and its relationship to the two gravel hills and the Walbrook. The most common urban teaching tool remains the 'sketch map to show the site of X', with a castle pleasingly situated on a natural strongpoint, and arrows curving off in all directions, obediently selecting gaps in the surrounding hills. Clearly, a consideration of physical siting must form an integral part of any study programme in urban geography; the internal morphology of a town is often otherwise inexplicable, and physical controls, especially the limiting effect of low and ill-drained land, may still be strongly in evidence. But within such programmes, it is surprising how often contemporary processes and problems are less prominent than the study of Anglo-Saxon fords and 'gap towns'.

Emphasis upon the historical component in urban studies partly reflects a concern for the traditional types of geographical explanation. If we focus upon the origins and growth of the city, it may be possible to demonstrate the operation of 'geographical' controls more vividly, than if we concede priority to current developments. Whatever else may be incorporated in a sequence of town study, the historical component is rarely missing (this also reflects the antiquarian flavour of most British topographical writing; it is sometimes easier to establish the dates of medieval buildings than those of post-war ward boundary changes). The use of historical hindsight to determine the environmental imperatives that produced towns and guaranteed their growth often ignores the element of arbitrary or personal decision that is present in very many cases. There are few towns in Britain without an element of planning, military or speculative (Beresford 1967), in their origins; the entire system of charters can be represented as an artificial protection from the competition of other 'central places'.

THE EMPHASIS ON MANUFACTURING INDUSTRY IN TOWNS

The controls model also accounts for another long-established feature in the conventional treatment of towns in school geography; a preoccupation with manufacturing industry. Lists of principal products are probably an even more common text-book ingredient than site-maps. Ever since the days of Celia Fiennes and Daniel Defoe, towns seem to have been primarily categorised by what their inhabitants make. 'On their arrival at any provincial town the first thing that both set out to discover was the particular staple commodity of the place' (Moir 1964). It is not difficult to find geography books that are virtually indistinguishable from the gazetteer type lists of earlier publications. 'Staffordshire has very important mining and manufactures. Stafford, county town, makes boots and shoes, Wolverhampton makes hardware, Burton-on-Trent has famous breweries, Stoke-on-Trent and Hanley have large potteries ...' (Cormack 1900). The poorer geography teaching has always been entirely descriptive, but where analysis is involved, the discussion of towns in terms of their industrial structure has again favoured the traditional types of explanation. The focusing of attention on the steel industry in Sheffield, the cotton industry in Bolton, enables environmental imperatives to be discerned concerning natural resources such as water power, fuel, iron ore, and so on. The concentration of population in large agglomerations is explained in terms of factory employment, which is in turn explained in terms of mineral resources, the raw materials available locally, and accessibility.

This preoccupation with the secondary sector of employment is increasingly unhelpful if we are seriously concerned to assist pupils towards an understanding of urbanisation in the second half of the twentieth century. In the first place, the selection of a few 'characteristic' activities wholly distorts the image of the town possessed by young pupils, for these 'major industries' rarely account for more than a small proportion of the urban workforce. Reading, regularly credited with specialisation in baking and brewing, actually has less than 5% of its workers* engaged in these trades, yet the temptation to focus on those industries which can be shown to result from contemporary or historical environmental imperatives (market centre of a productive agricultural region, and so on) is normally too strong to be resisted, especially as the traditional industries are often visually prominent in the inner urban landscape.

More significantly, any model of contemporary urbanisation which relies upon the growth of manufacturing industry is seriously deficient. In 1966 only 35% of the labour force in England and Wales was employed in manufacturing industry and this is a rapidly declining proportion in all advanced industrial economies. In the Reading employment area, only 28% were involved in the secondary sector, and even this figure may be regarded as inflated by the Standard Industrial Classification, which groups the clerical workforce of a factory under manufacturing (Rodgers 1965). This tendency to consider urban employment primarily in terms of factories may be seen in the history of the New Towns, where 'factory employment has formed the vanguard of the decentralisation movement' (Thomas 1969); the social balance of these towns was, temporarily, affected by the somewhat tardy realisation that most of the 'growth industries' were in the service sector, and that the location of office employment required an interventionist apparatus similar to that already established for factories by the Industrial Development Certificate mechanism.

Of course towns *do* specialise in certain economic activities (though to a lesser degree than is customarily taught); but this is most effectively brought out not by stressing the numbers of workers involved but by the use of *comparative* devices such as the *location quotient*. The number engaged in a particular industry is expressed as a percentage of the total local workforce (figures are readily available from Department of Employment and Productivity offices, though the area concerned is normally rather more extensive than the town itself). This percentage figure is then compared with the national equivalent; if the resulting location quotient is 1·00, the DEP region reflects the national pattern with relatively little specialisation or under-representation. Although only 8,747 people were employed in 1968 in SIC order XIV (timber, furniture, etc.) in the High Wycombe employment area (out of well over 60,000), this produces a location quotient for

* This figure relates to the DEP area, consisting of Reading and fifty adjacent parishes.

this sector of 10·95, indicating an exceptionally high degree of specialisation, in the national context. The location quotient is a simple tool which should be a staple ingredient of urban studies at the secondary school stage (Rodgers 1965, Graves and White 1971).

IMPORTANT FEATURES OF URBAN GEOGRAPHY

Our own economic history seems to have obscured for us the important truth that there is no necessary relationship between urbanisation and industrialisation. An entirely agricultural society will generate a network of central places, which will be essentially urban, though possessing little or no secondary industry. A consideration of towns in pre-industrial societies, whether medieval or Third World, would confirm that 'cities do not grow up of themselves, countrysides set them up to do tasks that must be performed in central places' (Jefferson 1931). For most of history, and over most of the world, these 'tasks' have concerned the provision of services (distributional, professional, administrative, cultural) rather than the provision of factory employment. Perhaps, with the increasing migration of industry to greenfield locations, the fundamental service function of urban settlements will again emerge more clearly.

Criticism of the high priority generally given to the question 'What does this town make?' must not be taken as eroding the central significance of the question which apparently tormented Chekhov; 'What kept these sixty-five thousand people going? That's what I couldn't see. Kimry got its living by boots, I knew. Tula made samovars and guns, Odessa was a port. But what our town was and what it did, I had no idea' (Chekhov 1895). The problem, rather, is that conventional school geography has tended to prejudge the answer to Chekhov's question. The distinction between basic and non-basic urban employment may be helpful here. Basic urban employment, in both manufacturing and services, is concerned with the needs of consumers living outside the urban area; those jobs concerned with serving and sustaining the urban population itself are classified as non-basic (Johnson 1967). Thus, in Reading, the staff employed at the Berkshire County Council offices would be basic, their counterparts at the Town Hall non-basic. Models of urban growth certainly ought to accommodate the linked notions that the addition of new basic jobs (e.g. a new factory, a new national or regional office) will generate extra non-basic jobs, and that a very large proportion of urban workers are engaged in the latter, or city-sustaining, sector. Of 4,430,000 jobs within the Greater London Council area in 1966, no less than 1,710,000 were concerned with providing for the living needs of the Greater London population (Luttrell 1970).

Increasingly, explanations of urban settlement patterns based upon physical site advantages and local materials for secondary industry seem intolerably simplistic and irrelevant. As E. A. Wrigley reminds us, 'the striking thing about the general study of the location of populations and of the industries which afford them employment has been the way in which it has underlined the point that populations are nowadays more and more their own justification' (Wrigley 1965). Wrigley's argument that we should invert the study-sequence Place–Work–People, advocated by Le Play, and 'begin with population distribution in order to explain the distribution of industry rather than vice-versa' is amply confirmed by recent empirical evidence. 'In choosing a new location, firms are predominantly influenced by labour availability; the availability of an industrial development certificate; Government inducements; local authority assistance; environmental factors; and accessibility to markets and supplies, to an existing plant, or to the place from which they came.... Transport costs, for instance, are generally less significant than they may have been in the past' (South-east Joint Planning Team 1970). One wonders how closely this ranking of location factors corresponds to those generally stressed in secondary geography.

If we are concerned to assist pupils to discern patterns, groupings and systems as they study human geography, there are several ways of considering and classifying towns which would be superior to the 'Northampton-shoes, Coventry-cars' approach. Regarding the essential urban function as the provision of services, we might examine ways of assessing the status of a town. This is one of the more profitable areas of urban study for schools, involving as it does a variety of practical exercises (Thorpe 1966, Everson and Fitzgerald 1969, Storm 1970). For the teacher, a particularly attractive feature of 'hierarchy studies' is the ease with which such tasks may be graded. Adopting Davies' useful categorisation of the main approaches to the study of centrality (Davies 1966) direct measurement may involve, at the simplest level, a listing of the number and type of services available. Or more sophisticated systems may be employed, involving the weighting of particular functions, according to their 'rarity' or centrality value, on a points system, or on the recognition of certain key 'marginal hierarchical goods'. Indirect measurement methods (in which the status of the central place is assessed according to the extent and nature of its surrounding 'field') may be similarly varied, ranging from the mapping of delivery, circulation and local transport areas (Waites 1970, Briggs 1970), to more detailed survey work in the surrounding rural area to determine the centres normally used.

Whatever the level of hierarchy studies attempted, it would seem vital that any teaching model should accommodate the 'nesting' nature of central place systems, accepting from the outset that individuals normally use a variety of service centres, travelling further for furniture than for newspapers, and so on. As with employment studies, a comparative context is essential in any ranking exercise (Carruthers 1967). Nor are central place systems immutable (Smith 1968), and the collection of data should form the basis for a discussion of trends such as the growth of one-stop out-of-town shopping centres (National Economic Development Office 1970). The practical relevance of such studies may be demonstrated by games or simulations involving the optimum location of retail outlets, or the design of 'rational' administrative units. All attempts to re-draw the local government map have made heavy use of the 'urban field' concept. 'The boundaries between adjacent city-regions would best be drawn along the 'watersheds' of lines of least friction between neighbouring units. These watersheds can be found mainly in areas of relatively sparse settlement, limited population growth, low rateable values, minimal pressures for land use change and with light traffic flows across the watershed' (Ministry of Housing and Local Government 1967). The Redcliffe-Maud report, with its wealth of maps and regional data, is only one of the more recent of a long series of government publications which appear to be strangely neglected as 'raw material' by the teacher; a study of local government boundary revision would illuminate the central concept of 'threshold populations' in a particularly dramatic way (Royal Commission on Local Government 1969, Davies 1967, Mackintosh 1968, Ministry of Local Government and Regional Planning 1970).

Whether we are considering employment structure, or status as a central place, a town's character can only be established in a comparative context. The census volumes can provide us with useful data on the town's socio-economic composition, age-structure, sex-structure, journey-to-work movements, modes of travel, and housing stock, but this sort of information only becomes 'live' if we link it to equivalent figures for other centres, for the region, or for the country. Nationally, there are 133 employers, managers and professional workers for every thousand occupied persons, but for individual towns the figures can range widely and instructively – Scarborough has 165, Billingham 59. Resorts show dramatically atypical demographic profiles; Bournemouth has 1,316 females for every thousand males, compared with the national figure of 1,067. New towns and town expansion schemes often show markedly asymmetrical age-structures; Bracknell has 30% of its population under 15, compared to Newbury's more normal 22%. There are also interesting variations in female employment, school-leaving patterns, household mobility, and a host of infrastructure indicators ranging from the critically important rateable value per capita (Brighton £72·3, Halifax £29·6) to the degree of overcrowding – but these can only be discovered and utilised in a comparative approach which places at least as much emphasis on the documentary aspects of urban study as on the recording of land use in the field.

If our image of the town as a place where people make things is seriously over-simple, so, for most regions, is an image of the town as a free-standing entity, dominating a clearly defined hinterland which sends both workers and customers into the town. Work movements are increasingly complex, resulting from the dispersal of employment and residence, and increasing mobility. Like the location quotient, the *job ratio* is a simple device for ranking the town according to whether it is a net importer of labour (an employment focus) or a net exporter (with 'dormitory' functions). The industrial tables will supply a figure for the number of jobs within the urban area, whilst the census occupational tables tell us the number of occupied population resident within the area (Rodgers 1965). Expressing the first as a percentage of the second gives figures typically ranging from 142 (Slough, a strong employment focus) to 67 (Marlow, with well-developed suburban attributes). A weakness of the job ratio is that a figure of 100, indicating an apparently ideal balance between resident occupied population and jobs available within the town (Maidenhead 99·7) can mask massive inward and outward movements. This can be remedied by using the *independence index*, which is the sum of all internal work-journeys within the urban area (i.e. the number of people resident in the area and also employed there) divided by the sum of all 'crossing' work-journeys (i.e. the number of people resident in the area and working outside, plus the number of people working in the area but resident outside) (Thomas 1969). The census workplace tables provide the material for this calculation; broadly speaking, an index of less than 1·00 indicates that the town is part of a complex 'labour market area' (Hunter 1969) whilst over 1·00 indicates a degree of 'self-sufficiency' (Windsor 0·78, Bracknell New Town 1·02). The workplace tables also provide invaluable information on the destinations of workers 'exported' and the origin of workers 'imported', as well as the types of transport used. The latter material can be particularly valuable in stimulating discussion. Why do only 28·7% of work journeys into Reading involve private cars, whilst the figure for Bracknell is 46·2%? Does this relate to the larger size of Reading, its greater congestion and parking problems? Or does it reflect Reading's better public transport network and Bracknell's spacious industrial zoning?

If the commonest forms of text book coverage of towns concern physical siting and manufacturing, urban field study is similarly dominated by land use and traffic surveys. Such activities have considerable value, involving detailed observation and the devising of effective ways of classifying, recording and communicating. Yet too often the work has a fundamentally static quality, mapping what is there but not analysing it. Adapting a classic maxim from another area of landscape study, one could argue that urban landscapes are a product of structure, process and stage. Just as the study of a drainage system would not confine itself to the first variable, so an urban investigation should be concerned with the processes of change and the stages reached. For instance, several recent publications have stressed the use of traffic survey information, collected in the field, as a basis for analysis, relating the data to official road recommendations or town size (Boaitt 1970, Morrison 1970).

Analysis is essential; take, for example, the model of urban growth commonly employed in schools. This tends to equate the visible spread of the built-up area with natural-increase population growth, often ignoring the very strong redistributional component in all settlement expansion. Without a close look at central population decline, a process established for at least a century in most towns of 50,000 upwards, and the related phenomena of 'sequent occupance' and outward movement (planned and spontaneous) the processes of urban growth must appear utterly mysterious, especially when one considers that the period of most rapid annual growth of the built-up area (the inter-war years) corresponds to a period of demographic stagnation. Studies which focus on residential densities can be a useful way of clarifying the processes involved (Storm 1965, 1971).

The conceptual framework for urban studies is often grotesquely inaccurate. On two occasions recently I have examined manuscript texts, proposed for school use, which took as a central theme increasing urbanisation, with more and more people flocking to live in the cities. This may be a reasonable description of Third World urbanisation, but as an account of the situation in developed economies it is totally misleading. All major cities can show a levelling-off or a decline in their population totals, and this is not simply a reflection of obsolescent municipal boundaries, but an indication of an ever more rapid dispersal, affecting both residence and employment. The heterogeneous group of social scientists and planners who contributed to a recent symposium on urban problems, established a remarkably solid consensus of opinion that we are moving towards 'a pattern of urbanisation which is more diffuse and less centred upon "place" than in the past' (Cowan 1970) and several contributors cited the seminal thinking of the American sociologist Webber, who has described the emergence of 'the non-place urban realm' and 'the ascent of amenity as locational determinant' (Webber 1964, Hall 1970). The *exurban* family, living in a 'village' twenty or thirty miles from job locations, and using a variety of centres, is an even more neglected phenomenon, in school studies, than its suburban counterpart.

CONCLUSION

The quality of urban geography undertaken in the schools depends ultimately upon the teacher being informed and enthusiastic about such topics. He must resist any temptation to squeeze urban geography into a Procrustean bed of environmental imperatives relating to river-crossings and industrial raw materials. He must be ready to use, and to mediate to his pupils, every form of documentation available for his area, from census reports to trade directories. He must be able to devise satisfying sequences of urban field study which incorporate discussion and analysis, as well as cartographic skills.

Above all, he must recognise that there is no urban-suburban area without its tensions and conflicts – concerning the conservation of historic buildings, the renewal and relocation of housing, the balance between vehicular access and amenity, and so on. With this in mind, he must hope that a suitably problem-orientated approach to urban studies – whether undertaken as 'geography' or under some more fashionably holistic label – will achieve that elusive 'relevance' which has come to be the holy grail of secondary education everywhere.

References

J. Archer and R. Dalton, (1968) *Fieldwork in geography*, Batsford.
A. Archer and H. G. Thomas, (1936) *Geography, first series*, Ginn.
M. W. Beresford, (1967) *New towns of the Middle Ages*, Lutterworth.
J. H. Boaitt, (1970) 'Making a study of communications', *Geography in the field*, K. S. Wheeler (ed.), Blond Educational.
J. Bradley, (1970) *Places for people*, Intertext.
K. Briggs, (1970) *Field work in urban geography*, Oliver & Boyd.
G. B. G. Bull, (1969) *A town study companion*, Hulton.
W. I. Carruthers, (1967) 'Major shopping centres in England and Wales 1961', *Regional Studies*, May 1967.
A. Chekhov, (1895) 'My Life' quoted in *Russian Writers and Society*, Weidenfeld & Nicolson, 1967.
J. Cormack, (1900) *Cormack's Merit Geography*.
P. Cowan (ed.), (1970) *Developing patterns of urbanisation*, Oliver & Boyd.
W. K. D. Davies, (1966) 'The ranking of service centres', *Transactions of the Institute of British Geographers*, December 1967.
(1967) 'Centrality and central place hierarchy', *Urban Studies*, February 1967.
M. Dilke (ed.) et al., (1965) *Field studies for schools*, Rivingtons.
J. A. Everson and B. P. Fitzgerald, (1969) *Settlement patterns*, Longmans.
N. J. Graves and J. T. White, (1971) *Geography of the British Isles*, Heinemann.
P. Hall, (1970) 'The Search for Environment', *New Society*, 16 May 1970.
(1970) 'Britain 2000', *Geographical Magazine*, June 1970.
L. C. Hunter, (1969) 'Planning and the Labour Market', *Regional and Urban Studies*, S. C. Orr and J. B. Cullingworth (eds.), Allen & Unwin.
G. James and R. Walford, (1969) *On the Spot Geographies*, Longmans.
J. H. Johnson, (1967) *Urban Geography*, chapter 4, Pergamon.
M. Jefferson, (1931) 'The distribution of the world's city folk', *Geographical Review*, vol. 21.
J. Lowry, (1960) *The British Isles*, Edward Arnold.
W. F. Luttrell, (1970) 'Employment in Greater London', *London under stress*, Town and Country Planning Association.
J. P. Mackintosh, (1968) *The devolution of power*, see especially pp. 49–50, Penguin.
Ministry of Housing and Local Government, (1967) *Written evidence submitted to the Royal Commission on Local Government*, HMSO.
Ministry of Local Government and Regional Planning, (1970) *Reform of local government in England*, Cmnd. 4276, HMSO.
E. Moir, (1964) *The discovery of Britain*, Routledge.
A. Morrison, (1970) 'Traffic Study as quantitative Field Work', *Teaching Geography*, no. 14, Geographical Association.
National Economic Development Office, (1971) *The future pattern of shopping*, HMSO.

H. B. Rodgers, (1965) 'Techniques of urban survey', *The purpose and organisation of field studies*, M. S. Dilke (ed.), Rivingtons.

Royal Commission on Local Government in England, (1969) *Report*, HMSO.

South-East Joint Planning Team, (1970) *Strategic plan for the South East*, HMSO.

R. D. P. Smith, (1968) 'The changing urban hierarchy', *Regional Studies*, September 1968.

M. J. Storm, (1965) *Urban growth in Britain*, Oxford University Press.
(1970) 'Shopping list', articles in *Teacher's World*, September 1970.
(1971) 'School and the community: an issue-based approach', *Bulletin of Environmental Education*, May 1971, Town and Country Planning Association.

R. Thomas, (1969) *London's new towns*, PEP.

D. Thorpe, (1966) *The geographer and urban studies*, Occasional Paper no. 8, University of Durham.

P. M. Turner, (1970) *Towns*, Macmillan.

B. Waites, (1970) 'Leicester: a provincial city', *Leicestershire landscapes*, Blond Educational.

M. P. Webber, (1964) 'Order in diversity: community without propinquity', *Cities and space*, L. Wingo (ed.), Johns Hopkins Press.

M. and L. White, (1964) *The intellectual versus the city*, Mentor Books.

E. A. Wrigley, (1965) 'Geography and population', *Frontiers in geographical teaching*, R. J. Chorley and P. Haggett (eds.), Methuen.

17 Networks

VINCENT TIDSWELL and KEITH HILTON

Perhaps the simplest definition of a network is that provided by Kansky (1963): 'a set of geographic locations interconnected in a system by a number of routes'. Since at present, the emphasis is upon the geometry in geography (Chorley and Haggett 1969), where we are concerned with the landscape as points, lines and surfaces, the linkages between these characteristics become especially important to the physical and human geographer alike.

The description and analysis of any network may be topographical, using existing maps and aerial photographs, or topological, employing transformations from this data. Topographical analysis are both time-consuming and limited in their scope. Topological transformations, (colloquially called rubber-sheet geometry), on the other hand, are easier to manipulate and more flexible in that they may be applied to networks upon any basis.

In teaching geography it is valuable to spend some time on a study of networks, firstly because it focuses on functioning spatial structures (the 'how' of things) and secondly because it allows a rigorous scientific mode of enquiry and description. Thirdly, it helps to integrate the physical and human aspects of geography, and finally it allows us to follow modern academic geomorphology in its concern with *process*.

DEFINITION OF TERMS

We need not here go into details of the mechanics of topological derivation and analysis since they are well presented elsewhere (Haggett and Chorley 1969), but the distinction between branching and circuit networks and that between planar and non-planar graphs should be explained.

Branching networks, such as those of river channels, are tree structures whose interconnecting lines do not form any complete loops. Circuit networks, such as many road systems, contain closed loops or circuits.

The term graph is used to mean the same thing as topological network. In a planar graph the arcs are on a two-dimensional surface, so that they can intersect and form nodes (e.g. two roads meeting at a junction). When arcs move in three dimensions (e.g. an air route) they may cross without intersecting and do not form a node. This is a non-planar graph.

The terminology is often confusing since differing words are used to describe the same feature. It may therefore be helpful to know that a node is synonymous with a vertex and edges with arcs.

BRANCHING NETWORKS IN FLUVIAL GEOMORPHOLOGY

The networks most easily studied in physical geography are the branching networks of rivers. Describing and analysing them as networks lets us see them as fundamental, widely recurring spatial patterns. Analysing them as functional systems involving the flow of water through the network allows us to examine the working of some fundamental processes.

An examination of almost any topographic map or aerial photograph, especially one taken from a satellite, shows the ubiquitous veination of river channels and valleys. The first step in analysing these branching networks is to isolate the pattern, and this is most conveniently done by means of a tracing.

The representation of a stream channel on a topographic map will of course vary with the scale of the map, the nature of the original ground, the aerial survey and so on. Although there are wide variations in the accuracy of the representation of stream channels (Leopold, Wolman and Miller 1964), the choice of one national survey and one scale normally permit reasonable comparison. In any case, the basic identification of the pattern and organisation of the network is little affected.

Once the pattern has been isolated it becomes possible to describe the network in terms of graphs – graphs being arrays of points, which are connected or not connected to one another by lines (Chorley and Haggett 1969). Although this involves losses of information, the higher level of abstraction is an advantage for discerning if there is any order in the organisation of the network.

Geomorphologists have been concerned with describing these patterns for some time. Descriptions such as straight and sinuous are ambiguous. Description by analogue (e.g. a dendritic or pinnate pattern) is equally subjective and in many cases such descriptions do not apply to the whole drainage basin under investigation. Applying

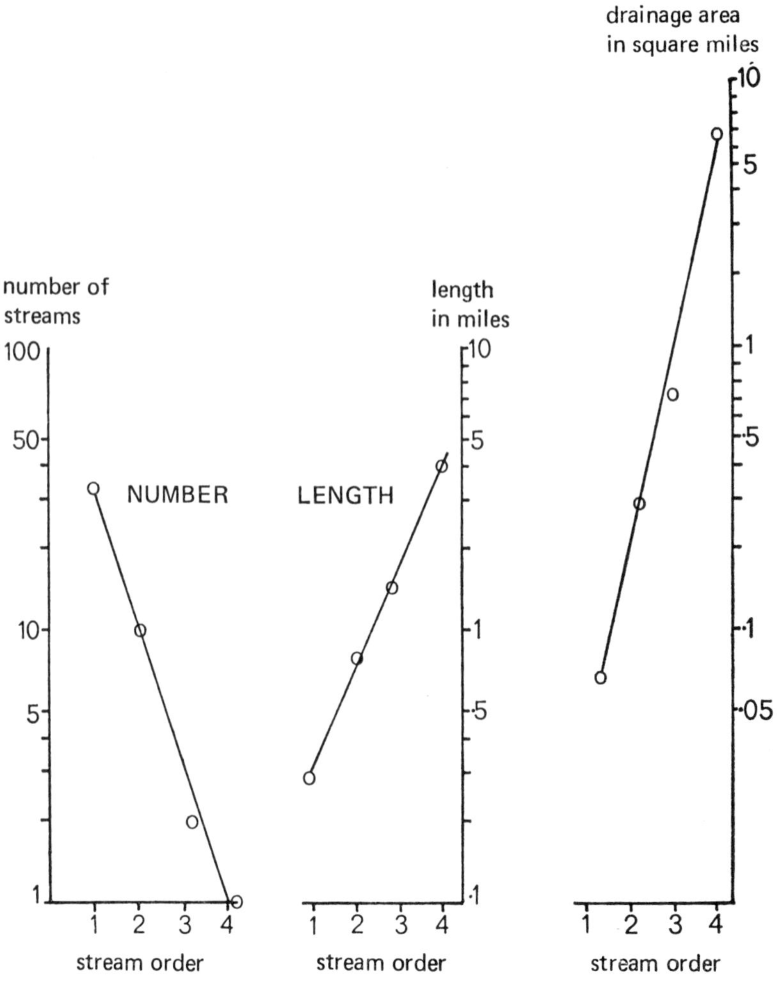

Relation of average length and number of streams to stream order.

Relation of stream order to drainage area.

Figure 1 Horton analysis of drainage networks. Drainage basin of Watts Branch, Maryland (after Leopold, Wolman and Miller) such terminology as consequent, obsequent and subsequent is also limiting. It involves some knowledge of the structural geology of the area, its lithology and its historical geology, and in addition it implies that streams are geologically or structurally controlled. All these ways of describing the network are attempts to identify its fundamental organisation, and the simplest way to describe and detect a network organisation is by numerical means.

Numerical description owes much to Horton's work (Horton 1945) but the simplest method of network analysis for a classroom is that devised by Strahler (1953). After the network has been isolated and the divides or watersheds inserted, the description of the streams may begin. (The most convenient way to distinguish them is by colouring a tracing.) In this system the unbranched tributary streams are designated first order. Where two first order 'fingertip' channels join, the segment downstream becomes a second order stream. A third order segment is identified when two second order segments join, a fourth order when two third order join and so on. If a second, or higher, order segment is joined by any number of first order streams its order remains unchanged, the stream channel segment only increases in order when two streams of equal order join. The basin magnitude equals the magnitude of the greatest link. (The system of numbering is shown in Figure 3.) At this stage it is convenient to collect other data such as the drainage basin area and the lengths of the stream segments of each order.

The next step, after isolating the pattern in this way, is to find a means of depicting its organisation. Planimetric tracings of drainage networks can be so diverse in scale and appearance that comparison is difficult. However, Horton was able to outline some basic and recurring order in the organisation of river networks which, from visual inspection, appeared very different. In a 'Horton analysis' stream order is seen to be related to the number of streams, the channel length and the drainage area by simple geometrical relationships – the so-called 'laws of hydraulic geometry'. These can be illustrated by plotting stream order against the variables on semi-logarithmic paper (Figure 1).

In teaching, the procedure might be as follows. Firstly, isolate the pattern, describe it verbally and show the limitations and imprecision of this type of description. Secondly, make a numerical analysis and present the results in a conventional Horton analysis.

Once this basic step of discovering order in the landscape has been taken – and quite small basins can show this order – additional

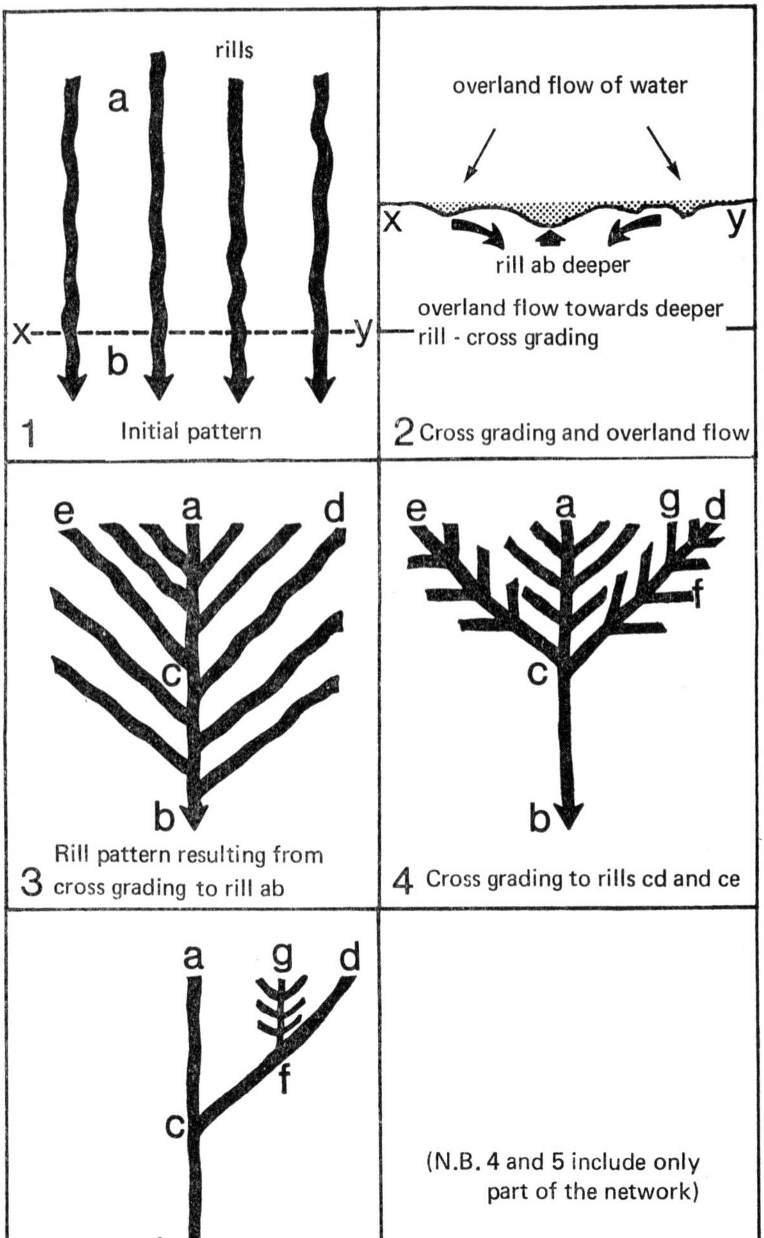

Figure 2 Drainage net development by cross grading (after Horton)

basin data can be examined and the general nature of the organisation appears naturally (Scheidegger 1966, Leopold et al. 1964, Morisawa 1962, Doornkamp 1967).

Horton developed a rational model to explain these geometric series in which number and length of streams of different order occur. The essence of his argument can be seen in Figure 2. Initially series of parallel rills develop on a slope. During periods of overland flow, when the water overtops the rills, water drains across the slope towards the longer and deeper rill *a b*. This new flow obliterates the earlier rills in a process known as cross grading. The new slope and rill system is in turn subjected to further cross grading towards the new positions of the longest length of overland flow and a new alignment of rills is produced. A complete network simulated in this way will have the same geometric properties as those observed in natural networks.

Shreve (1963), on the other hand, has suggested that the development of streams is a random process. He believes that Horton's law is simply a 'statistical relationship resulting from random development of drainage networks, rather than from orderly evolution' and that, looking at all possible sets of stream numbers, the most probable in nature are those with stream numbers close to an inverse geometric series (Shreve 1966). Simulations have been made of drainage networks produced by random procedures, but these networks bear little visual resemblance to natural networks although they do display the same type of organisation as revealed by statistical analysis (Leopold et al. 1964).

These two models of stream development can be demonstrated easily in teaching. The Horton model can be illustrated by examining the rills on a local spoil heap. The random (or 'stochastic') model can be produced by making a hexagonal grid and throwing dice to initiate drainage from the hexagons (Figure 3), return paths and circuits naturally being forbidden. Such an exercise can be undertaken with small areas, the resulting nets analysed in Hortonian terms and the similarity of organisation between the stochastically produced net and reality noticed.

The rational approach to drainage evolution, with its argument about cross grading, leads to the development of a net in which the geometric proportions follow those of natural drainage basins. The same geometrical properties can result from a random process producing the most favourable configuration. Neither model explains how the net evolves.

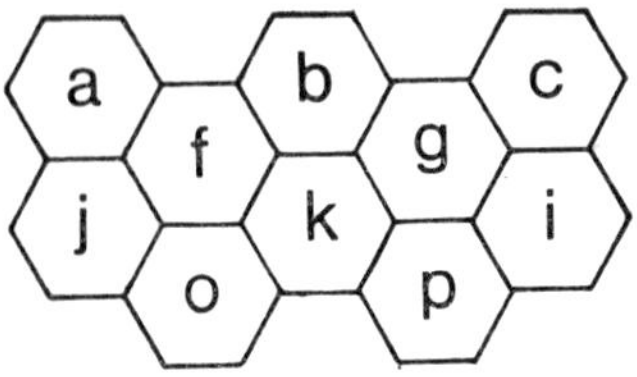

1 Section of area to be drained. Each hexagon will generate a channel.

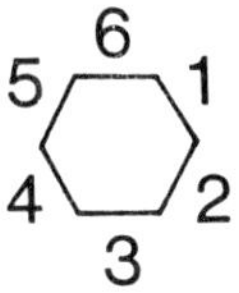

2 Possible drainage directions 1 to 6. Determined by dice throw.

3 Insertion of drainage directions after dice throw for each area. a = 1, b = 2, c = 5.

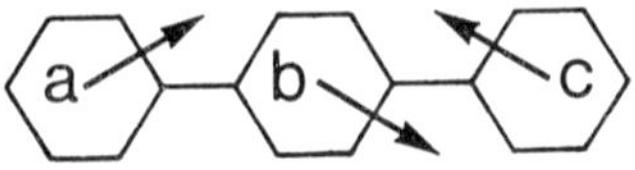

4 Drainage continues. f = 4, g first throw 5 invalid as it was a return flow, second attempt 3 direction inserted, j = 6, k = 1, i = 6, o = 1, first throw 5 invalid as it generated a loop, second attempt direction 6 channel inserted.

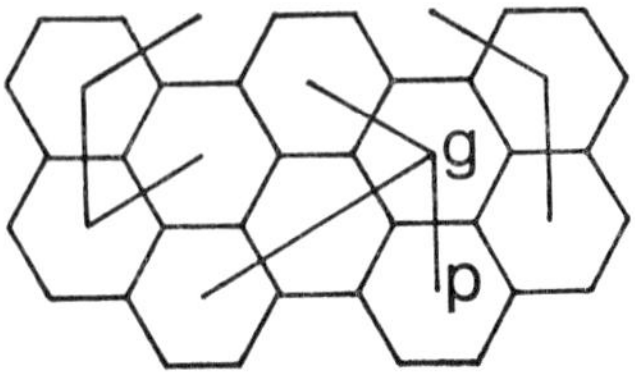

5 Each unit area drained. No return loop (internal drainage) or circuits

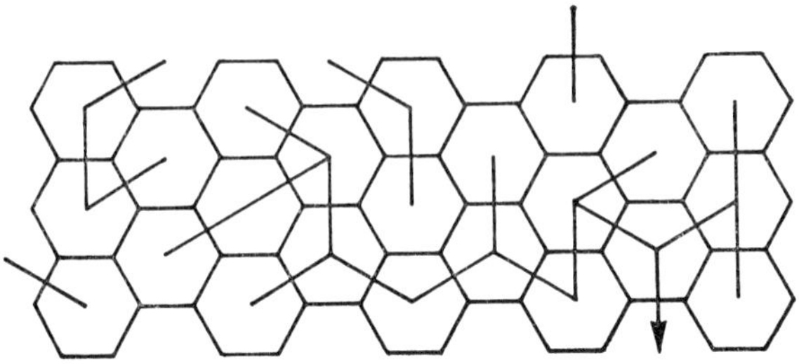

6 Network isolated and numerically described.

(The channel segments are given Strahler order)

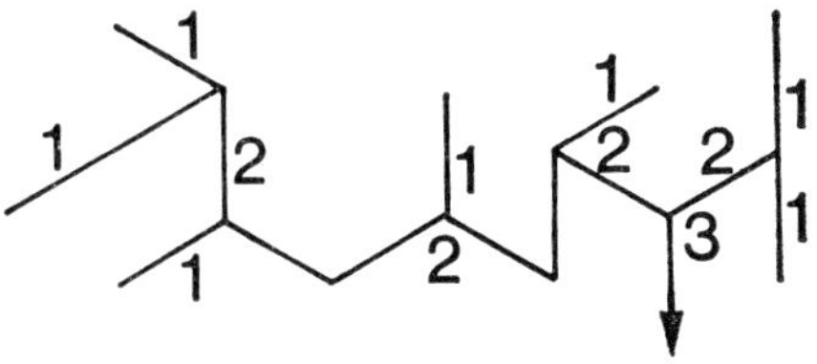

Figure 3 Random networks

The evolution of drainage nets is discussed in Haggett (1969) and Leopold et al. (1964). The latter authors use data provided by Ruhe, who studied drainage evolution on five glacial till sheets in the Mid West of the USA, and they believe that the data suggests that drainage density and stream frequency increase with time systematically, and also that the net is not continually changing; development might be quite rapid at first but later changes are slower and the 'geometrical properties appear then to represent a kind of equilibrium condition appropriate to the available processes, erodibility and structure of the region' (pp. 427–28).

Network analysis using the procedure outlined above can lead to more rigorous regional geomorphological studies. Chorley and Morgan (1962) compared the morphological features of the Unaka Mountains, Tennessee, with Dartmoor, and concluded that differences in rainfall intensities operating over time were the major cause of morphometric differences. Drainage density (that is, the total stream length in a basin divided by the area of the basin) can show wide differences between regions (Dartmoor, for example, has 3·45 miles of channel per square mile and the Unaka Mountains 11·8).

The explanation of such differences easily lends itself to the scientific method of enquiry when such factors as geology, lithology, precipitation characteristics, biogeography and human land use are critically reviewed. In addition, the realisation of the existence of order in the river networks naturally leads into attempts at discerning order in the whole of the fluvially linked landscape.*

Hence, in teaching fluvial geomorphology, we suggest that teachers introduce students to:

1 Strahler's system of stream numbering and basin magnitude. This is most conveniently done from 1:50,000 scale maps.
2 The graphical relationships between stream order and (*a*) number, (*b*) length and (*c*) area of the basin. This could be done firstly for the basin studied; additional data to illustrate the general applicability of these 'laws of hydraulic geometry' could be provided later.
3 The calculation of drainage densities in networks as a basis for comparing networks and seeking an explanation of the differences through investigations into climate, lithology and geomorphological history.

* See Strahler (1958) for a method of doing this by hypsometric analysis.

The network has been treated in this section as an inert spatial structure, some of whose characteristics have been described. Ideally the network should be vitalised and this can be done when its function of conducting flows of water is investigated. The flow of water in the stream channels and the general characteristics of hydraulic geometry are reviewed in Leopold et al. (1964). They also offer wide opportunities for field and classroom investigation and problem solving.

CIRCUIT NETWORKS IN SOCIO-ECONOMIC GEOGRAPHY

In this section we shall examine how network analysis has been used within a regional framework, and then explore the possibilities of studying networks *per se* as a conceptual mode of learning and as an approach to that branch of the discipline which is generally known as Human Geography. In both instances such analysis helps the search for order in the landscape.

The importance of the role of transport in the economic development of countries has long been assumed. Despite this, while modes of transport received some attention from the traditional regional geographer, the network as a whole was almost completely ignored. Now that a relationship has definitely been proven between railroad connectivity (i.e. the degree to which towns are interlinked) and degree of economic development as measured by per capita income (Yeates 1968), transportation studies, and in particular transportation networks, may become a focal point for regional analysis.

One of the earliest attempts to measure the impact of a network upon economic activity was the study by Garrison (1960) of the connectivity of the Inter-State Highway System. This network was superimposed on the existing network much as the British motorway system was. Other common elements are limited access points and the essentially national character of both systems (i.e. they were designed to link large metropolitan areas). Other towns which incidentally benefit merely receive chance emoluments. A complex method of analysis is used to identify changes in accessibility, reductions in transport costs and the general economic implications of these changes. A very much simplified exercise based upon the motorway network of Central England is contained in the G.A. *Teaching Geography* Series, Number 15.

An incisive study investigating the relationship between accessibility (i.e. ease of movement between places) as determined by transport networks and the economic structure of the Republic of Ireland has more recently been undertaken by O'Sullivan (1968). His discussion of the problems associated with selection and definition is helpful to the teacher in solving similar problems when attempting this kind of exercise for other regions. O'Sullivan's conclusions supported those of Yeates, for he found 'a functional relationship between the intensity of economic activity and accessibility on the transport networks'.

These studies were made at macro scale or national level, whereas work in schools may be centred upon the smaller region or immediate locality. A parallel investigation to that of O'Sullivan was undertaken for Cornwall by Westaway (1970). The methodology is similar but the findings have little in common with O'Sullivan's work. The reasons for this immediately involve the geographer in examining conventional regional data and force him to place them in perspective against the total national picture. In experimenting with his local area, therefore, the teacher should not become discouraged when unexpected results occur, but use those results to isolate problems to be further investigated. This can lead to genuine on-going, open ended work with children, and especially with sixth formers.

The dynamic processes operating upon the landscape are evident in changes in transport networks. This has already been intimated in Garrison's paper. Two further articles are relevant: one dealing with evaluating a change which has taken place and one predicting priorities for change.

Burton applied graph theory to the regional highway network in northern Ontario to predict the increased accessibility each additional link in the network would provide. This is a good example of how geography can be truly predictive and may be applied in actual planning. An example of Burton's method may form the springboard for further similar studies of relevant areas.

Figure 4 shows the motorway network for Italy, north of Naples. Suppose it is proposed to build three new links in this network, our problem is to establish how much the network as a whole will benefit from such links and so establish an order of priority for building. Alternatively it may be necessary for economic planning to establish which towns will benefit most from road improvements, and this too may establish an order of priority, but using a different criterion.

Before attempting to improve the network it is helpful to evaluate it in terms of connectivity or integration. This is usually expressed as the Beta Index and is obtained by dividing the number of links (edges)

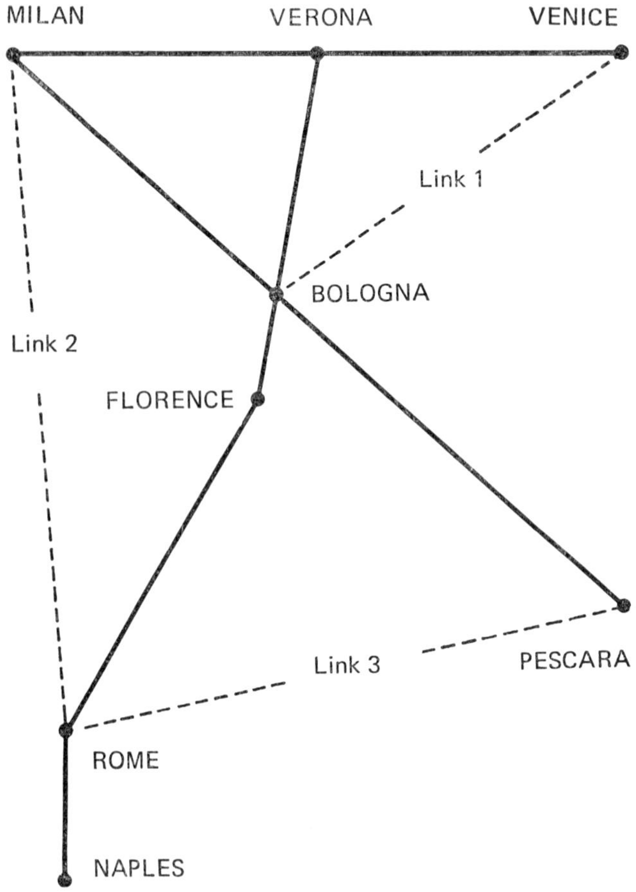

Figure 4 Topological representation of the motorway network of Italy north of Naples

by the number of towns (nodes). In Figure 4 this value is 1·0 (8/8). If one link is added, the value is increased to 1·12, if two links to 1·25 and finally to 1·37 (11/8) when all three links are incorporated. The significance of this increase will be appreciated later.

However, the problem is to establish an order of priority for building, and the first step is to establish the accessibility of each town by constructing a shortest path matrix, as in Table 1. This shows the number of links traversed when travelling between towns by the shor-

	Milan	*Verona*	*Venice*	*Bologna*	*Florence*	*Pescara*	*Rome*	*Naples*	*Accessibility Index*	*Rank order*
Milan	0	1	2	1	2	2	3	4	15	4
Verona	1	0	1	1	2	2	3	4	14	3
Venice	2	1	0	2	3	3	4	5	20	7
Bologna	1	1	2	0	1	1	2	3	11	1
Florence	2	2	3	1	0	2	1	2	13	2
Pescara	2	2	3	1	2	0	3	4	17	5
Rome	3	3	4	2	1	3	0	1	17	5
Naples	4	4	5	3	2	4	1	0	23	8
Gross accessibility index (dispersion of network)									130	

Table 1 Shortest path matrix in original network of motorways of Italy

test available path. The associated number of a place is the largest number of links required to travel to another town in the network (e.g. for Rome 4 and for Venice 5). Although this reflects accessibility (low numbers) or inaccessibility (high numbers), the total number of links traversed in order to go to all other towns in the network is a much stronger one. The rank order of accessibility can be deduced from Table 1 for all the towns in the Italian network. The total number of links traversed by the entire number of journeys, in this case 130, is known as the gross accessibility index and is a measure of the dispersion of the network. The lower the number, the less dispersed the network, and the greater the ease of movement within it.

Using similar methods it is now possible to evaluate the improvements when links 1, 2 and 3 (and combinations of these) are introduced in turn. The results are summarised in Table 2 which reveals that,

	Original network	*Links* *1*	*2*	*3*	*1 & 2*	*1 & 3*	*2 & 3*	*1, 2 & 3*
Milan	4	4	1	5	2	6	1	2
Verona	3	3	3	4	3	4	4	4
Venice	7	4	7	7	6	6	8	7
Bologna	1	1	1	1	1	1	1	1
Florence	2	2	4	2	4	2	5	4
Pescara	5	6	6	2	7	2	5	4
Rome	5	6	4	5	4	4	1	2
Naples	8	8	8	8	8	8	7	8

Table 2 Rank order of accessibility resulting from improvements in linkage

whatever happens, Bologna remains the most accessible central place and Naples the least accessible. Rome and Milan markedly improve when links 2 and 3 are added. Clearly it is possible to evaluate the effect of linkage improvements on any town. The desirability of any particular improvement would depend on the economic feasibility, or demand, and this is what gives importance to the gravity model explained later.

If all the towns are regarded as of equal importance, then the effect of additional links on the overall network may be deduced from Table 3. It will be recalled that as links were added so the degree of integration increased and it may now be seen that accessibility also increases (i.e. the gross accessibility index is reduced from 130 to 100). In establishing an order of priority for building, link 2 clearly offers the greatest single advantage. Since Milan (Table 2) also gains very substantially, the economic motive may also be present to stimulate such building.

	Accessibility index	*Gain*	*Rank order*	*Gain per link*	*Rank order*
Original network	130	—	—	—	—
plus link 1	120	10	6	10	4
link 2	114	16	5	16	1
link 3	122	8	7	8	7
links 1 and 2	109	21	3	10·5	3
links 1 and 3	112	18	4	9	6
links 2 and 3	106	24	2	12	2
links 1, 2, 3	100	30	1	10	4

Table 3 Gross accessibility indices resulting from improvements in the network

Cooper has assessed the improved accessibility on the underground network of Central London resulting from the construction of the Victoria Line. His methods use conventional graph theory and are remarkably easy to handle at school level. Using the underground network is advantageous in that it always appears as a topological map and younger children are familiar with it since they know no other presentation. By comparing the accessibility of nodes both before and after the incorporation of the Victoria Line (as explained in the Italian network above) it is possible to evaluate in quantitative terms the percentage gain in accessibility for any individual place and to determine the rank order of that place within the complete network. For example, Victoria improves its rank order by 31·5 places, Oxford Circus by only 1, whilst Cannon Street goes down by 4 places in the network as a whole.

Studies of this kind, are, of course, concerned with the efficiency of a network and therefore with route minimisation. Determining the optimal route is mathematically complex, but once again the solution is possible in the computer age. English Electric Leo Computers Ltd offer a route planning programme which takes into account six diverse variables such as ten different vehicle capacities, daily time for delivery and collection, and visits to be made first or last during the trip. Simple problems of minimisation to be solved by trial and error are contained in *New Ways in Geography* by Cole and Beynon (1969). Route minimisation for the builder of roads can be dramatically presented by means of hardware models, simple to construct and operate. Surface tension from a soap solution indicates the optimal route on perspex. Comprehensive instructions for this model, devised by Dr Morgan, are contained in *Models in Geography* (1967).

The gravity model, which was mentioned above, is used in forecasting traffic flows. (Examples can be found in the literature already cited but the most comprehensive account in an applied context is contained in the study by Starkie (1967) of traffic generation and spatial interaction.) The gravity formula states that the interaction between two towns can be predicted by multiplying together the populations of the towns and dividing by the distance between them. Recent work by Briggs (1971) has shown a close correspondence between telephone calls actually made and those predicted by this formula for a study area in Lancashire. One of the most helpful ways the gravity formula may be used is to generate hypotheses of traffic movement which may be tested by normal census methods and the results correlated and evaluated.

Although each of the studies so far considered was carried out in an isolated regional framework, many of the authors sought principles that could be generally applied. A formalised sequential model of network extension in relation to economic development has been established for Ghana and Nigeria by Taaffe, Morrill and Gould (1963) who recognised six stages in a progressively more integrated network. This has been further analysed by Yeates and applied in a different regional context, that of Malaya, by Ward (1970). The apparent repetitive pattern and sequence is in tune with a model aiming at generalisation. Similar approaches to the development of networks from the seaboards of the USA and Australia could provide a refreshing and stimulating way of introducing regional studies of these two popular areas. Equally one could search for this sequential pattern in the evolution of the motorway networks of Europe and Britain.

NETWORKS AS A SYSTEMATIC STUDY

It was stated earlier that networks could be considered in either a regional or a purely systematic context. The latter facilitates a conceptual approach. This does not, however, mean that such a mode is devoid of facts, but rather that they are used to identify and convey the concepts of the discipline. Few educationists would now doubt the value of the conceptual approach to learning. An attempt has been made by Ambrose (1969) to identify these concepts and a further effort has been made by the authors of this chapter to develop a series of conceptually based units of work or modules, concerned with the systematic branches of the discipline. Figure 5 shows the structured sequence of the basic idea and Figure 6 the primate concepts, second order concepts and skills involved when implemented for transport networks. It will be deduced from Figure 6 that inter-relationships form a key goal. It is the desire to be able to compare in a valid statisti-

Region	*Relief Index*	*Rank*	*Detour Index*	*Rank*	*d*	d^2
Cumberland and Westmorland	91·9	9	230	9	0	0
Yorkshire	9·0	4	117	1	3	9
Gloucestershire	11·3	5	156	7	−2	4
Devon	34·0	8	282	10	−2	4
Staffordshire	3·0	1	118	2	−1	1
Oxfordshire	4·9	2	145	6	−4	16
Nottinghamshire	6·8	3	137	4	−1	1
Denbighshire	98·0	10	211	8	2	4
Kent	15·0	6	125	3	3	9
Sussex	22·0	7	142	5	2	4

Mean Relief Index = 29·6
Mean Detour Index = 166·3

Table 4 Relief and detour indices for ten regions of England and Wales

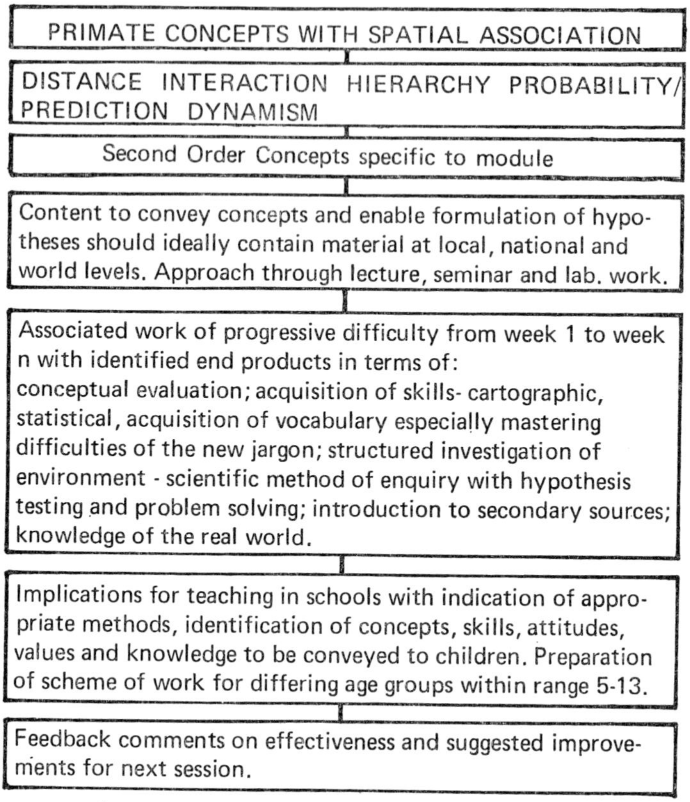

Figure 5 The structure of a hypothetical module as used in a College of Education.

cal way one network with another which underlies the work of Kansky (1963), and thus arrive at an appreciation and understanding of order in the landscape.

Table 4 shows the comparative figures for two variables, relief and accessibility, for ten study regions within the British Isles. Detailed instructions for the derivation of these indices are contained in *Quantitative Methods* (Tidswell and Barker 1971) and it is merely intended here to show how one could establish whether or not the two variables are related and the strength of any such relationship. The Spearman Rank Correlation yields a value of +0·68 whilst the regression line using a log/log transformation is shown in Figure 7. A tentative conclusion to be drawn from the results of these two techniques is that the

Distance	*Interaction*	*Hierarchy*	*Probability/ prediction*	*Dynamism*
Barriers to movement – physical and human	Journey to work patterns	Density	Route minimisation	Growth of motorways
		Integration	Route improvement	
	Gravity models	Accessibility within networks	Gravity model	Contraction of railways Bridge building
Simple measurement	Flow line maps	Hypothesis formulation	Matrices	
Cross sections			Resection	
Relief indices		Test via correlation	Critical path analysis	Matrix manipulation
Topological transformation	Field testing			
Detour and accessibility indices		Establish relationships		

Inter-relationships of primate concepts and implications in regional studies
Real World Networks: local, national and world scales; canal, rail, road and air media

Figure 6 Outline of transport module showing relationship between concept, skill and content

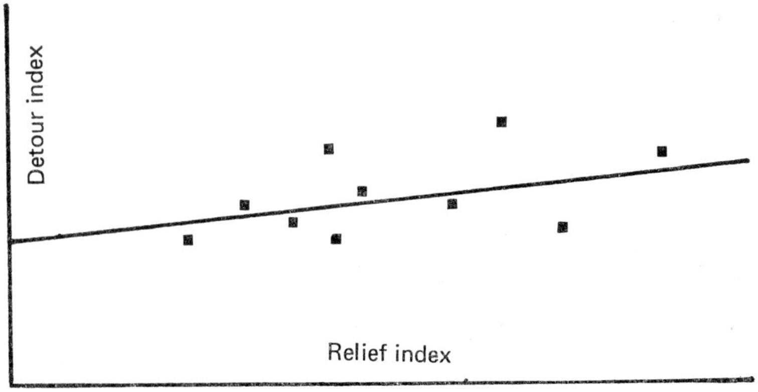

Figure 7 The relationship between relief and detour indices

positive correlation between relief and inaccessibility, whilst existing, is by no means as strong as many hitherto imagined. Certainly in regions of other than physical extremity it is essential to look at other variables such as population density and economic structure as forces contributing to the establishment of an efficient network.

CONCLUSION

In conclusion, the ubiquitous nature of networks must be stressed. The chain store network and its series of interacting hinterlands, although intangible, is just as real as the more overt networks such as the hierarchical one of Christaller settlement patterns as revealed by rank size rule. Ambrose (1969) sums up the importance of networks both in geography and education when he writes: 'Clearly networks are vitally important and because they always have a spatial dimension they are of particular interest to geographers. If the concept of a network is introduced at an early stage of training, using very simple examples, the task of understanding progressively more difficult techniques of network analysis becomes that much easier.'

Geography teaching at the present time lays stress on acquiring facts. It is less good at teaching more sophisticated cognitive skills such as the ability to classify, correlate and critically manipulate data, and it is especially weak in problem posing and solving. Once we realise that the aims of geography teaching are wider than the professional training of geographers, we can undertake a more rigorous programme of inquiry, especially if we are ready to discard superfluous factual content. A programme of that kind should be concerned with establishing general statements and the understanding of systems, and in it the study of networks can take a valuable place.

References

P. J. Ambrose, (1969) *Analytical human geography*, Longmans.

K. Briggs, (1971) Unpublished work achieved with sixth form, Canon Slade School, Bolton.

I. Burton, (1962) *Accessibility in N. Ontario: an application of graph theory to a regional highway network*, Toronto University.

R. J. Chorley and P. Haggett, (1967) *Models in geography* (ch. 17), Methuen.

R. J. Chorley and M. A. Morgan, (1962) 'Comparison of morphometric features, Unaka Mountains, Tennessee and North Carolina, and Dartmoor, England', *Geological Society of America Bulletin*, vol. 73.

J. C. Cooper, (1970) 'A graph theoretic analysis of the effect of the Victoria Line on the underground network of Central London', *Horizon*, vol. 19.

J. C. Doornkamp, (1967) 'The morphometric analysis of drainage basins illustrated by some examples of third order basins in Uganda', *Bulletin of Quantitative Data for Geographers*, no. 13, University of Nottingham.

W. L. Garrison, (1960) 'Connectivity of the inter-state highway system', *Papers and procedings of the Regional Association*, vol. 6; reprinted in *Analytical human geography*, P. J. Ambrose, Longmans 1969.

P. Haggett and R. J. Chorley, (1969) *Network analysis in geography*, Edward Arnold.

R. E. Horton, (1945) 'Erosional development of streams and their drainage basins: hydrophysical approach to quantitative morphology', *Geological Society of America Bulletin*, vol. 56.

K. J. Kansky, (1963) 'Structure of transport networks: relationship between network geometry and regional characteristics', *Research paper* no. 84, University of Chicago Geography Department.

L. B. Leopold, M. G. Wolman and J. P. Miller, (1964) *Fluvial processes in geomorphology*, Freeman.

M. E. Morisawa, (1962) 'Quantitative geomorphology of some watersheds in the Appalachian Plateau', *Geological Society of America Bulletin*, vol. 73.

P. M. O'Sullivan, (1968) 'Accessibility and the spatial structure of the Irish economy', *Journal of Regional Studies*, vol. 2, no. 2.

A. E. Scheidegger, (1966) *Theoretical geomorphology*.

R. L. Shreve, (1963), "Horton's Law" of stream numbers for topographically random networks', *Transactions of the American Geophysical Union*, vol. 44.
(1966) 'Statistical law of stream numbers', *Journal of Geology*, vol. 74.

A. N. Strahler, (1953) 'Revision of Horton's quantitative factors in erosional terrain', *Transactions of the American Geophysical Union*, vol. 34.
(1958) 'Dimensional analysis applied to fluvially eroded landforms', *Geological Society of America Bulletin*, vol. 69.

D. N. M. Starkie, (1967) *Traffic and industry* (LSE Geographica Papers no 3).

E. J. Taafe, R. L. Morrill and P. R. Gould, (1963) 'Transport expansion in underdeveloped countries: a comparative analysis, *Geographical Review*, vol. 53.

W. V. Tidswell, (1971) *An introduction to the analysis of road networks*, Teaching Geography series no. 15, Geographical Association.

M. W. Ward, (1969) 'Progress in transport geography', *Trends in geography*, R. U. Cooke and J. H. Johnson (eds.), Pergamon.

E. J. Westaway, (1970) 'Accessibility and the spatial structure of the economy of Cornwall', *Horizon*, vol. 19.

M. H. Yeates, (1968) *An introduction to quantitative analysis in economic geography*, McGraw-Hill.

18 Statistical techniques

PETER DAVIS

Recent trends in the approach to the study of geography at both university and school level have placed considerable emphasis upon the use of quantitative techniques. Greater publicity seems to have been given to this aspect of the subject's development during the past decade than to many others. To many teachers, particularly those with little or no specialised mathematical training, the prospect of using statistical techniques within the classroom may appear somewhat daunting. Some may fail to see their relevance to the teaching of geography in schools, whilst others are almost certainly discouraged from experimenting with new ideas and new methods by the apparent difficulty of the statistical computation involved (Gregory 1969). To a certain extent this may be due to the present limited amount of published material which deals specifically with the statistical treatment of geographical material, although several works are available (Cole and King 1968, Gregory 1963, Theakstone and Harrison 1970). There would appear to be a need for more practical illustrations of the way in which actual techniques can be applied, with benefit, to real classroom situations. This chapter suggests some possible applications for some of the more commonly used techniques.

At this stage it is necessary to consider briefly the role of statistical techniques in modern geography. The recent increase in the use of such techniques, labelled by many as the 'quantitative revolution', has not, of course, been an isolated development. Essentially it represents a response to other changes of a more fundamental nature which have very largely transformed the methodology of the subject. These changes have been well-documented and need little description here (Bunge 1966, Chorley and Haggett 1967, Cole and King 1968). However, two aspects are particularly important; the first is the much greater emphasis which has been placed upon the drawing of generalisations from factual information, and which has resulted in the formulation of certain theoretical concepts and the construction and use of models. The second aspect is the adoption of a more scientific approach to the collection and use of factual material, within the context of setting up and testing hypothetical statements of a generalised nature against reality. Figure 1 illustrates the main steps which are involved in working through a problem-solving situation of this kind (Cole and King 1968, Everson 1969). One value of this type of approach is that it defines clearly the function of statistical techniques in geography, not as ends in themselves, but as an essential means of reaching meaningful conclusions from the analysis of factual information collected in numerical form.

Obviously the effects of important methodological developments are felt initially at the higher levels of education. Opportunities for research and development are greater in universities than in schools, and the introduction of new ideas is easier within a more advanced academic environment. However, there are important reasons why at least some of the recent changes in approach to the subject should find their way as quickly as possible into school geography courses.

Firstly, and perhaps most important of all, the careful use of games and models to illustrate the operation of certain simple concepts offers a structured theoretical framework from which to consider the complexity of the real world. Secondly, the use of hypotheses, which can be formulated and tested within the classroom using statistical methods, encourages original thought and contribution on the part of the class, whether as a whole, or in groups, or as individuals. Together these two innovations stimulate the pupil into taking a more active role in learning, by requiring him to search for explanations of what he discovers, rather than being content with mere factual description. This approach contrasts rather strongly, of course, with some more traditional methods of teaching geography in schools, which require little more than the straightforward collection and storage of large amounts of factual information (Crisp 1969).

If the changes which are gradually taking place in the teaching of geography at school level are to be fully effective, it is essential that pupils should be able to deal confidently with numerical information. They should also be familiar with the application of some simple statistical tests, and know the reasons for applying them. A few text books are already available which make use of carefully selected data and fairly simple exercises to guide pupils into searching for, and recognising, obvious regularities which might indicate an underlying relationship (e.g. Cole and Beynon 1968, Everson and Fitzgerald 1969). The same principle, or concept, can be applied more than once, of course, within a form of spiral curriculum (Bruner 1960), allowing the degree of explanation and formalisation to be increased step by step. At the same time more sophisticated techniques of analysis can be introduced to increase the degree of objectivity achieved. Thus a simple exercise involving little more than the ranking in order of two sets of figures by 10-year-olds, with the object of relating a farmer's crop layout to distance from his farm, might be developed into a full-scale correlation exercise to illustrate the operation of the von Thünen principle that land use may be a function of distance from a central place, by the time that the same pupils reach the sixth form. In this type of situation, the stimulus for the setting up and testing of some form of hypothesis is provided largely by the observation of factual information given to the pupil in prepared form. As an alternative approach, it is quite possible for the stimulus to be some theoretical concept, the operation of which is to be tested against reality. In formulating a hypothesis to be tested, the teacher may be able to exploit the intuitive notions of the class, based on their own everyday observation and experience. In this case factual information is not provided, and must be collected by the class before processing can begin. There is an important role here for fieldwork, particularly in the local area (Chapallaz 1970).

Exercises of this type, involving the use of statistical methods, help to make the pupil aware that the ability to analyse and explain the characteristics of the information with which he is dealing is a valuable asset in learning geography. With practice, and depending upon their age and ability, pupils may be able to develop and test their own hypotheses, making use of information which they have collected themselves, perhaps through their own fieldwork. For some, experience gained in the careful use of quantitative techniques in problem-solving situations at school level, will undoubtedly ease the transition to higher education.

If the testing of hypotheses is to be successful, however, the teacher must be careful to select the most suitable statistical techniques for his purpose. A number of factors govern this choice:

1 Techniques must be kept simple enough to be within the mathematical capability of the group using them. It is doubtful whether the application of techniques merely by rote has any real value. A reasonable understanding of what the test is designed to do is highly desirable.

2 The amount of arithmetical computation must be kept fairly small. How much is acceptable must depend on the facilities available (log tables, desk calculators, etc.) and the level of study; but too much computation is time-consuming and boring. Many techniques really demand a computer.
3 The techniques should allow the teacher to make full use of a problem-orientated approach. They must be chosen to suit the nature of the hypothesis being tested.
4 All techniques, especially those involving tests of significance must be applied vigorously. They should not be used if conditions attached to them cannot be met.

Usually only one or two techniques will appear relevant to a particular situation, and the choice is a fairly simple one to make.

The following examples are intended as practical illustrations of the way in which statistical techniques can be employed in the classroom within the context of hypothesis testing. By describing the application of a few commonly used techniques, it is hoped to show how varying degrees of complexity and objectivity can be introduced to suit age and ability, whilst dealing with the same basic information. The situations chosen represent only a fairly limited field of geographical study, and it should be emphasised that the statistical methods involved are capable of much wider application, even at school level, than is necessarily implied here.

SEARCHING FOR RELATIONSHIPS

The first exercise involves the use of fairly simple techniques which can be applied and understood by 15-year-old pupils of moderate ability, and also perhaps by able 14-year-olds. As part of an elementary course on settlement geography in the first term of their fourth year, pupils carried out some work on the characteristics and functions of market towns, developing by investigation and discussion an awareness of their importance as centres providing essential goods and services for the surrounding area. The 'problem' was to discover why some market towns should be larger than others, and again discussion prompted the suggestion that perhaps this had something to do with how large an area they served, and thus how accessible they were as centres. This suggestion was formalised slightly to produce the hypothesis that 'variation in the size of market towns can be explained in terms of variations in their accessibility as centres'.

This type of hypothesis, postulating the existence of a causal rela-

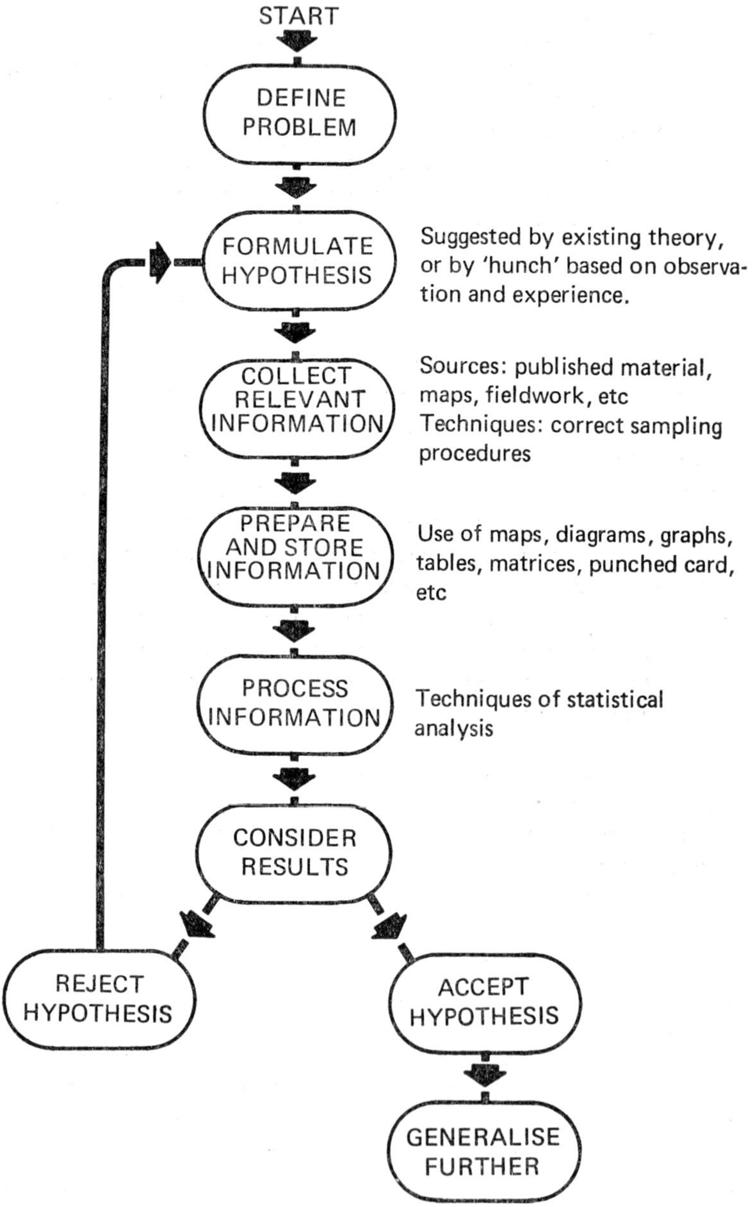

Figure 1 The problem-solving approach in geography (after J. A. Everson, from an idea of J. P. Cole)

tionship between two spatially distributed variables (in this case accessibility and size), is frequently employed in solving geographical problems. It is important, of course, that the suggested relationship should be a meaningful one, capable of logical explanation. A little care is also needed to ensure, as far as possible, that the two factors being tested for relationship are not 'co-variables', both dependent on a third underlying factor which has not been specified.

The next step in the sequence suggested in Figure 1 is the collection of information against which to test the hypothesis. In this example, only the data collected for market towns in East Anglia (Norfolk and Suffolk) will be considered, although the size of the form enabled a much wider area to be covered. Obviously two sets of information were required, one relating to the size of the market towns, and the other to their accessibility. Population was taken as a simple indicator of size, but it was more difficult to find a definition of accessibility in terms which could be easily measured. After some discussion it was decided to count the number of 'A' and 'B' class roads which led into each centre. Information was collected for all market towns – literally defined – in the area studied, so that sampling was unnecessary.

After the data had been collected, a certain amount of preparation was necessary to manipulate the information into a form suitable for testing. It was agreed that, as 'A' roads were likely to carry considerably more traffic than 'B' roads, they should be given a weighting of 2. Using this principle, an 'accessibility index' was worked out for each town, and the complete set of data tabulated as shown in Table 1.

Two techniques were used in processing the information, in order to test the validity of the hypothesis:

(*a*) *Scatter plotting* The two separate sets of data, one relating to each variable, were plotted graphically against each other on a 'scatter diagram'. The position of each town in turn was fixed by plotting its own pair of values as a point on the graph. As the postulated causal factor, or 'independent variable', accessibility was scaled along the horizontal axis, whilst population, as the resultant factor, or 'dependent variable', was scaled along the vertical axis. Because of the large range of population figures involved, from just over 1,000 to well over 100,000, it was decided to use a logarithmic scale on the vertical axis, whilst retaining a normal arithmetic scale on the horizontal axis. The graph was thus a 'log-normal' one. No special graph paper was used, although this would have been possible, and so the pupils were

Name of town	*Population*	*Number of 'A' roads*	*Number of 'B' roads*	*Accessibility Index*
Attleborough	3,027	2	2	6
Aylsham	2,635	2	4	8
Beccles	7,332	5	2	12
Brandon	3,344	2	3	7
Bungay	3,582	5	0	10
Burnham Market	1,211	0	4	4
Bury St Edmunds	21,179	7	2	16
Cromer	4,892	5	0	10
Diss	3,681	3	3	9
Downham Market	2,835	5	0	10
East Dereham	7,199	2	5	9
Eye	1,583	0	4	4
Fakenham	3,753	4	3	11
Framlingham	2,005	0	5	5
Great Yarmouth	52,970	4	1	9
Haverhill	5,445	3	1	7
Hingham	1,388	0	2	2
Holt	2,061	2	3	7
Ipswich	117,395	8	1	17
King's Lynn	27,536	7	1	15
Lowestoft	45,730	3	1	7
Mildenhall	7,132	5	1	11
Newmarket	11,227	5	3	13
North Walsham	5,014	2	4	8
Norwich	120,096	9	5	23
Stowmarket	7,795	3	2	8
Sudbury	6,642	5	2	12
Swaffham	3,202	5	1	11
Thetford	5,399	6	2	14
Watton	2,462	0	7	7
Wickham Market	1,283	2	4	8
Wymondham	5,904	2	2	6

Table 1 Summary of data for exercise on East Anglia

required to look up the logarithm for each population value before they could start plotting. The completed scatter diagram is shown in Figure 2.

This technique is a very simple one, and can easily be used with younger age groups, although without the complication of logarithmic scales. The construction of such a scale is not difficult, but needs a

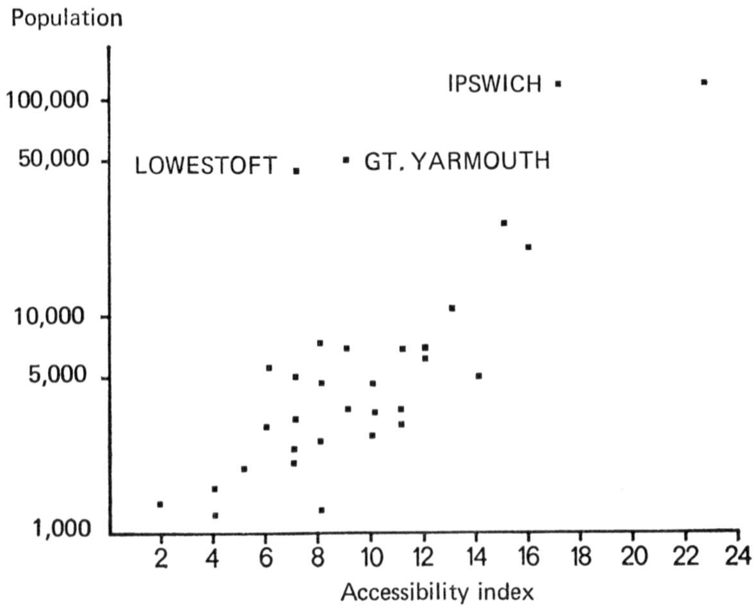

Figure 2 Scatter diagram showing relationship between population and accessibility

little practice. It should be within the capabilities of most fourth-year pupils. The method used is illustrated in Figure 3. Arithmetic graph paper can be used but it is the logarithm of the number (the number expressed as a power of 10) that is plotted and not the number itself. For reference purposes the scale can be marked on in ordinary number form, as in Figure 2, but it will of course appear distorted. The effect of such a logarithmic transformation is to compress the upper end of the scale, by progressive steps, relative to the lower end.

Scatter plotting can hardly be described as an objective test of the relationship between two variables, but it can usefully provide an initial indication of the nature and extent of such a relationship, and may help in deciding whether further testing, using more objective methods, is likely to be worthwhile. In this context a number of points may be noted:

1 A perfect relationship, capable of precise mathematical description, would be indicated if all points on the scatter diagram were positioned in a straight line. In practice this will not occur, since

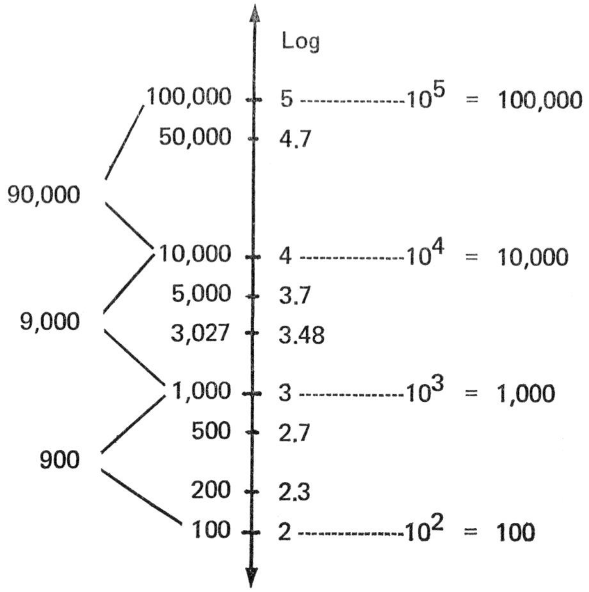

Figure 3 The construction of a logarithmic scale

geographical phenomena cannot be fully explained in terms of one factor only.

2 If there is very little or no relationship between the two variables, the diagram will reveal nothing more than a scatter of points, forming no identifiable trend in their pattern (see Figure 4).

3 A degree of relationship is indicated by the existence of a definite trend in the distribution of points on the scatter diagram. If a 'belt' of points can be identified, its width can give some idea of the strength of the relationship (see Figure 4).

4 A direct or 'positive' relationship, in which an increase in the value of one variable is associated with an increase in the value of the other, can be recognised as an upward trend of points from left to right. An indirect, or 'negative' relationship, in which an increase in one variable is associated with a decrease in the other, is indicated by a downward trend from left to right (see Figure 4).

Referring to Figure 2, it can be seen that in this instance the scatter diagram implies a reasonable positive relationship between accessibility and population. It was therefore decided to go on to the next stage of processing the information.

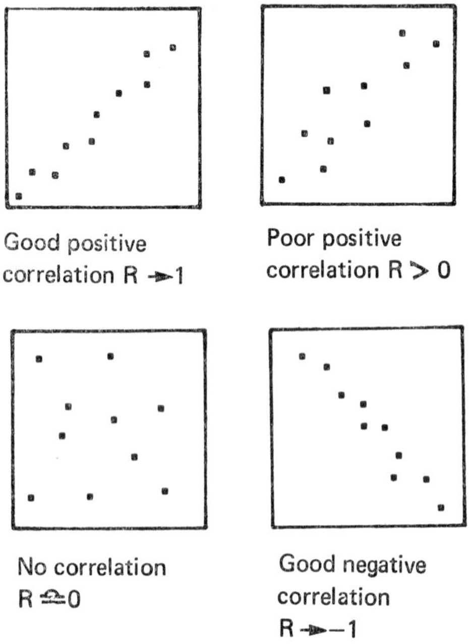

Figure 4 Examples of scatter diagrams

(*b*) *Rank correlation* This technique allows the degree of relationship between two variables to be assessed objectively, and expressed in precise numerical form as a 'correlation coefficient'. The test is 'non-parametric'; that is, it is not concerned with the actual numerical values of either variable, but only with their position in a ranked list. For this reason the values of both population and accessibility for the market towns in East Anglia were ranked in order, from highest to lowest. (This test is not so useful if the total number of items to be ranked is small, e.g. less than 10.) The appropriate population rank and accessiblity rank were then allocated to each town, as shown in Table 2. Several towns were found to have the same accessibility index, and were therefore ranked equal on this variable. A simple rule governs the procedure in a situation such as this, where two or more values are the same. Suppose that the values, ranked in order, are

13 12 12 11 11 11 10 ...

The two values of 12 occupy second and third positions on the list, but must obviously be ranked equal. Adding ranks 2 and 3 gives 5, and

Name of town	*Population Rank*	*Accessibility Rank*	*D*	D^2
Attleborough	23	27·5	4·5	20·25
Aylsham	25	19·5	5·5	30·25
Beccles	9	7·5	1·5	2.25
Brandon	21	24	3	9
Bungay	20	13	7	49
Burnham Market	32	30·5	1·5	2·25
Bury St Edmunds	6	3	3	9
Cromer	17	13	4	16
Diss	19	16	3	9
Downham Market	24	13	11	121
East Dereham	10	16	6	36
Eye	29	30·5	1·5	2·25
Fakenham	18	10	8	64
Framlingham	28	29	1	1
Great Yarmouth	3	16	13	169
Haverhill	14	24	10	100
Hingham	30	32	2	4
Holt	27	24	3	9
Ipswich	2	2	0	0
King's Lynn	5	4	1	1
Lowestoft	4	24	20	400
Mildenhall	11	10	1	1
Newmarket	7	6	1	1
North Walsham	16	19·5	3·5	12·25
Norwich	1	1	0	0
Stowmarket	8	19·5	11·5	132·25
Sudbury	12	7·5	4·5	20·25
Swaffham	22	10	12	144
Thetford	15	5	10	100
Watton	26	24	2	4
Wickham Market	31	19·5	11·5	132·25
Wymondham	13	27·5	14·5	210·25
			$\Sigma D^2 = 1811{\cdot}5$	

Table 2 Calculation of rank correlation coefficient

in order to keep this total both values are given a rank of 2·5. In the same way the three values of 11 occupy fourth, fifth and sixth positions. This time the addition gives a total of 15, and the three values are therefore ranked equal fifth. It is most important that ties of this nature are handled correctly, since the accuracy of the technique depends upon it. In the example given the final rankings should be

1 2·5 2·5 5 5 5 7 . . .

Once the data had been ranked, the next step involved the calculation of a value 'D', defined as the difference between the population rank of each town, and its accessibility rank. The difference was taken to be positive in each case, since the next step was to work out D^2, and the sign was unimportant. Once calculated, D and D^2 were tabulated with the rest of the information, as illustrated in Table 2. The D^2 column was then summed, and the total entered at the foot of the column.

The value of the correlation coefficient was calculated using Spearman's formula:

$$R = 1 - \frac{6\Sigma D^2}{n^3 - n}$$

where R is Spearman's Rank Correlation Coefficient, ΣD^2 is the sum of all the values of D^2 and n is the total number of values.

Thus, substituting actual values in the formula,

$$\begin{aligned} R &= 1 - \frac{6 \times 1811 \cdot 5}{32^3 - 32} \\ &= 1 - \frac{10869}{32736} \\ &= 1 - 0 \cdot 332 \\ &= 0 \cdot 67 \text{ (to 2 decimal places)} \end{aligned}$$

The value of R has a possible range of between -1 and $+1$. A value of $+1$ implies perfect positive correlation, and a value of -1 perfect negative correlation. If there is no correlation at all between the two variables, then R is equal to zero. Thus values of R approaching one, whether positive or negative, indicate good correlation, whilst low values are a sign of poor correlation. A number of scatter diagrams illustrating different possible values of the correlation coefficient are shown in Figure 4.

By squaring the value of R, and multiplying by 100, it is also possible to arrive at a figure which indicates, as a percentage, how much of the variation in the value of the dependent variable has been successfully explained by variations in the value of the independent variable. This measure, known as the 'coefficient of determination', is therefore a useful standard by which to judge the success of the hypothesis which is being tested.

In the case of the East Anglian exercise, it was agreed that a value of 0·67 for the correlation coefficient indicated a fairly good relationship between the two variables. About 45% of the variation in the size of market towns could be explained in terms of variations in their accessibility, and the hypothesis was therefore accepted. The availability of this information in numerical form enabled comparisons to be made between East Anglia and other parts of the country, where different correlation coefficients had been found. This prompted discussion about other factors which might be important in determining the size of market towns, and the class gained a good impression of the distorting influence of non-service functions. By referring to their scatter diagrams, pupils were able to discover which towns appeared to have larger populations than would be expected on the basis of their accessibility alone. Many of these, in addition to being market towns, were found to belong to other categories such as industrial towns, ports, or resorts. The characteristics of these could then be discussed in greater detail.

It must be emphasised that the methods used in this exercise in searching for a relationship between two separate variables represent only one approach to the testing of a hypothesis of this kind. The advantages of rank correlation are that it is reasonably simple to apply, easy to understand, and can be worked through quite rapidly. On the other hand, the coefficient it produces is only an approximation to the true value, which can only be obtained by using more complicated techniques. Further work on the scatter diagrams is also possible, as part of more advanced regression analysis. Of course the far greater complexity of these techniques, whilst matched by greater objectivity, makes them difficult to apply, even at sixth-form level, and also requires a great deal more time to be spent on tedious calculation in order to produce a result. It is doubtful whether, at school level, the effort is worth it, unless very good calculating facilities are available.

TESTING FOR SIGNIFICANCE

It is always possible, although often unlikely, that patterns which have been observed, or relationships discovered, are due more to the operation of chance than to some valid geographical factor. This is particularly so in cases where chance variation may have been introduced by sampling error. A variety of tests are therefore available to assess the probability that chance may have influenced the results of an investigation, thus enabling the degree of confidence that can be given to its conclusions to be specified. The test described here is a fairly simple one, although a considerable amount of computation may be involved. It can quite easily be handled by sixth-formers with no special inclination to mathematics.

The exercise in which the test was used resulted from fieldwork carried out by sixth-formers in the Norwich area. The basic problem was to try to explain certain aspects of the urban geography of Norwich in terms of the operation of a number of related concepts. The idea for one of several hypotheses tested came from an established theory, that of the sector layout and growth of towns proposed by Hoyt (1939). It was postulated that significant variations in character would exist between different sectors of the city. However, since all significance tests work on the basis of assuming a 'null hypothesis', it was necessary to take the opposite point of view and put forward the hypothesis that: 'Any variations in character which exist are merely the result of chance, and therefore are not significant.'

Since Hoyt's theory related specifically to the characteristics of residential areas, it was decided to test the null hypothesis using data referring to the social characteristics of the population, collected from the 10% census of Norwich conducted in 1966. This represented a stratified random sample of the population, and provided information on the distribution of inhabitants between five specified 'social classes' within each enumeration district. The city was divided arbitrarily into

Class / *Sector*	1	2	3	4	5	*Row total*
North	40	221	692	175	88	1216
East	55	189	913	218	114	1489
South	80	238	708	244	99	1369
West	24	112	722	261	143	1262
Column total	199	760	3035	898	444	5336

A Observed frequency matrix

Class / *Sector*	1	2	3	4	5
North	45	173	693	205	101
East	56	212	847	251	124
South	51	195	779	230	114
West	47	180	718	212	105

B Expected frequency matrix

Table 3 Comparison of observed and expected frequencies (Class 1 Professional occupations; 2 Intermediate; 3 Skilled: 4 Semi-skilled; 5 Unskilled)

four sectors, in the form of right-angled wedges radiating outwards from the centre. The enumeration districts falling wholly or largely within each sector were listed, and their social class data added together to form totals for each sector. This gave the number of people in the sample belonging to each class within each sector. This information was tabulated in matrix form as shown in Table 3.

The processing of the data was undertaken by means of the 'chi-square' test. This is another non-parametric technique designed for application in cases where the information is available in the form of frequencies within a number of specified classes. The first step was to construct a matrix of expected frequencies which could then be compared with the observed frequency matrix already tabulated. The observed frequencies were summed to provide row and column totals, and an overall total (see Table 3). Expected frequencies were calculated by applying simple rules of probability, as shown in the following example:

Probability of person living in northern sector $= \dfrac{1216}{5336}$

Probability of person being in class 1 $= \dfrac{199}{5336}$

$\therefore$ Probability of person living in northern sector and being in class 1 $= \dfrac{1216 \times 199}{5336^2}$

$\therefore$ Expected number of persons in class 1, living in northern sector $= \dfrac{1216 \times 199}{5366^2} \cdot 5336$

$$= \frac{1216 \times 199}{5366}$$

$= 45$ (to nearest whole number)

In general, the expected frequency in any box of the matrix is given by

$$\frac{\text{Row total} \times \text{Column total}}{\text{Overall total}}$$

The chi-square (χ^2) test was then applied, in order to assess whether or not the differences between the two matrices could be regarded as statistically significant, or whether they were the result of chance factors. The value of χ^2 was calculated by using the formula

$$\chi^2 = \sum \frac{(O - E)^2}{E}$$

where O represents an observed frequency and E represents the corresponding expected frequency. Each box of the two matrices was taken in turn, and the calculation involved recorded as shown in Table 4.

O	*E*	*O–E*	*(O–E)²*	*(O–E)²/E*
40	45	5	25	0·56
221	173	48	2304	13·31
692	693	1	1	0·14
175	205	30	900	4·39
88	101	13	169	1·67
55	56	1	1	0·18
189	212	23	529	2·50
913	847	66	4356	5·14
218	251	33	1089	4·34
114	124	10	100	0·81
80	51	29	841	6·56
238	195	43	1849	9·48
708	779	71	5041	6·47
244	230	14	196	0·85
99	114	15	225	1·97
24	47	23	529	11·26
112	180	68	4624	25·68
722	718	4	16	0·02
261	212	49	2401	11·32
143	105	38	1444	13·75

$$\sum \frac{(O-E)^2}{E} = 120{\cdot}40$$

Table 4 Calculation of the value of χ^2

Before any conclusions could be drawn from the value of χ^2, it was also necessary to calculate the number of 'degrees of freedom' possessed by the original matrix. This value is an expression of the degree of choice available in allocating frequencies to individual boxes of the matrix, given the actual row and column totals. In this case each row had 4 degrees of freedom (one less than the total number of boxes in the row) and each column had 3. The total number of degrees of freedom for the whole matrix was therefore 4×3, or 12.

By referring to a set of statistical tables (e.g. Lindley and Miller 1968), it was found that a χ^2-value of 120·4, with 12 degrees of freedom, indicated a probability of less than 0·1% that the null hypothesis was correct. In other words, differences of the magnitude discovered between observed and expected frequencies would be expected to occur by chance on less than one occasion in a thousand. The null hypothesis was therefore rejected. The original and alternative form of the hypothesis, that variations in social class data between sectors were not the result of chance, was accepted at the 99·9% level of confidence. This was well above the minimum level of 95% required if the results were to be declared significant. This meant that the differences between the two matrices could be considered in more detail, enabling certain conclusions to be reached. For instance, the southern sector was characterised by an unexpectedly large number of people belonging to the 'higher-income group' represented by classes 1 and 2. The western sector, on the other hand, had relatively few people in these two classes, but a larger number than expected in classes 4 and 5, representing a 'lower-income group'. These and other observations resulted in suggestions for the development and testing of further hypotheses.

The information value of this exercise could obviously have been improved by increasing the number of sectors, and by taking greater care over the decision of where to locate the sector boundaries. Alternatively a series of concentric zones, rather than sectors, could have been used to test the relevance of another theory of urban structure (Garner 1967). It is as well to bear in mind, however, if the use of more classes is contemplated, that there is a direct relationship between the number of boxes in the matrix, and the amount of computation involved in arriving at a value for χ^2.

No attempt has been made here to cover anything like the range of statistical techniques available to the geographer, although the methods described are, perhaps, some of the most suitable for application at school level. Emphasis has been placed upon the processing of information rather than its collection, and upon the analysis of data rather than its description. This is not to imply, of course, that these other aspects of quantitative work are any less important than those dealt with, but it is felt that they have been given fuller treatment in the past (Gregory 1963, Thompson 1969). The use of sampling procedures, questionnaire surveys, and simple methods of representing numerical information in cartographic form can, of course, be incorporated with statistical analysis in project work of all kinds. No amount of description of these or any other techniques can substitute for practical experience of their use.

It is not being suggested that statistical techniques provide an immediate or simple solution to all geographical problems. Used in moderation, however, they can add realism and precision to many aspects of geographical enquiry, and thus help to increase the degree of motivation which pupils derive from problem-solving situations. There is obviously a danger that what starts as a challenge can become a chore, and for this reason techniques must be kept simple and purposeful. Carefully and successfully applied, they can afford a high degree of satisfaction to both teacher and pupil alike.

References

J. S. Bruner, (1960) *The process of education*, Vintage Books.

W. Bunge, (1966) 'A geographic methodology', *Theoretical Geography*, Gleerups.

D. P. Chapallaz et al., (1970) *Hypothesis testing in field studies*, Teaching Geography series, Geographical Association.

R. J. Chorley and P. Haggett, (1967) 'Models, paradigms and the new geography', *Models in geography*, Methuen, University Paperback 1968.

J. P. Cole and N. J. Beynon, (1968) *New ways in geography*, Blackwell.

J. P. Cole and C. A. M. King, (1968) *Quantitative geography*, John Wiley.

J. A. A. Crisp, (1969) 'New approaches to teaching geography', *Geography*, vol. 54.

J. A. Everson and B. P. Fitzgerald, (1969) *Settlement patterns*, Longmans.

J. A. Everson and B. P. Fitzgerald, (1969) *Settlement patterns*, Concepts in Geography series, Longmans.

B. J. Garner, (1967) 'Models of urban geography and settlement location', *Models in geography*, R. J. Chorley and P. Haggett (eds.) Methuen, University Paperback 1968.

S. Gregory, (1969) 'Models and quantitative techniques in teaching – attitudes, opinions and prejudices', *Geography*, vol. 54.

(1963) *Statistical methods and the geographer*, Longmans.

H. Hoyt, (1939) *The structure and growth of residential neighbourhoods in American cities*, Washington.

D. V. Lindley and J. C. P. Miller, (1968) *Cambridge elementary statistical tables*, Cambridge University Press.

W. H. Theakstone and C. Harrison, (1970) *The analysis of geographical data*, Heinemann.

D. Thompson, (1969) 'A selective bibliography of quantitative methods in geography', *Geography*, vol. 54.

Notes on contributors

Notes on contributors

Trevor Bennetts was until recently Head of the Geography Department, Queens School, Bushey, Herts.

John Carnie is Deputy Principal of Charlotte Mason College of Education, Westmorland. Until recently he was in charge of post-graduate courses at Coventry College of Education where he had considerable contact with immigrant communities in the west Midlands.

Peter Davis is Assistant Geography Master at St Dunstan's College; he has contributed to the *Teaching Geography* series published by the Geographical Association.

Norman Graves is Head of the Geography Department at the University of London Institute of Education; previously he taught in a grammar, a technical and a comprehensive school. Author of *Geography in secondary education*, and co-author (with John Talbot White) of *Geography of the British Isles.*

David Harvey is teaching in the Department of Geography and Environmental Engineering, Johns Hopkins University. He has previously taught at the University of Bristol, Pennsylvania State University and the Australian National University. Author of *Explanation in geography.*

Keith Hilton is Lecturer in Geography at Hereford College of Education and Visiting Professor at Calgary and Saskatchewan Universities.

Gerald Hones is Lecturer in Education at the School of Education, University of Bath. He has lectured at Southern Connecticut State College, with a Fulbright Award.

Dennis Milburn is Associate Professor of Education in the University of British Columbia. He was formerly Senior Lecturer in Geography at the Fröbel Institute of Education, and from 1969 to 1971 Adviser on Education to the Government of Chile. Author of *A first book of geology.*

Terence Moore is Lecturer in the Philosophy of Education at the University of London Institute of Education.

Michael Naish is Lecturer in Education with special reference to the teaching of geography, at the University of London Institute of Education.

William Rhys is Principal Lecturer and Head of the Education Department, Kesteven College of Education.

Herbert Sandford taught in a variety of schools before joining the staff of S. Mark and S. John College of Education as a lecturer in geography. He has acted as adviser to publishers of school atlases.

Graham Stevens is Head of the Liberal Studies department, Forest Hill School, London.

Michael Storm is Principal Lecturer and Head of the Geography department, Berkshire College of Education. Author of *Urban growth in Britain.*

Vincent Tidswell is Principal Lecturer and Head of the Geography department, Hereford College of Education. Author of *An introduction to the analysis of road networks*, and *Quantitative methods: an approach to socio-economic geography.*

Thelma Veness was Professor Educational Psychology at the University of London Institute of Education. Author of *School leavers: their aspirations and expectations.*

Rex Walford is Principal Lecturer in Geography and Senior Tutor at the Maria Grey College, Twickenham. Author of *Games in geography.*

John Talbot White is Senior Lecturer in Geography at the Rachel McMillan College of Education, London. Co-author (with Norman Graves) of *Geography of the British Isles.*